SUPERFIGHTERS

The Next Generation of Combat Aircraft

General Editor
Mel Williams

AIRtime Publishing Inc.

United States of America • United Kingdom

Published by AIRtime Publishing Inc.
USA: 120 East Avenue, Norwalk, CT 06851
Tel (203) 838-7979 • Fax (203) 838-7344
email: airpower@airtimepublishing.com
www.airtimepublishing.com
UK: CAB Intl. Centre, Nosworthy Way, Wallingford OX10 8DE
Tel +44 (0)1491 829230 • Fax +44 (0)1491 829334
email: airpower@btinternet.com

Copyright © 1999, 2000, 2001, 2002 AIRtime Publishing Inc.

ISBN 1-880588-53-6

General Editor
  Mel Williams

Contributing Authors
  Piotr Butowski
  David Donald
  Andrey Fomin
  Henri-Pierre Grolleau
  Jan Gunnar Jørgensen
  Jon Lake
  Bill Sweetman

Artists
  Mike Badrocke, Piotr Butowski, Zaur Eylanbekov,
  Aleksey Mikheyev, Mark Styling, Andrey Zhirnov,
  Vasiliy Zolotov

Designer
  Zaur Eylanbekov

Editorial Production
  Jill Brooks, Natalie Raccor

Controller
  Linda Deangelis

Publisher
  Mel Williams

Special thanks to Eric Hess and Tom Kaminski

Color Reproduction by Chroma Graphics, Singapore

PRINTED IN ITALY

Much of the material in this book has previously has appeared in
International Air Power Review or *Combat Aircraft*. Where possible
it has been updated and expanded.

To order more copies of this book or any of our other titles call
toll free within the United States 1 800 359-3003, or visit our
website at: *www.airtimepublishing.com*

Other books by AIRtime Publishing include:
United States Military Aviation Directory (Jun 2000)
Carrier Aviation Air Power Directory (Dec 2001)
Phantom: Spirit in the Skies Updated and Expanded Edition (Aug 2002)
Russian Military Aviation Directory (Dec 2002)

Retail distribution via:

Direct from Publisher
AIRtime Publishing Inc.
PO Box 5074, Westport, CT 06881, USA
Tel (203) 838-7979 • Fax (203) 838-7344
Toll-free 1 800 359-3003

USA & Canada
Specialty Press Inc.
39966 Grand Avenue, North Branch, MN 55056
Tel (651) 277-1400 • Fax (651) 277-1203
Toll-free 1 800 895-4585

Dealer inquiries are welcome

Photo and illustration acknowledgements
Jacket Mikhail Kuznetsov (1), Lockheed Martin (8), Katsuhiko Tokunaga (1),
Eurofighter (4), Saab (2), Luigino Caliaro (2), François Robineau (1), Henri-
Pierre Grolleau (2), Sergey Skrynnikov (1), Hugo Mambour/AviaScribe (1)
Page 4-6 Lockheed Martin **Page 7** Mark Styling (Art), Lockheed Martin
Page 8-11 Lockheed Martin **Page 12-13** Mike Badrocke (Cutaway) **Page
14-15** Lockheed Martin **Page 16** Jim Dunn (1), Lockheed Martin (2) **Page
17** Lockheed Martin, Jim Dunn **Page 18-24** Lockheed Martin **Page 25**
Lockheed Martin (1), Pratt & Whitney (1), Zaur Eylanbekov (Line art) **Page
26-27** Lockheed Martin **Page 28** Lockheed Martin (1), Zaur Eylanbekov (Art)
Page 29-49 Lockheed Martin **Page 50** BAE Systems **Page 51** BAE
Systems (2), Eurofighter GmbH (1) **Page 52** Clive Bennett (2), BAE Systems
Page 53-55 BAE Systems **Page 56-57** Mike Badrocke (Cutaway) **Page 58**
Eurofighter, Mel Williams **Page 59-69** Eurofighter **Page 70** Zaur Eylanbekov
(Line art) **Page 71** BAE Systems **Page 72** Saab **Page 73** Saab, Luigino
Caliaro **Page 74** Clive Bennett (2), Gary Bihary (1), Jan Jørgensen (2) **Page
75** Saab **Page 76** Saab (2), Gary Bihary (1), Luigino Caliaro (1) **Page 77-79**
Saab **Page 80-81** Mike Badrocke (Cutaway) **Page 82** Saab **Page 83**
Saab/BAE Systems (Art) **Page 84** Luigino Caliaro **Page 85** Saab **Page 86**
Luigino Caliaro **Page 87** Gary Bihary, Saab **Page 88** Piotr Butowski **Page
89-91** Saab **Page 92** Frédérick Lert **Page 93** Katsuhiko Tokunaga (1), Clive
Bennett (1), François Robineau (1) **Page 94** François Robineau **Page 95**
François Robineau **Page 96** Frédérick Lert, Dassault **Page 97** Henri-Pierre
Grolleau (1), François Robineau (2) **Page 98-99** Mike Badrocke (Cutaway)
Page 100 François Robineau **Page 101** Henri-Pierre Grolleau (1), Frédérick
Lert (1), David Donald (1) **Page 102** Thales **Page 103** Dassault, François
Robineau, **Page 104** François Robineau, Katsuhiko Tokunaga/Dassault **Page
105** Frédérick Lert, François Robineau **Page 106** Henri-Pierre Grolleau (2),
François Robineau **Page 107** François Robineau **Page 108** François
Robineau **Page 109** François Robineau, Jelle Sjoerdsma **Page 110** François
Robineau, Frédérick Lert **Page 111** Zaur Eylanbekov (Art) **Page 112** Henri-
Pierre Grolleau, Zaur Eylanbekov (Line art) **Page 113** François Robineau
Page 114 Hugo Mambour/AviaScribe **Page 115** Sergey Sergeyev (1), Hugo
Mambour/AviaScribe (1), Aleksey Mikheyev (1) **Page 116** Hugo
Mambour/AviaScribe (2), Sergey Skrynnikov (1), Vasiliy Zolotov (Art) **Page
117** Sergey Skrynnikov (2), Hugo Mambour/AviaScribe (1), Aleksey Mikheyev
(1) **Page 118** Sergey Skrynnikov (1), Hugo Mambour/AviaScribe (1), Mark
Styling (Art), Sukhoi (4) **Page 119** Hugo Mambour/AviaScribe (1), Sebastian
Zacharias (1), Sukhoi (4) **Page 120** Mikhail Kuznetsov (1), Sergey
Pashkovskiy/Sukhoi (1), via Sergey Skrynnikov (1) **Page 121** Mikhail
Kuznetsov (1), Hugo Mambour/AviaScribe (1), via Sergey Skrynnikov (1)
Page 122 Hugo Mambour/AviaScribe (1), via Sergey Skrynnikov (1), Mikhail
Kuznetsov (1) **Page 123** Andrey Zhirnov (Art) **Page 124-125** Aleksey
Mikheyev (Cutaway) **Page 126** Aleksey Mikheyev, Sukhoi **Page 127** Sergey
Skrynnikov **Page 128** Sukhoi, Hugo Mambour/AviaScribe **Page 129** Vasiliy
Zolotov (Art), Aleksey Mikheyev **Page 130** Sergey Skrynnikov **Page 131**
Andrey Zhirnov (Art) **Page 132** Sebastian Zacharias, Piotr Butowski **Page
133** Aleksey Mikheyev, Sebastian Zacharias **Page 134** Piotr Butowski (2),
Sebastian Zacharias (1) **Page 135** Zaur Eylanbekov (Art) **Page 136** Sergey
Skrynnikov, Clive Bennett **Page 137** Mikhail Kuznetsov **Page 139** Piotr
Butowski (Line art)

INTRODUCTION

Tremendous technological advances in the field of electronics are fundamentally reshaping modern combat aircraft and the nature of air warfare. Smarter computer chips and ever more sophisticated software are revolutionizing avionics and weapon systems to bring crews and commanders precision surveillance and attack capabilities never before available to them. Coupled with these developments have been radical new approaches to warplane funding, concept and design — driven by tighter defense budgets, more demanding military requirements and global competition. The result has been the emergence of a new-generation of warplanes unlike any that have gone before in terms of versatility, capabilities — even appearance. This book examines these aircraft, their development, systems, weaponry and production prospects.

CONTENTS

CHAPTER 1

Lockheed Martin F-22A Raptor

DEVELOPMENT & FLIGHT-TESTING

While the Lockheed Martin F-22A Raptor is the most expensive fighter ever built, it also promises to be the best ever deployed. The type is of critical importance both militarily and industrially since, without it, the USA will have no credible competitor to the new generation of 'super-fighters.' Despite much hype to the contrary, aircraft like the F-15 and F-16 are older-generation platforms unable to match new fighters like the Rafale, Gripen and Eurofighter, however much new equipment is incorporated in ambitious upgrades. Furthermore, they are increasingly likely to struggle against well-flown, upgraded types like the MiG-29, Su-27 and Mirage 2000. The F-22A, on the other hand, will outclass every other aircraft flying or under development, provided it can be afforded in sufficient numbers. Yet, despite its undeniable excellence and pivotal importance, its future can hardly be described as secure.

Although the Raptor is now widely referred to as the Air Dominance Fighter (ADF), it was originally known as the Advanced Tactical Fighter (ATF) — an acronym first used in 1971 when the former Tactical Air Command began drawing up a new concept of operations for a type that would replace the

A-10 and F-16, both still entering service at that time. The advent of the MiG-29 'Fulcrum' and Su-27 'Flanker' dented American faith in the long-term ability of the new F-15 and F-16 to stay ahead of the threat, and an emphasis on the air-to-ground role gave way to a dual-track approach. In the early 1980s work began in earnest on the ATF and a study was made to determine whether air-to-air and air-to-ground requirements could be filled by a single platform. It also sought to ascertain which role had the higher priority in the event both missions could not be handled adequately by one aircraft. With funding tight, the study was eventually put out to industry and manufacturers were asked to provide proposals. Ideas for a common type, related variants or entirely separate designs were called for. Fairchild and Vought chose not to respond to the Air Force's request for information but Boeing, General Dynamics, Grumman, Lockheed, McDonnell Douglas, Northrop and Rockwell came back with diverse proposals. Northrop offered a featherweight concept, whereas Lockheed proposed a monster design weighing almost 120,000 lb (54431 kg) that would cruise at Mach 2.8.

By 1982, USAF interest was focused on the air-to-air mission. At that time, the F-111 showed no sign of needing to be replaced and the top secret F-117A was about to enter service.

Conceived for beyond-visual-range (BVR) combat through a combination of stealth, advanced avionics and 'smart' weaponry, the F-22A still possesses good agility for close-in engagements.

The initial test flight of the first prototype (PAV1) was undertaken on 29 September 1990, exactly one month after it was rolled out at Lockheed Martin's Palmdale facility in California. The aircraft was fitted with General Electric YF120 power plants whereas the second and only other YF-22 was fitted with competing Pratt & Whitney YF119s, the latter ultimately winning the engine contest. After Lockheed Martin was declared the winner of the fighter competition in 1991, the first prototype was retired from flight duties.

Furthermore, derivatives of the F-15 and F-16 promised to fill the gap as interim strike/attack aircraft. This pushed the USAF towards a compromise platform that would be an F-15A/C replacement primarily, able to go to the target and beat the enemy wherever it was found. In turn, this drove the ATF's performance requirements, size, weight and range, and led to the imposition of some specific requirements. The latter included utilization of very high-speed integrated circuits (VHSIC), an active-camber wing, non-flammable high-pressure hydraulics, conformal antennas for the sensors and an integrated flight control/propulsion control system. The USAF originally specified voice control for certain systems and a degree of STOL capability (with thrust reverse) but these requirements were later relaxed.

Boeing, General Dynamics, Grumman, Lockheed, McDonnell Douglas, Northrop and Rockwell again responded to a request for proposals based on the refined specifications, and all were awarded concept definition contracts. All submitted proposals

for a DemVal phase and the hope was that this would lead to a competitive fly-off between two pairs of prototypes. Requests for proposals for a Joint Advanced Fighter Engine were issued to General Electric and Pratt & Whitney at much the same time, and the YF120 and YF119 prototype power plants came about as a direct result.

In 1986, the ATF program took on added importance when the US Navy announced it would use a derivative of the selected air force ATF (to be called the NATF) as an eventual replacement for its Grumman F-14 Tomcat. This promised to take production to well over 1,000 aircraft, with as many as 750 ATFs going to the USAF and 546 NATFs to the Navy. Suddenly, the competition looked worth winning in commercial terms and some of the contenders formed teams. They agreed to work together no matter which team member's design was chosen, on the basis the winning member would become the prime contractor. Lockheed teamed up with Boeing and General Dynamics, while McDonnell Douglas entered into a similar arrangement with Northrop. Lockheed's submission was placed first and Northrop's second, followed by General Dynamics, Boeing, McDonnell Douglas, Grumman and Rockwell, in that order.

The Lockheed and Northrop teams were each awarded contracts on 31 October 1986 to build a pair of prototypes. One of the aircraft, in each case, was to be powered by YF119 engines and the other by YF120s, and full avionics rigs were to be produced as well. All three companies in the team took responsibility for different parts of the aircraft with Lockheed looking after the nose, forward fuselage, cockpit, core avionics and radar stealth. General Dynamics was responsible for the mid-body, IR stealth features, logistics and flight controls, whereas Boeing was to produce the rear fuselage, wings and flying laboratory. The design was 'frozen' in May 1988.

Although the prototypes did not have operational equipment, they were required to match the planned production aircraft in key performance areas. Furthermore, for the purpose of durability testing they did not have full applications of radar absorbent material (RAM). Instead, just a few patches were applied. The first Northrop/McDonnell Douglas YF-23 (fitted with YF119 engines) made its maiden flight on 27 August 1990, and the first YF-22 (powered by YF120 engines) followed on 29 September. The second YF-22 (fitted with YF119 engines) took to the air on 30 October and the second YF-23 flew for the first time four days earlier. Informally, the YF-23 was known as the 'Black Widow,' after Northrop's most famous fighter, while the YF-22 was briefly and unofficially referred to as the 'Lightning II,' echoing Lockheed's wartime P-38.

The YF-22 completed its flight-test program on 28 December

Superfighters

Lockheed Martin equipped the prototypes with very large vertical tails because the designers had no wish to experience the kind of problems encountered with the F-117A, due to its early fins being too small. However, such generously sized surfaces were unnecessary and production aircraft will be fitted with fins 20-30 percent smaller.

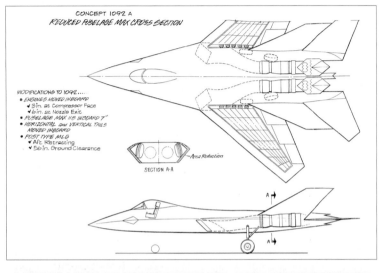

1990, after making 74 flights and accumulating 91.6 flying hours. During this phase the aircraft exceeded Mach 2 and sustained Mach 1.58 without afterburner. The aircraft also fired AIM-9 and AIM-120 missiles from internal weapons bays and flew at a 60° angle of attack (AoA, or high-Alpha), although these tests had not been requested or required. The YF-23s amassed 65 hours but did not fire any weapons or conduct any high AoA testing. However, they did demonstrate an ability to 'supercruise' at more than Mach 1.6 (the actual speed achieved remains classified). The type promised to be faster than the YF-22 and offered a lower radar cross-section (RCS). Wind tunnel tests suggested it would have no Alpha limits and would be extremely agile. Conceptually, the Northrop design placed greater emphasis on stealth and very high speed, aiming always to destroy hostile aircraft before they could close to visual range. Lockheed favored a compromise approach, whereby agility was to be taken into account.

The Lockheed ATF team was declared the winner in April 1991, partly due to the strength of its derived NATF design, which promised to marry the YF-22's fuselage with a two-seat cockpit and a variable-geometry wing. Ironically the NATF program was abandoned within months of the ATF decision. In addition, Pratt & Whitney's more conservative YF119 engine was selected over the variable-cycle YF120 to power the production F-22A. This was because of the company's thrust vectoring experience, the engine's relative lack of complexity and lower risk this carried.

The Lockheed Martin production F-22A differs from the YF-22 prototype in several respects. After the problems the company initially encountered with the F-117A, due to insufficient fin area, it played it safe with the YF-22. Ultimately, the contractor was able to reduce the size of production aircraft tail fins by 20-30 percent. Leading-edge sweep was reduced by about 6° and stealth considerations prompted a redesign of the wing's trailing edge and shape of the stabilators. Finally, the cockpit was moved forward a short distance to provide a better view over the nose, while the engine intakes were moved aft to give the pilot a better downward view and to either side. The YF120-engined YF-22 was subsequently retired for use as an engineering mock-up, while the second YF-22 aircraft flew another 39 sorties and amassed 61.6 flying hours in follow-up testing. However, this aircraft suffered a serious landing accident on 25 April 1992, after severe pilot induced oscillations

The line drawing depicts one of the configuration concepts created during evolution of the 090P design for ATF improvement, while the middle plan view shows the shape that emerged for the YF-22 demonstrator. The design differences between the YF-22 and F-22A (bottom) are clearly visible. The production aircraft has its cockpit positioned farther forward and air intakes placed farther back, to improve the pilot's field of view. The wings have an increased span, lower sweep and a different contour, while smaller vertical and larger, reshaped tail surfaces are apparent.

Lockheed Martin F-22A Raptor (Serial 91-4001, Construction No. 4001)
Raptor 01 entered the test program at Edwards AFB on 18 May 1998
and was used primarily for flight envelope expansion tests.

(PIO) were encountered. Thereafter, it was used for antenna testing after receiving a production-representative F-22A wing and empennage, and never flew again.

The EMD contract originally called for seven single-seat F-22As and two twin-stick F-22Bs, as well as two non-flying static test airframes. Under the contract the first flight was expected by mid-1996, and the first full-production F-22A was to fly by mid-1999. The first operational squadron was supposed to be active by 2003. Limited funding quickly caused these dates to slip, however. On 9 April 1997, the first F-22A ('Spirit of America') was rolled out and officially designated the Raptor during a high-profile ceremony. It made its maiden flight from Dobbins ARB in Marietta, Georgia, on 7 September of that year. In the meantime, the two-seat F-22B had been officially postponed on 10 July. The second F-22A joined the flight-test program on 29 June 1998 and these heavily instrumented EMD F-22As were complemented by several test bed aircraft. Flight control software was developed using the VISTA F-16D, while an entire cockpit and avionics system was installed in a modified Boeing 757 Flying Test Bed (FTB).

A representative F-22A forward fuselage/radome was mounted on the B757 in August 1997, and a dummy wing section, complete with conformal antennas, was mounted above its flight deck in December 1998. With 25 technicians and extensive test equipment aboard, the modified airliner is capable of employing the F-22A's avionics against representative targets in real time. This is particularly useful since the first three EMD F-22As lack full mission avionics. There is also a full-scale communications, navigation and identification (CNI) model atop a tower in Fort Worth, Texas, consisting of a scale replica of the forward section of an F-22A, with partial wings attached that house conformal antennas.

After initial flight-testing by the company, the F-22As have been transferred to Edwards AFB in California, one by one, where the Combined Test Force (CTF) is located. Test program participants include the Air Force Flight Test Center (AFFTC), the Air Force Operational Test and Evaluation Center (AFOTEC), Air Combat Command (ACC), Pratt & Whitney, the F-22 System Program Office (F-22 SPO) and Lockheed Martin Tactical Aircraft Systems. The first aircraft was delivered aboard a C-5B Galaxy on 5 February 1998 and the second aircraft flew to Edwards under its own power on 26 August of that year. The third F-22A, the first with a fully representative internal structure, flew for the first time on 6 March 2000 and arrived at the base on 15 March.

Slowness in delivering development aircraft has delayed the program considerably. Of the nine EMD models, only 4002 made its first flight on time while the others were late by up to a year and more. In political circles there was much grumbling over the state of the program and, in July 1999, the US House of Representatives shocked the Pentagon and contractors alike by voting to eliminate all F-22A production funds for fiscal year 2000 (FY00) — the sum of $1.8 billion. That would have caused havoc within the program had funds not subsequently been restored, albeit with strings attached, before low-rate initial

production (LRIP) could begin. Conditions included delivery of the Block 3.0 software; carrying out AIM-9 Sidewinder and AIM-120 AMRAAM separation tests, including a guided AMRAAM launch; and commencement of RCS and radar performance testing. With generally satisfactory progress during the past two years, LRIP has proceeded while the USAF has extended its test schedule. Under the new plan, dedicated operational test and evaluation (DIOT&E) will begin in April 2003 even though EMD will not be finished by then. Up through that date, the emphasis will be on those elements essential to DIOT&E, like structural envelope testing. Although weakness in the vertical tails was identified early on, it was too late to impact the construction of 4002. Consequently, only 4003 is a fully instrumented structures test aircraft today.

The first EMD aircraft, 4001, ended its flight duties in late 2000 and has since gone to Wright-Patterson AFB in Ohio for use in live-fire testing. Initially earmarked for structural testing, 4002 is being used for weapon-separation tests instead. It carries the spin recovery parachute. Raptor 4003 is performing the role described above, while 4004 has been modified for climate testing and 4005, 4006 and 4007 are currently being used to verify the avionics systems. Reports suggest the F-22A's overall performance has been good, with 'supercruise' and the F-119 engine exceeding expectations.

Late delivery of most of the aircraft needed for EMD testing at Edwards has seriously delayed completion of this phase. In order to make up some of the time lost, a decision was made to begin dedicated operational test and evaluation in April 2003, even before EMD ends. Below, Raptor 01 is accompanied by aircraft from Edwards' 412th Test Wing.

Superfighters

AVIONICS

For the DIOT&E phase, the F-22A should carry avionics and software representative of the initial operating capability (IOC) standard. The hardware and software first underwent comprehensive testing at the the avionics integration laboratory (AIL) at Boeing Field near Seattle, after which they were installed on the Boeing 757 FTB. While the FTB cannot replicate the agility of the F-22A, no surprises have been reported in terms of the way the radar and electronic warfare system responds versus FTB experience. It appears to be working well at moderate *g* levels. Version 3.1 of the software is already in use and two more releases are expected before the start of DIOT&E. During the summer of 2002, 3.1.1 will be installed and used to train pilots for this evaluation phase, whereas 3.1.2 will be the standard for DIOT&E and initial operational service. This release will include all major radar, electronic warfare, and communications, navigation and identification (CNI) functions.

deleted in the DemVal phase and have not been reinstated.

The APG-77's specifics are still classified but the smaller Raytheon APG-79, which is under development for the Super Hornet, is thought to be capable of tracking targets at ranges in excess of 115 miles (185 km) — almost twice the range of many radars in service today. The APG-77 is more powerful and has more transmit/receive (T/R) modules — perhaps one and one-half times the number in smaller radars. The AESA is efficient in that it does not have to waste energy scanning sky that has been found clear of targets already and can, instead, concentrate on tracking previously detected targets. It also offers new small-target detection capabilities like track-before-detect, and the detection threshold can be set at a low-enough level to pick up false alarms as well as genuine targets. When the radar encounters a suspicious return, the beam dwells on the target to confirm if it is genuine. Returns that exceed the threshold, but cannot be confirmed, can still be matched from scan to scan and if they turn out to be targets, the radar already has track data on them.

Beneath its skin, the F-22A is an extremely sophisticated aircraft, possessing a highly integrated avionics system. This is built around a pair of common integrated processors (CIP) that act as the aircraft's 'brain.' Rather than having traditional communications and navigation equipment, such as a global positioning system (GPS) and instrument landing system (ILS), modules within the CIP emulate the CNI system. Each CIP holds 66 separate modules that are capable of automatic reprogramming, enabling one to take over from another in the event of a malfunction or failure. The heart of the weapons system is the Northrop Grumman/Raytheon AN/APG-77 radar, an active, electronically scanned array (AESA) suite that is probably the most advanced of its kind in production today. It first flew on 21 November 1997. The CIP also functions as the processor for the radar and EW systems.

A unique advantage of an AESA is that its design reduces radio-frequency (RF) losses. It can offer several times greater sensitivity than a conventional radar, partly because the receiver is coupled almost directly to an amplifier in each module. As a result, there is little opportunity for interference or noise to enter the signal before it is amplified, resulting in a very clean signal reaching the processor. One less desirable characteristic — at least in a conventional nose-mounted radar with a fixed array — is the radar field of regard. This is restricted to 60° either side of the boresight. The F-22A has provision for side radar arrays in its forebody, but the arrays themselves were

While the avionics and warfare systems carried by the Raptor will offer capabilities and sophistication not seen in current fighters, particular effort is being devoted to maximizing pilot situational awareness. This is achieved through sensor fusion to provide a clear tactical picture and minimize workload.

Offering a reduced RCS, an AESA is important to an aircraft's ability to maintain stealthiness. A mechanically driven antenna has a complex shape and is difficult to shroud, and no known stealth aircraft has ever been built or even proposed with a mechanically scanned radar. The APG-77 array is installed with a slight-upwards tilt which deflects the head-on main-lobe reflection up and away from any likely receiver. Furthermore, backscatter from the edges of the radar array is masked by the use of RAM on the perimeter of the array.

If AESA technology has one 'killer application' for stealth aircraft, it is low probability of intercept (LPI). AESA greatly expands the number of LPI techniques that can be used to ensure a stealth platform does not betray its position and identity through radar emissions. The agility of the radar makes it possible to reduce peak power adaptively so that as a target gets closer, radar power can be decreased rapidly to a point where an intercept receiver cannot detect it. An AESA radar can also search simultaneously with multiple beams and because each beam searches only a small sector, it dwells longer on a

Possessing very large air intakes, the F-22 also features a highly blended wing that has a pronounced camber, as is evident in this view. To serve its various avionics systems, more than 30 sensors equip the Raptor — all of which are flush with the surface of the aircraft to preserve stealthiness.

given spot. Thus, it is capable of achieving similar probability of detection with less power. Another feature of AESA technology fielding sufficient processing power is that it can confuse an interception system. It does this by varying almost every characteristic of the signal, apart from its angle of arrival, from one pulse integration to the next. It can change its pulse width, beam width, scan rate and pulse-repetition frequency (PRF), all of which are essential identifying characteristics for interception systems.

Another important LPI technique is to leave the radar turned off. One system that helps in this respect is the BAE Systems (formerly Sanders) ALR-94, perhaps the most technically complex system carried by the Raptor. The ALR-94 is a passive receiver system having greater capabilities than simple radar warning receivers (RWR) fitted to most fighters. It features multiple antennas covering several bands and can detect side-lobes as well as main lobes, and accurately locate and track any emitting target. In all likelihood, it uses the radar's AESA as a sensitive and accurate adjunct receiver. Information from the ALR-94 and other non-emitting sources like the fighter's datalink is used automatically to cue the radar, which cuts down on electronic emissions. The ALR-94 can track in real time high-priority emitters, like fighter aircraft at close range, and in this mode (called narrow-band interleaved search and track / NBILST), the radar is used only to provide precise range and velocity data to set up a missile attack. In fact, an enemy aircraft's radar might provide the ALR-94 with nearly all of the information necessary to launch an AIM-120 AMRAAM air-to-air missile and guide it to impact. This would make the AMRAAM act more like an anti-radiation AAM.

Another important aspect of the F-22A's avionics suite is its ability to identify targets in a beyond-visual-range (BVR) engagement. Not only is within-visual-range (WVR) combat becoming increasingly dangerous, imposing visual identification deprives the F-22A of most of its capabilities in the air-to-air arena. Pretty much any fighter with a high-off-boresight missile and helmet-mounted display (HMD) could prove as

capable as an F-22A close in, so avoiding such encounters is crucial. Destroying enemy aircraft in BVR, preferably at extreme range, is where the Raptor's strengths really lie. Rules of engagement (ROE) set the conditions under which an unseen target can be attacked, and while these vary from situation to situation, a basic principle is that the target should be 'declared' by multiple independent channels. The F-22A has at least four channels available — identification friend-or-foe (IFF) functions in the CNI suite, offboard identification provided by the datalink, the ALR-94 and the radar.

The ALR-94 should rapidly be able to identify a target if it is using its radar, while the APG-77 radar, with its ability to generate a very narrow, focused beam, should be able to deploy several non-cooperative target recognition (NCTR) modes. One is jet engine modulation, which relies on detecting characteristic patterns in the radar pulse caused by rotating compressor blades. While the F-15 and F/A-18 have employed this since the 1980s, more advanced NCTR is based on high-range resolution (HRR). The radar measures the signature of range cells along the length of the target, and compares the signature to a template. The exact range at which a target can be recognized has not been revealed but, as a general principle, identification at greater distances requires more energy.

The use of a datalink, though, may be the biggest single change to offensive fighter tactics. The F-22A's intra-flight datalink (IFDL), which uses narrow pencil beams to defeat interception, ties the sensors of several F-22As together. Fighters in a datalinked flight no longer need to stay in visual contact and can spread out across many miles of sky. Another basic use of the datalink is 'silent attack'. An adversary may be aware that he is being tracked by a fighter radar that is outside missile range but may not be aware that another, closer fighter is receiving that tracking data and is preparing for a missile launch without using its own radar. Again, the way in which the F-22A is designed to exploit this datalink is classified in detail but the potential uses of linked radars have been outlined by the developers of the Swedish JAS 39 Gripen, the most datalink-intensive aircraft in service today. For example, if the radars or ESM systems on two fighters detect the same target, they can locate it instantly by triangulation. The datalink results

Superfighters

in better active radar tracking with fewer signals. Usually, three plots or echoes are needed to track a target in track-while-scan. The datalink allows the radars to share plots, not just tracks. Even if none of the aircraft in a formation gets enough plots on its own to track the target, they may do so collectively. While each radar plot includes Doppler velocity, which provides the individual aircraft with range-rate data, on its own the data does not yield the velocity of the target. Using a datalink, two fighters can take simultaneous range-rate readings and thereby determine the target's track instantly, reducing the need for radar transmission.

Improvements to this formidable capability are already being studied – and could lead to an F-22 that can hit multiple ground targets with precision weapons. The first wave of changes to the design, however, is intended to deal with the mundane but tricky problem of out-of-production components. In the late 1980s, just before the YF-22 and YF-23 prototypes were flown, the USAF was sponsoring advanced-technology programs to develop 384-kB memory chips — at a time when few thought of onboard data storage needs measured in megabytes. By the time the program began, technology had reached a point where the CIP could use commercially available Intel I-960 chips. Those processors are now out of production and 8 MB is the standard for a $100 pocket organizer rather than a $100 million fighter.

The prototype Boeing 757-200 was specially converted by Boeing and supported the YF-22's DemVal phase as the Avionics Flying Laboratory. Subsequently, after undergoing major modifications in 1998, it became the F-22 Flying Test Bed and was used to carry out significant aspects of the F-22's EMD-phase avionics testing. The B757 was fitted with a representative Raptor forward fuselage, a special 'wing' above and behind the flight deck housing the electronic warfare and CNI antennas, an APG-77 radar in its nose and separate stations for software engineers. The FTB allowed significant progress to be made towards verifying crucial aspects of the F-22's avionics software package, despite the fact initial EMD examples (01, 02 and 03) were not fully instrumented or integrated.

Moreover, the semiconductor industry is no longer interested in producing chips in the relatively tiny quantities required for defense projects. In fact, the problem of diminishing manufacturing sources affects most military electronics programs.

The answer to DMS is to switch, as far as possible, to commercial-off-the-shelf (COTS) components. One goal is to accommodate COTS components in modules or cards that protect the commercial chip from vibration, heat and cold, electromagnetic pulse (EMP) and other features of the fighter environment. The second is to enable ever-changing COTS chips to work with the 'fixed core' of the fighter's avionics system, to avoid difficult and expensive changes to power, cooling and data functions. Thus, no two F-22As might be to an exact common configuration, even though the differences would be entirely invisible to the pilot and maintainer. The first low-rate production batch of F-22As will have a new CIP with fewer modules and a different backplane design, better adapted to the power and cooling needs of modern processors.

The first of the full-rate production F-22As in 2005/6 will be delivered with a new radar, using similar technology to the F-35 JSF and the APG-80 for the Block 60 F-16. Gallium-arsenide microwave monolithic integrated circuit (MMIC) chips of the kind used in the T/R modules are now being produced for commercial communications applications, ranging from satellites to broadband wireless modems for computers. The current F-22A radar uses specially developed processors, but the APG-80 uses Mercury Computer Systems' RACE system, based on multiple commercial-type processors. The new F-22A radar will work better and cost less than today's system, and opens the way to an important expansion of the F-22A's mission.

Inside the cockpit, the Raptor's primary display is a BAE Systems wide-angle HUD, almost identical to that found in the Eurofighter. It provides a field of view extending 30° horizontally and 25° vertically. The instrument panel is dominated by six color LCD multifunction displays (MFD) and the ICP is located just below the glare shield. The latter is the pilot's primary means for manually entering autopilot, communications and navigation data — plans for touch-sensitive screens having been dropped at an early stage of F-22A development. The Raptor is also fitted with full hands-on throttle and stick (HOTAS) controls that feature a BAE Systems-designed and manufactured side stick, and texture-and-shape-coded buttons on the stick and throttle.

The US Air Force elected not to incorporate a voice recognition system as a means of controlling onboard systems, even though direct voice input (DVI) technology is being incorporated into other advanced jets like the Eurofighter. Instead, it has elected to develop this technology for the JSF program. DVI is especially useful when assigning targets to aircraft within a formation and for confirming or modifying the weapon system computer's recommended priorities. It has been calculated that in the seconds before missile launch, as opposing formations accelerate and climb to try and reach an optimum weapon release point, DVI could make a crucial difference by preventing the 'friendly' team from assigning the same target to two aircraft within the formation, and by ensuring every hostile is properly targeted. Furthermore, DVI can dramatically reduce cockpit workload, thereby improving pilot situational awareness.

Lockheed Martin F-22A Raptor

Successful completion of Block 3 software represents a crucial milestone in the F-22A program. The software integrates the aircraft and its weapon, navigation, countermeasures and communications systems, and evidence of a successful flight of Block 3 was mandated by the US Congress in 1999 before construction of additional aircraft could be permitted. Block 3.1 (the DIOT&E standard) made it first flight aboard Raptor 06 on 25 April 2002.

Two 3 x 4-inch (76 x 102-mm) upfront displays (UFD), located to the left and right of the ICP display, integrate caution/advisory/warning (ICAW) information and serve as the standby flight instrumentation group and fuel quantity indicator (SFIG/FQI). Although presented on the LCD display, the SFG provides the pilot with basic information needed to fly the aircraft, like the artificial horizon. It is connected to the aircraft's primary electrical system, which is often referred to as the 'Essential Bus.' This approach differs from that incorporated into the Eurofighter, which relies on miniature conventional instruments as get-you-home backups. An 8 x 8-inch (203 x 203-mm) LCD located in the center of the instrument panel serves as the Raptor's primary multifunction display (PMFD). It displays navigational information and situational awareness data while three 6.25 x 6.25-inch (159 x 159-mm) secondary multifunction displays (SMFD) provide offensive and defensive tactical information, as well as non-tactical data like checklists, engine-thrust output and the status of subsystems and stores. Two flank the PMFD while the third is located between the pilot's knees.

The Air Force opted not to include an emission-free, long-range target detection, acquisition and tracking system in the F-22A because it felt it offered poor detection-range performance. This was decided upon despite the fact that an infrared search-and-track system (IRSTS) is being installed on the latest Russian and European fighters. The lack of an IRSTS forces the Raptor pilot to rely on the other means previously described. The risk is that its emitting systems can easily betray the fighter's position and alert an enemy to its intentions. The lack of an IRSTS could be of particular concern if AWACS support is not available.

Lockheed Martin is justifiably proud of the Raptor's highly integrated displays and sensor fusion. The computer feeding the pilot's primary display receives information in the form of track files from the radar and offboard sensors, and carefully compares and matches the different target tracks. It then prioritizes and displays them, even mixing inputs from different sensors to give the most accurate picture. ESM, for example, may give the best angular bearing for a target, whereas an AWACS might provide the fighter with the target's best range

and speed. Tracks are displayed collectively but without their origins (radar, AWACS, ESM, etc.) so the display remains simple and intuitively easy to interpret. One consequence, of course, is that there is no indication as to how a particular target has been detected, so it may be hard to judge the reliability of the information being displayed or the possible effects of hostile jamming.

For the future, the USAF is reported to have identified three priority upgrade programs for the F-22A. The first is a synthetic aperture radar (SAR) mode, to be introduced with the new radar. The second is a transmit mode for the Joint Tactical Information Distribution System (JTIDS) datalink, and the third is incorporation of new weapons that can exploit opportunities brought about by the other two changes.

LOCKHEED MARTIN F-22 RAPTOR

1. Composite radome
2. Northrop Grumman/Texas Instruments AN/APG-77 multimode active electronically scanned radar antenna
3. Canted radar mounting bulkhead
4. Pitot head
5. Air data sensor system receivers, four positions
6. Radar equipment bay
7. Missile launch detector windows
8. Cockpit front pressure bulkhead
9. Forward fuselage machined aluminium alloy sidewall panel
10. Underfloor avionics equipment bays
11. Avionics equipment modules, downward-hinging for access
12. Electro-luminescent formation lighting strip
13. Composite fuselage chine skin paneling
14. Rudder pedals
15. Instrument console housing six multifunction full-color LCD displays
16. GEC-Marconi Avionics head-up display
17. Upward-hinging cockpit canopy
18. McDonnell Douglas ACES II (modified) ejection seat
19. Starboard side console panel with sidestick controller for digital fly-by-wire flight control system
20. Port side console panel with engine throttles
21. Off-base boarding ladder stowage
22. Cockpit sloping rear pressure bulkhead
23. Electrical power equipment bay
24. Battery bay
25. Nosewheel doors
26. Landing and taxiing lights
27. Forward-retracting nosewheel
28. Torque scissor links
29. Port engine air intake
30. Titanium intake frame
31. Intake bleed air spill duct
32. Inlet bleed air door/spoiler panel
33. Bleed air door hydraulic actuator
34. Datalink support antenna, microwave landing system antenna beneath intake
35. Air-cooled flight-critical equipment (ACFC) cooling air intake in boundary layer diverter duct, blower for ground operations
36. Boundary layer diverter spill duct
37. On-board oxygen-generating system (OBOGS)
38. No. 1 fuselage fuel tank
39. Canopy hinge point
40. Canopy actuator, electrically-powered
41. Starboard engine air intake
42. Intake spill and boundary layer bleed air ducts
43. Lateral avionics equipment bay
44. Missile launch detector window
45. Datalink antenna
46. ACFC cooling air exhaust ducts

47. Forward fuselage production joint
48. Composite intake duct
49. Canopy emergency jettison control
50. Lateral missile bay doors
51. Missile launch rail
52. Launch rail trapeze arm
53. Hydraulic rail actuator
54. Environmental control system equipment bay
55. Fuselage main longeron
56. Ventral missile bay
57. L-band antenna
58. No. 2 integral fuselage fuel tank
59. Machined fuselage main frame, typical
60. Illuminated inflight refuelling receptacle, open
61. Airframe-mounted auxiliary equipment gearbox, shaft-driven from engines
62. Intake overpressure spill doors
63. Global positioning system (GPS) antenna
64. Ammunition feed chute, 480-round ventral fuselage transverse magazine
65. M61A2 six-barrel, lightweight rotary cannon
66. Cannon barrels
67. Cannon muzzle aperture beneath flip-up door
68. Wing-root EW antenna
69. Communication/Navigation/Identification (CNI) UHF antenna
70. CNI Band 2 antenna
71. 600-gal (2271-lit) external fuel tanks

72. Starboard leading-edge flap, lowered
73. Flap drive shaft and rotary actuators
74. ILS localizer antenna
75. Carbon-fiber composite wing skin panel
76. Starboard navigation light, above and below
77. Wingtip EW antenna
78. Starboard aileron
79. Formation lighting strip
80. Aileron hydraulic actuator

© Mike Badrocke

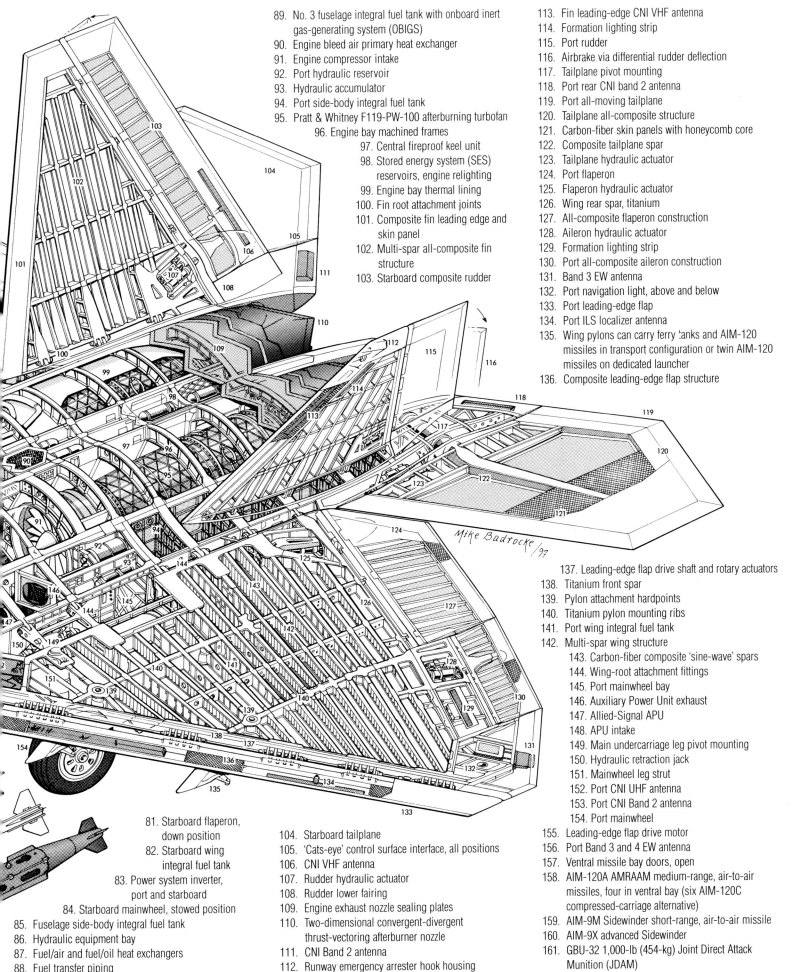

89. No. 3 fuselage integral fuel tank with onboard inert gas-generating system (OBIGS)
90. Engine bleed air primary heat exchanger
91. Engine compressor intake
92. Port hydraulic reservoir
93. Hydraulic accumulator
94. Port side-body integral fuel tank
95. Pratt & Whitney F119-PW-100 afterburning turbofan
96. Engine bay machined frames
97. Central fireproof keel unit
98. Stored energy system (SES) reservoirs, engine relighting
99. Engine bay thermal lining
100. Fin root attachment joints
101. Composite fin leading edge and skin panel
102. Multi-spar all-composite fin structure
103. Starboard composite rudder

113. Fin leading-edge CNI VHF antenna
114. Formation lighting strip
115. Port rudder
116. Airbrake via differential rudder deflection
117. Tailplane pivot mounting
118. Port rear CNI band 2 antenna
119. Port all-moving tailplane
120. Tailplane all-composite structure
121. Carbon-fiber skin panels with honeycomb core
122. Composite tailplane spar
123. Tailplane hydraulic actuator
124. Port flaperon
125. Flaperon hydraulic actuator
126. Wing rear spar, titanium
127. All-composite flaperon construction
128. Aileron hydraulic actuator
129. Formation lighting strip
130. Port all-composite aileron construction
131. Band 3 EW antenna
132. Port navigation light, above and below
133. Port leading-edge flap
134. Port ILS localizer antenna
135. Wing pylons can carry ferry tanks and AIM-120 missiles in transport configuration or twin AIM-120 missiles on dedicated launcher
136. Composite leading-edge flap structure

137. Leading-edge flap drive shaft and rotary actuators
138. Titanium front spar
139. Pylon attachment hardpoints
140. Titanium pylon mounting ribs
141. Port wing integral fuel tank
142. Multi-spar wing structure
143. Carbon-fiber composite 'sine-wave' spars
144. Wing-root attachment fittings
145. Port mainwheel bay
146. Auxiliary Power Unit exhaust
147. Allied-Signal APU
148. APU intake
149. Main undercarriage leg pivot mounting
150. Hydraulic retraction jack
151. Mainwheel leg strut
152. Port CNI UHF antenna
153. Port CNI Band 2 antenna
154. Port mainwheel

81. Starboard flaperon, down position
82. Starboard wing integral fuel tank
83. Power system inverter, port and starboard
84. Starboard mainwheel, stowed position
85. Fuselage side-body integral fuel tank
86. Hydraulic equipment bay
87. Fuel/air and fuel/oil heat exchangers
88. Fuel transfer piping

104. Starboard tailplane
105. 'Cats-eye' control surface interface, all positions
106. CNI VHF antenna
107. Rudder hydraulic actuator
108. Rudder lower fairing
109. Engine exhaust nozzle sealing plates
110. Two-dimensional convergent-divergent thrust-vectoring afterburner nozzle
111. CNI Band 2 antenna
112. Runway emergency arrester hook housing

155. Leading-edge flap drive motor
156. Port Band 3 and 4 EW antenna
157. Ventral missile bay doors, open
158. AIM-120A AMRAAM medium-range, air-to-air missiles, four in ventral bay (six AIM-120C compressed-carriage alternative)
159. AIM-9M Sidewinder short-range, air-to-air missile
160. AIM-9X advanced Sidewinder
161. GBU-32 1,000-lb (454-kg) Joint Direct Attack Munition (JDAM)

WEAPON SYSTEMS

Studies suggest that against a notional 'Flanker'-based threat, and given parity in radar and missiles, an F-22A would win about nine out of 10 one-on-one air combat engagements. By comparison, those same studies suggest the Eurofighter would win between eight and nine of every 10 engagements, and an aircraft like the F-15 would lose more often than it won.

Since it was designed as an air superiority fighter, the F-22A's primary armament reflects this mission. A centerline weapons bay can accommodate four AIM-120A or six AIM-120C

The first firing of an AIM-120 AMRAAM was undertaken on 20 December 1990. The medium-range missile is the Raptor's primary air defense weapon and the second prototype was the platform for this important program milestone. To help maintain stealthiness, the F-22A carries all of its ordnance within its fuselage section. For maximum combat persistence, however, the F-22 can also carry missiles under its wings at the expense of stealthiness.

AMRAAM missiles, while two smaller bays in the intake walls can carry two AIM-9M or AIM-9X Sidewinders. With a view to making the F-22A a more valuable asset, the USAF directed Lockheed Martin in 1994 to develop a nominal air-to-surface capability for the aircraft, as well. The main weapons bays have been modified and can now accommodate two 1,000-lb GBU-32 Joint Direct Attack (JDAM) guided weapons, displacing four of the six AIM-120Cs. In addition, the company plans to add underwing hard points that will allow additional payload to be carried at the expense of stealthiness. However, the Raptor currently lacks dedicated air-to-ground weapons aiming systems such as a FLIR, laser designator or spot tracker, but the proposed new SAR mode will enable the aircraft to carry out radar-bombing. Air-to-ground weapons options will include other autonomous precision-guided munitions, and there is also the possibility of a dedicated strike/attack variant being developed, akin to the F-15E. This is sometimes referred to as the FB-22, seen as a potential replacement for the F-117A Nighthawk and Strike Eagle. However, expanded air-to-ground capabilities will not be available until Block 5, for which deliveries will not begin before 2006.

Weapon trials have gone smoothly and a great deal of testing to support the AIM-120 AMRAAM has used an instrumented test vehicle (ITV), a non-releasable missile simulator carried in the weapons bay. In some ways the ITV is said to provide better data than that gained from live missile launches. The vehicle uses electronics that read the datalink transmissions from the fighter to the missile. The first two guided AMRAAM

launches took place in September 2001, and both were successful. In one case, the missile guided close enough to the target to have 'killed' it had it been fitted with a warhead, and in the other the AMRAAM skewered the BQM-74 drone and 'killed' it by impact alone. Needless to say, it was the missile and its active radar that performed the final intercept.

The first guided AIM-9 firing is due in 2002 but there is a clear consensus within the F-22A program that the AIM-120 will be the primary weapon. Significantly, there has been a delay in incorporating the Joint Helmet Mounted Cueing System (JHMCS) because of integration problems between the JHMCS tracker and the active noise reduction system in the F-22A helmet. The JHMCS has been deferred until the system is mature and is seen as less critical to the aircraft because, in any event, the Raptor has been designed primarily to fight in the BVR arena.

The F-22A's 'supercruise' capability and agility are seen as important assets in both offensive and defensive close-in engagements. Unlike a supersonic fighter, a subsonic airplane is easily targeted by fighters from the stern, aft quadrant, beam and front. As one fighter pilot describes it, attackers approaching from the stern have a relatively good standoff capability, since their missiles don't need to go so fast to run down the fighter. As the targeted airplane exceeds the speed of sound, however, it greatly reduces any stern firing opportunities. Similarly, aft-quadrant shots are denied because they lack the energy to complete the fly-out, and beam shots fail because missile seekers exceed gimbal limits when they attempt to pull the proper amount of lead for an intercept. Front quarter shots are limited because of the higher line-of-sight rates created by a high-speed target, and all shots are complicated by thin air at high altitude, where the F-22A flies comfortably. Chief test pilot Paul Metz notes that launching an AIM-120 AMRAAM at supersonic speed, with an altitude advantage over the target,

In combat configuration, the F-22A can operate to an altitude of 60,000 ft (18288 m), giving it a distinct edge over current fighters, which typically operate to 50,000 ft (15240 m). Compared with other fighters, the Raptor is particularly large — having a wing span that even exceeds that of the F-15 Eagle, the type it primarily is intended to replace.

increases its range by 50 percent. If a hostile fighter launches an AMRAAM against the F-22A, the latter can perform a super-sonic turn or 'cranking' maneuver, presenting the missile with a rapid and unpredictable change in line-of-sight and thereby decreasing its effective range.

Pilots working on new-generation fighters believe that the process of tactical change — which is traditionally slow except in combat — should be accelerated by the use of full-mission, multiple-player simulators. A former F-15 pilot now working on an advanced fighter team notes that a new aircraft is flown like the old one until pilots figure it out, and says that it took 10 years to employ the F-15 like an F-15, rather than like an F-4. With simulation, the same ground could be covered in four to five years. The development of tactics will be a key to exploit-ing the 'black world' capabilities of the F-22A and recently released details about the aircraft and its subsystems help to put together a picture of those capabilities, which are based on a combination of speed, stealth and avionics.

In terms of air-to-ground capabilities, the USAF now has its sights set on a new weapon for the F-22A, the Small Diameter Bomb (SDB). The SDB is a product of a mid-1990s project called the Miniature Munitions Technology Demonstration (MMTD) for which the goal was to exploit the fact that a small, accurate bomb can be as effective as a larger weapon with a greater miss distance. Specifically, the researchers set out to show that a weapon weighing around 250 lb (110 kg), with GPS/inertial guidance, a modern warhead and fuse design, and precise control of impact angle, could defeat hardened targets that

The Raptor's BVR capabilities means the pilot can largely avoid close-in air combat. However, the Raptor will be equipped to carry Sidewinders (ultimately the AIM-9X) for short-range defense, and with the introduction of Block 4 avionics software, helmet-mounted weapons cuing will be possible.

previously could be attacked only by bombs in the 2,000-lb (900-kg) class.

From the outset, it was seen that the MMTD could be very useful for stealth aircraft with internal weapons bays. The stan-dard Mk 80 low-drag general purpose (LDGP) bomb was designed in the 1950s for external carriage, and its elliptical profile gives it a large maximum diameter. A cylindrical shape is more efficient for internal carriage and the SDB will resemble the MMTD prototypes in shape and size. It will also have wings (as demonstrated by Boeing in 2001, under the Small Smart Bomb Range Extension program) and will be cleared for super-sonic release from the F-22A. Boeing's SSBREX demonstrator incorporated the Alenia Marconi Systems DiamondBack wing design and Russian-type lattice tail surfaces, which fold forwards for internal stowage. The USAF's minimum require-ment is that the smart rack should carry four SDBs, but both competitors are trying to meet the service's goal of six weapons per rack. This would give the F-22 the ability to carry 12 SDBs, in addition to a pair of AMRAAMs and a pair of AIM-9s. Launched from the F-22's cruising speed and altitude, the SDB would have a range of 56 miles (90 km).

Superfighters

Boeing and Lockheed Martin were awarded contracts to develop SDB designs in September 2001 and one of the two will be chosen to produce the weapon in September 2003. It is due to become operational on the F-15E in 2006 and the Raptor thereafter. The first version is to have a jam-resistant GPS/INS guidance system, whereas the second, to be operational from 2010, will have a seeker that uses radar or IR technology and is capable of searching a defined area for targets. The SDB will be a complete, integrated weapon rather than one built up in the field like the JDAM, and an integral part of the system will be the 'smart rack.' It is to be compatible with the F-22, F-35 Joint Strike Fighter and for external carriage, incorporating non-pyrotechnic ejectors and a databus that will connect the SDBs to the aircraft's avionics system.

In Lockheed Martin simulations, the F-22A uses its EW system and offboard targeting information to detect and locate SAM sites. Synthetic aperture radar scans the site and detects launchers, radars and control vehicles. The pilot selects multiple targets, releases SDBs at maximum range and breaks away in a 5g supersonic turn. While the F-35 has a similar weapons and avionics suite, the Raptor's unique advantage in this mission will be its speed, high-speed maneuverability and altitude performance. Speed and altitude increase the range of the gliding weapon — while speed, altitude and maneuverability combine to reduce the effective range of the SAM. An F-22A, therefore, can win a shoot-out against a SAM, while a subsonic, lower-flying F-35 would have to venture within the weapon's lethal radius in order to attack, and could not escape as quickly.

Speed and weapon range also allow an F-22A to respond more quickly to a new threat than a slower aircraft. For example, an air component commander may want to ensure that his forces can target any hostile emitter within a fixed time after the first signal. In that case, a Raptor can cover a much greater distance than a subsonic aircraft. With a JTIDS transmit function, too, the F-22A will distribute information from its sensor suite to other aircraft in the theater. For example, the Raptor will be able to confirm that it has located targets in the SAM site and launched weapons against them.

Integration of the SDB may not be the end of the F-22's metamorphosis into a bomber. In early 2002, Lockheed Martin briefed the USAF on a radically modified version of the fighter, with a delta wing, longer body and greater range and payload. A company-funded study of the so-called FB-22 will continue until the end of 2002. The proposed variant is clearly a bomber. Operations over Afghanistan drove home the fact that bases close to many potential targets may never be open to US combat aircraft. Apart from extreme-range operations by F-15Es, USAF fighters have been relatively little used in the theater — much of the burden instead being carried by B-52 and B-1 bombers. However, the USAF has no bomber replacement plan and previously expected to defer service entry of a new bomber until the 2030s. This depends on some very optimistic projections concerning the survivability and operational lifetime of the B-52 and B-1. Some members of Congress have pressured the USAF to buy more B-2s, but the USAF does not want to do this because the bomber is expensive to buy and maintain. One reason the service may consider the FB-22 is that it demonstrates how seriously it is taking the need for a new bomber, despite a lack of interest in more B-2s.

While some details of the FB-22 remains confidential, to some extent it is reminiscent of two earlier Fort Worth projects: the F-16XL and the delta-wing F-16 proposed to the United Arab Emirates in 1995. Both these aircraft were based on the F-16 but had no separate tail, a much larger wing and a stretched fuselage. The result was a very different, heavier aircraft with a much bigger fuel fraction. Despite the airframe changes, however, many elements of the aircraft like avionics, cockpit and systems remained similar to the original.

The FB-22's longer body accommodates larger weapon bays for nearly 30 SDBs, according to some reports. This would suggest it could carry an alternative load of six to eight JDAMs, or a mix of SDBs and larger weapons. The FB-22 would have no horizontal tail and a more sharply swept, longer-chord wing. However, the span is not likely to increase very much because the aircraft should still be capable of fitting into a 48-ft (14.6-m) wide hardened aircraft shelter. With a longer chord and deeper section, however, the FB-22 wing would accommodate much more fuel and there would be more tankage in the stretched fuselage, as well.

It is reported that aerodynamics work has been done on the new wing, which would use a complex camber variation to combine low drag with high volume and good low-speed characteristics. Another possibility is a completely tailless FB-22. Fort Worth has carried out much research into tailless designs with three-axis controls built into the wings but whether the FB-22 would retain the same 'supercruise' performance as the basic F-22A is uncertain, as of yet. The engine might have to be 'tuned' to match the wing, and the bomber might have to use the more powerful, more efficient (at subsonic speed) and markedly cheaper F135 or F136 engines from the JSF program. Some reports credit the FB-22 with an operating radius in the 2,175-mile (3500-km) range.

Serial 91-4001, which made its first test flight at Edwards AFB on 17 May 1998, was delivered to the desert base from Lockheed Martin's facility in Marietta, Georgia, aboard a C-5B Galaxy. The second Raptor to join the test program, 91-4002, arrived under its own power on 26 August 1999. Serial 91-4003, the third EMD aircraft joined the other two at Edwards on 15 March 2000.

FLIGHT CHARACTERISTICS

The F-22A was designed from the outset to be capable of 'supercruising' or sustaining supersonic speed without using its afterburners. While this capability is not unique to the Raptor, it has obvious significance in that it allows the aircraft to cruise at very high speeds without excessive fuel consumption, and enables it to fly through hostile airspace quickly. Where the Raptor's impressive thrust and low drag are most significant is in conferring extremely rapid supersonic acceleration. This allows it to impart maximum possible velocity to its air-to-air missiles, so long as launches from the internal weapons bays are not airspeed-limited. This is important because, the more velocity a missile has on launch, the farther it will travel — something of huge importance in a head-on BVR engagement.

Some defenders of the Raptor have dismissed the type's relative lack of very-high-Alpha capabilities, compared with some Russian aircraft, as tactically irrelevant 'circus stunts' that bleed precious energy. To some extent this is true but it ignores the occasional utility of high-Alpha maneuvering, which can be useful in snapping an aircraft's nose gun or missile seekers onto a target in a turning fight, or in a slow-speed vertical rolling scissors. Some analysts also ignore the benefits of the 'soft limits' of some Russian aircraft, which allow their pilots to deliberately make brief excursions into extreme areas of the flight envelope. In such circumstances departure from controlled flight becomes progressively more likely and the pilot risks overstressing the aircraft. However, allowing the pilot to maneuver in such a way to defeat a missile or avoid flying into a hillside has obvious benefits. In contrast, western fly-by-wire (FBW) control philosophies impose hard limits that cannot be overridden, with flight control system computers programmed to protect the pilot by preventing excessive placard g or Alpha limits.

High-Alpha testing officially has been limited to a 60° AoA and the aircraft has already demonstrated a number of maneuvers and rates at that angle. These include bank-to-bank rolls at 80 kts (148 km/h) flown for a full minute without loss of control and with only slight buffeting, roll rates of 100° per

With no dedicated new bomber program currently under way that would ultimately replace aircraft like the B-1B and B-52H, the US Air Force has expressed interest in a possible bomber version of the Raptor, dubbed the FB-22. The service is exploring the idea of using the platform to deliver the new Small Diameter Bomb (SDB), a highly accurate weapon that, while small, can be as effective as a larger weapon with a greater miss distance.

When Lockheed Martin won the ATF competition, the decision was partly influenced by the Navy's interest in a naval version of the fighter. As it happened, such plans were soon dropped.

second and pitch rates of 60° per second. Although the F-22A's agility will be impressive, the type has yet to fully show what it can do.

Lockheed Martin likes to stress the F-22A's low-observability or stealth characteristics, presenting it as the world's only truly stealthy air defense fighter. The 'Have Blue' and 'Senior Trend' (F-117A) programs have given the contractor more experience than anyone else in the design and production of stealth airplanes and much of this knowledge is incorporated into the F-22A. The Raptor cannot be considered a stealth platform like the F-117A, however. The Stealth Fighter was effectively designed to be invisible to enemy radar, through incorporation of a tiny RCS and a sophisticated flight planning system that allows the Nighthawk to slip through gaps in enemy radar coverage. Such gaps exist because the aircraft can be detected only when it is very close to an enemy's radar and because the pilot has complete flexibility when planning the mission. The aircraft can be routed to get it over the target at precisely the planned time.

For the F-22A pilot, the situation is quite different. The fighter might have to escort non-stealthy attack aircraft over a route chosen by those crews, or may be tasked with looking for enemy fighters. As a consequence, it cannot remain invisible to enemy radars by steering around them or by slipping through radar coverage gaps. Needless to say, having a small RCS is extremely useful and the smaller that is for the F-22A, the longer it will take for an enemy radar to detect it. Thus, a small RCS provides a measurable tactical advantage. The F-22A has been tailored for low observability with a faceted and chined configuration, and a shape designed to avoid RCS spikes. It has what is referred to as a 'bow-tie' RCS pattern (with the smallest

RCS at the nose and tail). Furthermore, RAM has been applied to selected edges and surface discontinuities, and care has been taken to minimize the number and size of access panels that need to be opened frequently (since they have to be self-sealing or sealed with RAM putty after being closed).

European manufacturers have chosen to follow a somewhat different philosophy with respect to stealthiness, reasoning that a low RCS is only really important from the frontal aspect — when opposing aircraft are approaching head on. The Rafale and Eurofighter have been designed with an extremely small frontal RCS, thus reducing the range at which they can be detected. The key to success in BVR combat is to see the enemy before he sees you, so a small frontal RCS is of paramount importance. In this respect, the F-22A, Eurofighter and Rafale are likely to be broadly comparable. Despite its larger size, however, the Raptor's stealthy design is likely to provide it with a distinct advantage because it returns a reduced RCS at all angles of intercept. In most engagements, the side-on RCS would be exposed only transiently to radar, and missiles have a hard time intercepting targets with high crossing rates.

The use of onboard radar in air combat is no longer inevitable. All modern fighters are fitted with RWRs that allow pilots to know when their aircraft are being 'looked at' by an enemy and detect when the hostile radar goes from search to

Knowledge gained by Lockheed Martin from its F-117A Nighthawk-related programs was put to good use by the contractor for its ATF. Low-observability is a key characteristic of the Raptor, not just from a head-on perspective (as is the focus of most other 'superfighter' programs) but from all angles, thanks to its shape and faceted and chined features.

tracking mode, and when it is supporting a missile in flight. RWRs also tell the pilot where the enemy radar is situated and, sometimes, how far away it is. The usefulness of an aircraft's radar is degraded by its ease of detection and many modern fighters tend to use off-board sensors like AWACS or passive sensors instead, to avoid giving away their presence. Alternatively, pilots make clever use of their radars by transmitting frugally.

As fighters having the capability to use other sensors for detection and tracking naturally include potential adversaries, a fighter like the F-22A needs to minimize all signatures, and IR has not been ignored. The Raptor employs IR-absorbent paint developed by Boeing and may also use fuel to cool its leading edges. It also is fitted with flattened two-dimensional engine nozzles that create a flatter exhaust plume to dissipate heat quickly. IR testing began in 2001 over Point Mugu, California, and the USAF says the type has a low all-aspect IR signature under sustained supersonic conditions. In any event, IR search and track (IRST) systems are not as all-powerful as stealth critics like to suggest. The very long detection ranges claimed generally assume the target is in afterburner, but the F-22A will use its thrust augmentors only transiently. Stealth protects the Raptor against detection and gives it the 'first look, first shot' advantage in an air-to-air engagement.

Through its reduced detection range, the F-22A is free to maneuver over a defended area and exploit its speed and mobility. Where it possibly is at a disadvantage is in the visual spectrum, being a big angular aircraft with a large wing area. Over the years, countless F-15 pilots have been picked up by their opponents at very long range due to the sheer size of their aircraft. For this reason, the Eagle is sometimes referred to as a 'flying tennis court.' In a visual-range fight, the F-22A is likely to be just as easy to spot.

Given the growing threat posed by Soviet fighters in the 1970s and 1980s, it is not surprising that high performance has been a crucial aspect of the F-22 program since the beginning. In fact, the type is the first to combine high performance with stealth. The F-22A's sustained supersonic speed without afterburning is now confirmed as Mach 1.7, which is 80 percent greater than any previous fighter. This means the F-22A has a

power reserve for maneuvering and acceleration at high supersonic speeds, unlike today's fighters and the planned JSF. The Raptor's operational altitude, formerly quoted as 'above 50,000 ft (15240 m)' is now confirmed as 60,000 ft (18288 m) — which is substantially higher than for other fighters limited to 50,000 feet for physiological reasons. If cockpit pressure is lost in a typical fighter, its pilot will lose consciousness before descending to an altitude where he or she can breathe sufficient oxygen. In the case of the F-22A, the anti-*g* ensemble includes positive-pressure breathing and functions as a pressure suit.

With afterburner, the USAF claims the Raptor has a maximum speed of Mach 2.0. This limit is probably governed by structural temperature considerations in the airframe and engines. The service has also quoted a ferry range of 1,800 nm (2,071 miles/3334 km) but has not revealed the combat radius. However, it has disclosed the aircraft's internal fuel capacity is 18348 lb (8323 kg), which is equivalent to a fuel fraction of 0.28 (28 percent of the mission takeoff weight is fuel). This is not unusually high and, unlike other fighters, the F-22A does not carry external fuel tanks on combat missions, which might suggest a somewhat limited range. However, in the past the USAF has indicated the Raptor will be able to 'supercruise' during half of an hour-long mission. If one assumes a supercruise speed of Mach 1.7 and a subsonic cruise speed of Mach 0.9, this equates to a 435-mile (700-km) unrefueled mission radius (with a 280-mile/450-km supersonic segment). The USAF has also repeatedly told the General Accounting Office that the F-22A is exceeding its specified combat radius.

In looking at the range equation, it has to be remembered that the F-22A does not fly and will not fight the same way a conventional fighter does. The Raptor carries no additional fuel in external tanks nor, therefore, does it suffer drag from tanks or pylons. Except indirectly through greater weight, weapons do not add to the fighter's drag either. Furthermore, in a typical mission, the F-22A will make less use of its afterburner than would a conventional fighter, significantly impacting its fuel consumption.

The first frontline F-22A operational site will be Langley AFB in Virginia and the first fighters are due to arrive there in late 2004 — ultimately equipping three squadrons. The highly sophisticated nature of the Raptor means potential export sales represent something of a dilemma for the United States, which is particularly sensitive about the export of advanced technology. Yet foreign orders for the jet could significantly help amortize its high development costs.

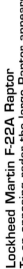

Lockheed Martin F-22A Raptor

To an opposing radar the large Raptor appears to be tiny, thanks to a careful blend of curves and straight edges designed to minimize radar reflectivity from all aspects (not just from head-on), a distinction that makes it a true stealth aircraft. Under the skin lies a very smart avionics system built around the APG-77 AESA sensor. More than just a radar, the APG-77 antenna array can be used in passive mode to pinpiont sources of radiation, feeding such data to the central computer.

Superfighters

PRODUCTION ORDERS

While the F-22 program originally called for 750 aircraft to be built at an estimated cost of $26.2 billion, this was subsequently cut back to 648 aircraft as cost estimates spiraled to $86.6 billion. The US Department of Defense's September 1983 Bottom-Up Review then cut planned production to just 438 aircraft, at a cost of $71.6 billion, before the number was further trimmed to just 339 under the Quadrennial Defense Review of May 1997. At that time, the estimated program cost was revised to $58.3 billion. However, in July 1999, proposals were made to delay funding of the six initial production aircraft for up to two years, in order to free up funds for pilot retention programs, other force commitments and more pressing programs. The justification for an aircraft program so costly was called into question many times and strong views about the project are still being expressed. Some believe the total number built might be as low as 125, making the Raptor little more than a 'golden bullet' to be augmented by advanced F-15s and JSFs. However, at the

The F-22A production line in Marietta, Georgia. The Raptor makes extensive use of composites, advanced metals and alloys — including welded and cast titanium, and heat-treated AirMet 100 steel for the undercarriage. Besides the two prototypes and two EMD static test vehicles, initial F-22 production calls for nine flying EMD aircraft, eight Lot 1/Lot 2 PRTVs and 10 Lot 1 Low-rate initial production (LRIP) examples. Total production requirements currently stand at 339 aircraft, with the USAF the sole customer.

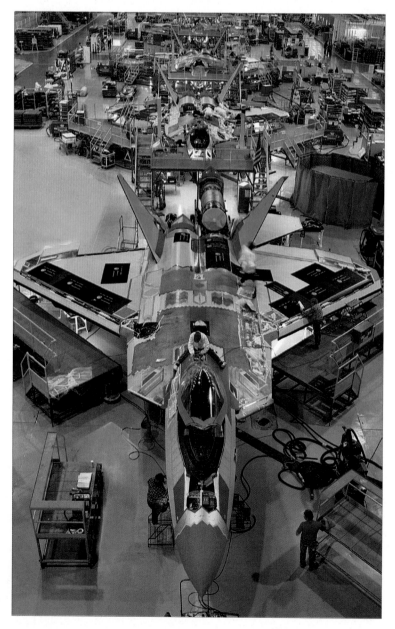

turn of the millennium, the planned procurement number stood at 322 full-production aircraft, to be delivered in 10 lots through 2011, in addition to the nine EMD F-22As, two PRTVs and six PRTV IIs — for a total of 339 aircraft.

Despite the USAF's unwavering commitment, these are uncertain times for the F-22 program still. Last August, the Pentagon's Defense Acquisition Board (DAB) authorized the start of low-rate initial production (LRIP), a program that will include more than 90 aircraft. However, as mentioned earlier, the start of operational testing has slipped by eight months (to April 2003) due largely to late delivery of development aircraft. If it slips further, the Pentagon will not be able to authorize the start of full-rate production, a decision that is due in 2004. With little slack left in the schedule, pressure to meet deadlines is being felt by the primary contractor and subcontractors alike.

The 2001 DAB review also delayed full-rate production and cut 36 aircraft from the USAF's planned force. Full-rate production, at 36 aircraft per year, will now start in FY2006 rather than FY2004. The first LRIP batch covers 10 aircraft, followed by 13 the year after, ramping up to 35 aircraft in FY2005. While the 1997 Quadrennial Defense Review had set the production at 339, this was nominally reduced to 331 aircraft because eight LRIP models (two ordered in December 1998 and two in December 1999) were re-designated PRTVs. The 2001 plan calls for a minimum of 295 aircraft in addition to eight PRTVs, although both the USAF and contractor still believe they will be able to implement cost savings that will make it possible for 331 examples to be built for the same money, once full-rate production starts. Key to the 2004 full-rate production decision will be the successful completion of DIOT&E, and this will depend heavily on timely delivery of aircraft. Four primary F-22As and a back-up are required, all close to production configuration. The four primaries are to comprise 4008 and 4009, the last two EMD aircraft, and 4010 and 4011, the first two PRTVs. The latter were ordered in FY2000 in a compromise that kept production moving despite the Congressional decision to delay LRIP. Only one of these aircraft is flying today and 4007 is the back-up.

At the height of the Cold War, continued fighter development by the other side could be taken for granted but in the years since the collapse of the Soviet Union, politicians and the public have become extremely sensitive about high-cost programs. Such projects draw accusations of extravagance and are viewed by some as irrelevant and anachronistic throwbacks to the old days. The military is expected to make do with cheaper, more cost-effective weapons, procured in smaller numbers. The F-22A program made a lot of sense in the spendthrift days of the Cold War, when production might have been extensive and few would seriously have questioned the need to provide US pilots with the best possible fighter. Now, there is the argument that a cheaper fighter might be enough to meet realistic threats.

At the end of the day, the US government probably has little choice but to push ahead with the F-22A, despite the hefty price tag. It would not be acceptable politically to buy a foreign

Currently undergoing testing is Block 3 software that is supposed to deliver full sensor fusion through enhanced electronic warfare and CNI functions. Block 3.1, flying in 4006 since 25 April 2002, integrates JDAM launch capability and JTIDS receive mode functions.

aircraft and, costs aside, it is simply too late to start a new tactical fighter program from scratch. As envisaged, the JSF will not be capable of filling the Raptor's mission as it is to be a fighter-bomber designed to cost and optimized for the air-to-ground role. As such, the JSF should be an excellent F-16 replacement but it will not be equipped to meet advanced fighters on even terms. Soldiering on with today's F-15s is not a credible option either. With aircraft like the Eurofighter and Rafale possibly entering the arsenals of potential enemies, the US might achieve parity with an upgraded version of the F-15. However, parity is considered an unacceptable option if US fighter pilots have to go to war, and it is a dangerously disingenuous suggestion in any event.

Arguably, aircraft like the Su-27, Su-30, Mirage 2000 and MiG-29 have already achieved parity with the F-15 family in many respects. It is the high quality and training of US pilots, coupled with overall air power superiority that allowed F-15s to achieve such impressive kill-to-loss ratios over Iraq and the Balkans. The F-15's success largely has been a result of air dominance. Without massive SEAD support and AWACS control, and the right pilot at the controls, an F-15 can be beaten by aircraft like the MiG-29 or even the lumbering Panavia Tornado, as exercises have demonstrated. The F-15 does not appear to exhibit any real advantage over the best of its contemporaries, especially when flown by equally well-trained pilots. The new generation of fighters typified by the Gripen, Rafale and Eurofighter are superior to the F-15, and if such aircraft were to fall into unfriendly hands, Eagle pilots would be at a distinct disadvantage. Some might suggest those new aircraft will never be exported to America's enemies but this cannot be guaranteed. In a rapidly changing world, today's friends might become tomorrow's enemies, and Europe's manufacturers are marketing their new aircraft with energy and aggressive determination around the globe.

Even if one disregards Europe's new fighters as threats, there are other potential dangers. Although Russian fighter development had been dormant it is showing signs of resurgence now that the Sukhoi-led LFI fifth-generation fighter program has been approved. If such aircraft could be fitted with advanced western avionics, perhaps from France or Israel, they could become serious threats. What is more, ongoing upgrades to existing Russian airframes will mean such aircraft could challenge today's F-15. If an enemy can provide its pilots with superior equipment, the unwritten contract between the United States and its servicemen might be called into question. No other nation in the world can rely on its forces to do its job motivated by such idealism. In return, only US servicemen comfortably assume that money will be no bar to their country providing them with the best possible equipment. What the

Air-to-air refueling of an F-22A was first undertaken on 30 July 1998 when serial 91-4001 hooked up with the 412th Test Wing's NKC-135E over California, at an altitude of 20,000 ft (6096 m). The cycle was completed midway through a three-hour test flight. The F-22A's refueling point is located on its spine, far behind the cockpit.

Superfighters

F-22A will provide to future US fighter pilots is a credible degree of superiority.

Quite apart from the increased risk to which USAF fighter pilots will be exposed if they are denied the F-22A, the US aircraft industry will suffer a terrible and humiliating failure if it is prevented from producing a viable competitor to the latest foreign fighters. This would lead to huge repercussions and the USAF would be left without an advanced air superiority fighter. The service has stated again and again that its willingness to take the low-cost, relatively low-capability JSF is predicated on having a sufficient number of F-22As. The JSF can operate as the cheap element in a 'hi-lo' platform mix and, according to the USAF, will rely on offboard sensors like the AWACS and Raptor to carry out its missions. It also should be remembered that the F-22 program is carrying much of the JSF program's risks and costs. Without the Raptor, development of certain avionics would fall directly to the JSF, causing that program's costs to rise. Furthermore, without the F-22A, the USA would be out of the advanced air superiority fighter business altogether.

Over time, the US government might have to consider accepting even higher costs in order to incorporate additional features now being showcased by competing advanced fighters. The Raptor will win few customers apart from the US Air Force but it can usefully serve as a flagship and capability-demonstrator for Lockheed Martin and the US aerospace industry as a whole. And, as previously stated, it is likely that its development will mean improved capabilities for the JSF.

Assuming the program moves forward without any major hitches, the first production F-22A (4018) should be with the 325th Fighter Wing at Tyndall AFB in Florida, in 2003. It is to be the training establishment for the new fighter, and

the Link Simulation and Training division of L3 Communications is due to deliver two full mission trainers and four weapon tactics trainers to the base by February. The first operational F-22A base will be Langley AFB in Virginia, adjacent to Air Combat Command headquarters, and the first F-22As are due to arrive there in September 2004. By 2009, three squadrons, each fielding 24 aircraft and six back-ups (a total of 78 Raptors) — should have replaced the F-15s at Langley.

While there is no doubt the F-22A should be the world's greatest fighter, whether it represents good value for money is a matter of conjecture. To a large extent its promised capabilities remain just that. While the risk of failure is becoming ever more slender that does not mean the program could not go awry even at this late stage. If everything works perfectly when the fighter enters service, will it represent the best use of US tax-payer dollars? The price tag continues to rise as the program is stretched out, and if total production costs of $39.8 billion are amortized over 339 aircraft, it will amount to $117.4 million each excluding weapons. This figure will not reflect the EMD bill of $18.9 billion nor the costs related to the DemVal and ATF evaluation phases, either.

Needless to say, the F-22A's high price will be compounded further if production for the Air Force is cut back again. Its price tag, coupled with the advanced technologies employed in the aircraft, means the Raptor is unlikely ever to be exported except, perhaps, to a close ally like Britain, Germany, Israel or Japan. Lockheed Martin is reported to have briefed Saudi Arabia and South Korea about the project but it is hard to imagine either nation having the resources to afford Raptors, even if the US government was to countenance such sales. Opportunities for further economies of scale look remote, although Lockheed Martin has embraced the 'lean manufacturing' concept with enthusiasm. Consequently, the Raptor 21 program should provide lowest-possible production costs. Ironically, however, the advantages the F-22A promises because of its advanced systems means it is unlikely a 'lite' version will ever come to market.

The USAF has made no secret of how important it views the F-22A to its future warfighting capability. The service has foregone other programs in order to free up sufficient funds to protect the project through what has been a stormy development, while some in the US Congress have questioned the air force's priorities. Keenly aware that the F-15 Eagle will not be able to hold its own against the world's new generation of fighters, the USAF wants the Raptor to be its 'top end' replacement.

SPECIFICATIONS

Wing span	44 ft 6 in (13.56 m)
Length	62 ft 1 in (18.92 m)
Height	16 ft 5 in (5.00 m)
Empty weight	Est. 30,000 lb (13608 kg)
Max. takeoff weight	Est. 60,000 lb (27216 kg)
Max. speed	Mach 2+ ('clean' at 36,090ft/11000 m)
Cruise Speed	668 kts (1237 km/h)
Operating Range	CLASSIFIED
Service ceiling	Est. 50,000 ft (15240 m)
Accommodation	Single pilot on zero-zero Aces ejection seat
Power plant	Two Pratt & Whitney F119-PW-100 turbofans with thrust vectoring, each rated at approximately 35,000 lb st (155.69 kN)
Armament	Internal – AIM-120C, AIM-9, GBU-32 JDAM; External – Provision for additional stores on four wing stations, M61A2 20-mm cannon

The Pratt & Whitney F119-PW-100 power plant — a twin-spool, augmented turbofan featuring a three-stage fan and a six-stage compressor — was selected for the F-22A. In the 35,000-lb st (155.69-kN) class, it has full-authority, digital electronic control (FADEC) and a two-dimensional vectoring nozzle.

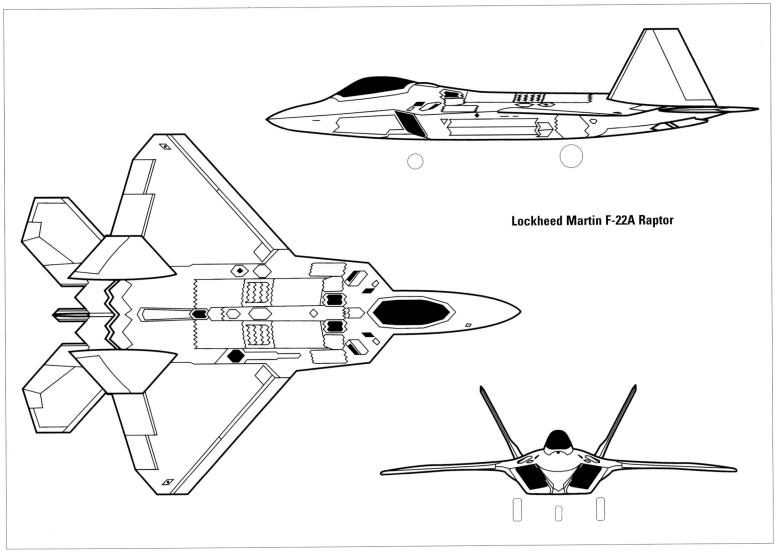

Lockheed Martin F-22A Raptor

CHAPTER 2

Lockheed Martin F-35 JSF

DEVELOPMENT

If the JSF program proceeds as planned, it will be the largest single defense project in history, with a potential market for 5,000-8,000 aircraft, and it will reverse the trend towards higher unit costs in military aircraft. The JSF will also be a breakthrough combat aircraft, not on account of its speed or agility but because of its blend of stealth, smart sensors, advanced displays and internal weaponry. Carrying two tons of precision-guided weapons, plus defensive air-to-air missiles, the JSF will still have much greater range than its predecessors and its pilot should be able to detect radar-guided threats long before they see the aircraft, giving a JSF formation the choice of avoiding or attacking them. The JSF's sensors have been designed from the outset in ways that reflect the designers' recognition that high-speed and secure datalinks will be essential in future conflicts. More than any other fighter, it reflects the concept of 'net-centered' warfare, in which communicating and gathering information and denying your adversary the ability to do the same may be as important as bombs and bullets.

The JSF family includes a STOVL derivative that should not increase the cost nor degrade the performance of its conventional siblings, a notion that nobody would have taken seriously for a second before 1990. The project takes aim at the idea that cost, in a military program, cannot be controlled as tightly as it is in the development of an airliner. This is true revolution. The JSF has already changed the way military aircraft are designed and built, being the first designed in an era when military requirements no longer set the pace of development in computing.

When President Clinton's first administration took office in early 1993, the USAF and Navy were developing two new fighters — the F-22 and the F/A-18E/F. Both services were also jointly planning a heavy attack aircraft (A/F-X) and the USAF was looking at an F-16 replacement. Both projects were cancelled in 1993 and less than three years later the Pentagon was working on a single new fighter to replace thousands of Navy and USAF aircraft, a version of which would be capable of replacing the Marine Corps' short-takeoff, vertical landing (STOVL) AV-8B. Serious design work on what became the JSF started in 1990-91, having its roots in technology studies that

had started several years earlier.

The JSF's predecessors owed their existence to two services, the US Marine Corps and British Royal Navy, which flew Harriers. In the early 1980s, both had started re-equipping with new versions of the type — the Royal Navy's Sea Harrier F/A.2 and the AV-8B — but the services recognized that they would need a new aircraft after 2000. Without a STOVL replacement, the Marines would go back to relying on the US Navy's carrier aircraft for air support, and would no longer be able to operate jet aircraft from the Navy's amphibious warfare ships. The Royal Navy's small carriers would not be able to operate conventional carrier-based aircraft at all, and would have to revert to being helicopter carriers.

In January 1986, an international joint agreement covering technology for a Harrier replacement was signed at NASA's Ames Research Center in California. The principal parties were NASA and the UK Royal Aeronautical Establishment — which later became part of the Defence Evaluation and Research Agency (DERA) — but they worked in close collaboration with the Marines and Royal Navy, and with US and UK industries. The agreement outlined a program that would compare several different STOVL designs against a draft requirement for a supersonic STOVL fighter. The plan was to select the most promising concepts for more detailed investigation and testing starting in 1988, and to start development of an operational fighter in 1995.

Of the four concepts selected for development, one was a derivative of the Harrier, using direct lift. To make the aircraft hover, the engine would be installed amidships and its thrust would be deflected downwards through swiveling nozzles. Another was called a 'remote augmented lift system' (RALS), which used an afterburner nozzle, fixed to point downwards, located in the fighter's nose and fed with bleed air from the compressor. A third concept, investigated by General Dynamics and de Havilland Canada, involved building large folding ejector ducts into the fighter's wing. The fourth, explored by Lockheed and Rolls-Royce, was a 'tandem fan' engine. This was like a conventional jet engine with an extra compression stage, mounted well ahead of the rest of the engine on an extension shaft. In straight-and-level flight, the engine worked like a conventional jet. All the air would pass through the inlets, the forward compression stage and the engine. For STOVL, the air through the front stage would be diverted to a pair of swiveling forward exhausts, and an extra set of inlets would open to feed the rest of the engine. In this mode, the engine acted like a high-bypass-ratio airliner engine, producing extra thrust.

By 1987, the Marine Corps had made a key decision. The Advanced STOVL (ASTOVL) aircraft would replace both its Harriers and its conventional F/A-18s. The service also refined

Declared the winner of the Joint Strike Fighter competition with Boeing, Lockheed Martin looks set to be the recipient of the largest jet fighter order in history — the USAF, US Navy, US Marine Corps, RAF and Royal Navy having already declared a requirement for a version of the recently designated F-35.

its requirement, calling for an aircraft no larger than the F/A-18 (in terms of empty weight) but with greater range and stealth — characteristics that have remained part of the specification to the present day. The USMC decision was important because it increased the potential size of the program to 700-plus aircraft — but it was the only good news surrounding ASTOVL.

All the chosen designs turned out to have major drawbacks. Problems caused by the interaction between the fighter's jet exhaust, the ground and its inlets proved more difficult than expected, ruling out the afterburner-equipped direct-lift system and RALS. [When Russia's Yakovlev brought its STOVL Yak-141 to the UK's Farnborough air show in September 1992, it hovered but did not land vertically because it would have wrecked any surface except a steel deck]. Control of a heavy, powerful aircraft in jet-borne flight was difficult and would extract a lot of power from the engine. Control during transition from wing-borne to jet-borne flight was particularly complex for the tandem fan and the ejector system. Some of the configurations were less compatible than others with stealth but that problem could not be discussed in detail because of security concerns.

By 1989, the ASTOVL program was dead in the water because none of the concepts under study showed any promise of

The tradeoffs each of the services had to accept in order to ensure a high degree of commonality across the JSF versions (and thus make the project a practical one), means the type will not offer many improvements in terms of maneuverability and speed, but it will be able to carry an exceptional weapons load and will possess highly capable avionics.

Superfighters

The Boeing X-32A (left and below) and the Lockheed Martin X-35A concept demonstrators essentially represented relatively 'high-risk' and 'low-risk' options, respectively — in terms of the different technologies they brought to the JSF project.

solving the many detail problems at an acceptable level of risk. It was at this inauspicious point in the program that the Defense Advanced Research Projects Agency (DARPA) started to look at STOVL. It had been DARPA, 15 years earlier, which had been the catalyst for the development of stealth technology. DARPA had been involved in the UK/US STOVL project and its managers saw, by the late 1980s, that it was in deep trouble. Convinced that, like stealth, ASTOVL could be made feasible with a more focused and more aggressive demonstration program, DARPA set new goals for the project.

Its leaders eliminated most hard requirements except for a 24,000-lb (10900-kg) maximum empty weight (a surrogate for cost); based the project on the powerful engines developed for the YF-22 and YF-23 Advanced Tactical Fighters; and laid out a program which started with the construction of a large-scale powered model (LSPM) — a non-flying vehicle with a complete propulsion system to be used for ground tests — and then proceeded directly to construction and testing of a manned prototype. The program was set up to ensure that no company would propose a solution unless it was confident that it could make it fly, and the testing of the LSPM would eliminate any approach which turned out to be a total dud. The memory of the Rockwell XFV-12A, a 1970s supersonic STOVL prototype that could not lift its own weight, was still fresh. Another principle, reflecting the agency's name and charter, was that preference would be given to new solutions that had not been tested before. The effects of this decision would ripple throughout the program and are still felt today.

Between 1989 and 1991, DARPA funded aircraft design studies by McDonnell Douglas, General Dynamics and Lockheed Advanced Development Company (the Skunk Works), together with propulsion studies at General Electric (which had produced the YF120 engine for the YF-22 and YF-23) and Pratt & Whitney (YF119). The studies concentrated on two basic problems with the earlier STOVL concepts. The first was that hot, high-velocity exhaust gas was no longer just a nuisance but a menace because of the greater size and power of the super-

sonic aircraft. The jet blast threatened to blow people and equipment off the deck like confetti, while creating a cloud of superheated air that would suck power out of the engine. Even if the challenge of hot-gas ingestion could be solved, operations on ship would be made impractical by the need to clear a large safety zone around a landing aircraft. The second problem was that stealth appeared to mandate a single, rear-mounted exhaust nozzle in up-and-away flight.

Both these problems could be solved if there was a way to move some of the engine's total energy forward, to balance the rear-mounted nozzle, while increasing the system's mass flow and reducing its jet velocity. Lockheed Skunk Works engineer Paul Bevilaqua devised such a method, which was patented in 1993. The new system evolved from the tandem fan but with three principal differences. The forward fan stream was separate from the core airflow at all times, the fan was shut down in cruising flight, and the fan was rotated so that its axis was vertical. It was a less complex system than the tandem fan and had a more easily controlled transition.

At the same time, General Electric dusted off the data on lift fan systems that it had built for the US Army in the 1960s. The GE fans had been driven by turbines fed by engine exhaust gas. Coincidentally, GE had developed a variable-cycle engine, the F120, as a candidate power plant for the Advanced Tactical Fighter (ATF). One attribute of this engine was that it could supply a great deal of high-pressure bleed air and continue to operate properly. By 1991, the Lockheed and GE fan-boosted systems emerged — in the view of the DARPA program managers — as the best hope for a practical system and, that same year, the agency persuaded the Navy to issue a draft requirement for a STOVL strike fighter, giving it the formal justification for a development program. DARPA called for proposals, announcing that it would pick two companies to build near-full-scale models in 1993. In 1995, the most promising candidate would be selected for a flight demonstration program.

As DARPA refined its requirements, another light bulb went on. Unlike the Harrier, the fan-lift STOVL designs had a

The JSF competition has revolutionized the thinking behind new combat aircraft programs, in a host of ways. It has redefined the state of the art in terms of avionics, construction techniques, commonality and affordability. For the first time, development of a fighter aircraft has been subject to the same kinds of disciplines that are applied to airliner development — with the price preset and the designers and builders charged with delivering the best product for the money. This has led to innovative approaches and successes that will impact military programs long into the future.

conventional internal layout with the engine in the back. If the fan and its hardware were removed, the area behind the cockpit would accommodate a large fuel tank, and the result would be a fighter with an unusually large internal fuel fraction and hence an excellent range. For the USAF, one of the lessons of Desert Storm was that it needed more range in its fighters if it was not going to fight in Central Europe. The DARPA planners started to see the ASTOVL aircraft as a potential replacement for the F-16 and, by the time it issued contracts to Lockheed and McDonnell Douglas in March 1993, the project was not only ASTOVL but also the Common Affordable Lightweight Fighter (CALF). The aircraft was to be designed and demonstrated in both STOVL and conventional takeoff and landing (CTOL) forms.

Two other companies joined the CALF effort in the subsequent 12 months, using independent research and development funds. Boeing had started looking at future fighters as soon as the ATF award went to Lockheed — with Boeing as a major team member — in April 1991. Having placed fourth in the ATF demonstration/validation contest in 1986, Boeing was determined to establish itself as a prime contractor for fighters. Certain that future budgets would be tight, Boeing focused on low cost. The company concluded that what was needed was a multi-service, multi-purpose fighter with an empty weight close to that of an F-16, a price far lower than the F-22, STOVL capability to replace the Harrier, and a better range than in-service fighters.

Boeing's concentration on cost and simplicity defined the AVX-70 design that emerged from a study of 30 configurations. It was a direct-lift design with no separate lift fan, but would be small and light enough to land vertically without lift augmentation. To minimize weight and accommodate a large fuel load, Boeing selected a delta-wing. Although it did not win either of the DARPA contracts, the company had enough faith in its concept to take part in the ground-test program with its own funds. Like McDonnell Douglas and Lockheed, the company would build a large-scale powered model and test it on a large outdoor rig.

Northrop Grumman announced its intention to bid on CALF in the summer of 1994. The company selected a lift-plus lift/cruise (LPLC) design. It had an F119 fitted with a vectoring nozzle, and a separate lift fan engine in the forward fuselage.

Superfighters

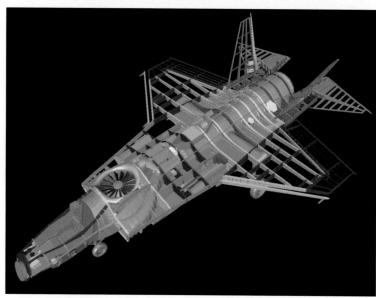

economy with the services having to increase pay to retain key people. The net result was that procurement and research and development funds became very tight. Tactical aircraft procurement almost ceased. Consequently, the USAF and Navy realized that they would need to buy aircraft at much higher rates in the 2000s in order to meet their requirements and, with projected budgets, these would have to be relatively cheap.

Many people thought that JAST would be an undisciplined collection of technology demonstrations and studies but what happened in the first few months of the office's existence was dramatic and unexpected. Under the leadership of Maj. Gen. George Muellner, a fighter pilot who had once commanded the 6513th Test Wing at Area 51 (Groom Lake), the JAST office assembled a massive program. Muellner's vision was of a 'universal fighter' that could cover all of the services' different needs in a largely common airframe. It would be made possible by precision weapons. Like the F-117, it would put two bombs in the right place and would not need a multi-bomb internal load like the A-12, and it would have advanced avionics. New manufacturing and design techniques would make it affordable and it would be based on the CALF designs.

Using the latest computer mission-modeling and campaign-level simulation techniques, the JAST office coordinated a tough session of trading among the three services. The Navy was persuaded to accept a single-engine, single-seat aircraft, after extensive studies showed combat and accidental loss rates would be comparable. The Air Force agreed to accept an aircraft that would be slower and less agile than the F-22 — in fact, not much faster or more maneuverable than the F-16. The result was an aircraft that accomplished the critical elements of the services' missions but was still small enough to form the basis

Rolls-Royce joined the team to work on the lift engine. The design featured an unusual 'hammerhead' wing planform, with a small canard attached to a large fixed leading-edge extension. Northrop did not intend to build a powered model, arguing that the risks of the lift-plus-lift/cruise configuration were small.

Upon the axing of the individual service's future fighter programs in 1993, the Pentagon established a new program called Joint Advanced Strike Technology (JAST), intended to look at weapons, avionics and other technologies for new-generation strike aircraft. Within a few months, a tidy-minded Congress had discovered CALF and transferred it from DARPA to the newly formed JAST office. The new administration's defense policy, it turned out, was defined by several factors. One was the desire to reduce or at least stabilize the budget. On the other hand, the Clinton team also wanted to use the military to support an inconsistently interventionist foreign policy, resulting in a series of expensive overseas deployments. The defense budget was also under pressure from a booming civilian

Lockheed Martin's Preferred Weapon Systems Concept (PWSC) design, submitted in response to the final JORD requirement, closely resembles the CDAs with some exceptions, notably the intakes. Evident in the cutaway is the STOVL's large lift fan assembly immediately behind the cockpit, and the 'roll post' ducts leading from either side of the engine to provide stability in hover. A fuel tank occupies the area taken up by the STOVL lift fan, in the other two versions.

of a practical STOVL aircraft. The industrial implications were enormous. The Marine Corps wanted to replace some 600 older aircraft, the Navy needed 300 aircraft and the USAF could replace almost 2,000 F-16s. Never had such a massive program been created so quickly. Moreover, JAST looked like the only US tactical aircraft program that would start before 2010 and was also being billed as the worldwide replacement for 2,000-plus F-16s and F/A-18s.

Back in 1986, seven companies had submitted proposals for the ATF Dem-Val phase and, by late 1994, four were ready to compete in JAST. Grumman had been acquired by Northrop, General Dynamics had been absorbed by Lockheed (which was itself in the process of merging with Martin-Marietta), and Rockwell had virtually left the military aircraft business. The two companies to be eliminated in 1996 would be out of the picture as combat aircraft 'primes.' As the JAST decision date loomed up, the contractors changed their designs and engaged in a mating dance. Lockheed and McDonnell Douglas had both proposed stealthy canard designs for the DARPA program. Under the area-rule principle, which holds that transonic and supersonic drag are lowest if the designer avoids a sharp increase in cross-sectional area towards the front of the aircraft, the canard was attractive because it moved the wing aft, away

Lockheed Martin looked at a pure delta-wing. At one point, the company was looking at a delta for the USMC, USAF and Royal Navy, and a tailed configuration for the US Navy but the final design echoed the F-22 — with four tails and a cropped delta-wing. One huge advantage of this design was that it drew on the extensive flight-validated database from the F-22 program. Data from the large-scale powered model unveiled in April 1995 and tested at NASA Ames was still applicable. McDonnell Douglas went through even larger changes. Late in 1994, Northrop Grumman agreed to collaborate with McDonnell Douglas and British Aerospace on JAST. The three companies formed a 'dream team' that encompassed all of the western world's STOVL experience, both surviving groups with carrier-based fighter skills, Northrop's stealth technology and Grumman's expertise in all-weather strike systems.

By mid-1995, however, clearly all was not well with the McDonnell Douglas team. McDonnell Douglas announced in June — only a year before the planned down-select date — that its JAST design would use Northrop Grumman's LPLC concept. The nearly completed large-scale powered model of the gas-driven lift fan design was mothballed. LPLC eliminated the coupling between the engine and the fan, and many studies showed that it was the lowest-weight solution. McDonnell

Hover pit testing of the X-35B began at Palmdale on 22 February 2001. On 10 March, the F119-611S power plant was run up to full dry power for the first time in hover configuration. Clearly visible behind the cockpit are the outward-opening spine doors that serve the lift fan.

from the inevitable bulge where the inlet ducts wrapped around the fan bay.

Unlike CALF, though, JAST had to land on a carrier. Such an aircraft must be able to fly slowly in a flat attitude, which implies a generous wing span and effective flaps, and must feature responsive and precise control at low speeds. As Lockheed Martin adapted the canard design to these requirements, the canard became awkwardly big. Also, Lockheed had relocated the JAST program to Fort Worth, where F-16 designer Harry Hillaker had long taught that 'the optimum location for a canard is on somebody else's aircraft.' In 1995, the canard Eurofighter Typhoon was sitting on the ground while its designers wrestled with flight-control problems, and the Saab Gripen's developers were dealing with a rash of handling gremlins. All in all, the Lockheed Martin team felt that there was enough risk in the JAST program without adding a canard to the mix.

Douglas could argue that its design would enter service with a thoroughly proven lift/cruise engine (a standard F119) and that the lift engine was little more complex than Lockheed Martin's lift fan. It had one substantial drawback, however: the Marine Corps logistics community hated the idea of a fighter with two different engines. In 1996, the company unveiled a previously secret, unmanned experimental aircraft called the X-36. It was clearly a cousin of the CALF design but while the latter had small vertical fins and a delta-wing, the X-36 had a swept wing with a kinked trailing edge and no vertical surfaces at all, and used yaw-axis thrust vectoring instead. Its technology was incorporated into the company's final JAST design. Boeing and Lockheed Martin had talked about teaming but neither wanted to give up its own design, so they competed with the McDonnell Douglas team. Boeing's JAST design was bigger than its original AVX-70 but apart from relocated vertical surfaces, on the after-body rather than the wingtips, it changed relatively little.

Also in 1996, the JAST office released a request for proposals for prototypes, with a deadline in early June. Shortly afterwards, the project name was changed from JAST to the Joint Strike Fighter, reflecting the fact it was backed by an

Superfighters

operational requirement. Most people expected Lockheed Martin and McDonnell Douglas would win. McDonnell Douglas had massive experience of STOVL and navy fighters on its side, together with Northrop Grumman's stealth expertise. Add up the total of manned supersonic aircraft, jet fighters and stealth aircraft built by Boeing and the number was zero. Unfortunately, however, it had taken McDonnell Douglas several months to organize its 'dream team', spread as it was from the UK to St. Louis to California. Lockheed Martin's design, with its close relationship to the F-22, looked like a low-risk solution. The McDonnell Douglas design was quite similar but the Boeing proposal was different and definitely riskier. In previous two-track flight demonstration programs, rival

winners had conformed to a pattern — different, with one a low-risk and the other a more adventurous solution. This logic prevailed and Lockheed Martin and Boeing were selected for the next phase of the JSF program in November 1996. McDonnell Douglas, facing the near-extinction of its commercial aircraft business and stunned by its defeat in JSF, negotiated a takeover by Boeing. Its fighter resources, including the ingenious innovators of the Phantom Works, were added to the latter's effort.

The first phase of the JSF program was planned as a four-year effort, starting with the issue of formal contracts in early 1997 and ending with the selection of one team to perform engineering and manufacturing development (EMD), planned for March 2001. There were three main strands of activity within this program. In the most visible part of the project, Lockheed Martin and Boeing each built two Concept Demonstration Aircraft (CDA). The CDAs had three principal tasks. The first was to

prove the design's 'up-and-away' performance characteristics (stealth characteristics were validated by model tests). The second was to demonstrate the low-speed performance required for carrier landings, and the third was to prove that the STOVL concept worked. It was clear the STOVL tests were the most critical and risky area of flight-testing. As a result, teams were required to build two sets of STOVL hardware and to design both of their CDAs so they could be modified into STOVL aircraft.

These were designated in the X-series, in alphabetical order, so that Boeing's JSF was the X-32 (re-using the CALF designation) and the Lockheed Martin aircraft was the X-35. The JSF office deliberately avoided using 'YF' designations in order to emphasize there was no 'fly-off'. There was no commitment to select the better-performing CDA. Ideally, the CDAs would demonstrate that either team's definitive JSF design would work and the Pentagon would then select a winner based on a balance of operational utility and cost. Both team's CDA prototypes were powered by Pratt & Whitney F119 engines, a selection made by default because the F119 is the only flight-rated engine with enough power to do the job, albeit with different and substantial modifications.

The second sector of JSF comprised a variety of technology programs and some elements of this work pre-dated JAST. For instance, the Joint Integrated Subsystems Technology (J/IST) demonstration had its roots in USAF research into electrical actuation for flight controls. Others, including much of the avionics activity, were launched in the early days of JAST when it was realized that their effect on cost was decisive. The third major part of the JSF definition phase was an iterative process in which the customer refined the requirements and the contractors designed their Preferred Weapon System Concept (PWSC). The PWSC had to include the design of an operational JSF, detailed proposals for production and support, and a plan for EMD.

In earlier programs, the customer set the requirement, the contractor tried to meet it and the cost was a by-product of this process. The JSF inverted this process. The cost could and

The Lockheed Martin X-35C (CV demonstrator) made its first flight on 16 December 2000, lifting off from Palmdale and landing at Edwards AFB (both in California) 27 minutes later.

would be controlled independently, and the contractor and customer would agree on what could be designed and built for the money. A cardinal rule was that the cost impact of any change to the requirements had to be fully evaluated. If any change resulted in a cost increase, an equal saving had to be found somewhere else. This trading process took place through a series of Joint Interim Requirements Documents (JIRD). JIRD I was produced in 1995 and focused on size, speed and stealth — the factors that determine the aircraft's shape. JIRD II was issued in June 1997 and looked at major trades between performance, cost and supportability, while JIRD III, released in the

take care of the most severe air-to-air threats. The USAF and US Navy do not require the JSF to be their primary air-to-air fighter, do not need to pay for such a capability and do not want it to be perceived as an alternative to the F-22 or Super Hornet. Although the 'F' stands for fighter, the initial requirement was 70 percent weighted towards air-to-ground missions. The Lockheed Martin X-35, for instance, has a lower thrust/weight ratio and higher wing loading than the F-22 and does not use vectored thrust in flight. Therefore, it will be less agile, will accelerate more slowly and will have less ability (if any) to 'supercruise.' The JSF's standard air-to-air missile is not the

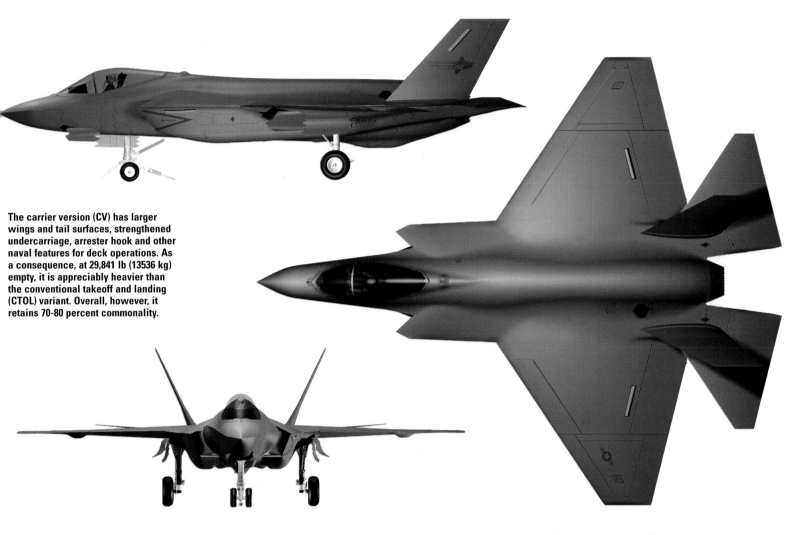

The carrier version (CV) has larger wings and tail surfaces, strengthened undercarriage, arrester hook and other naval features for deck operations. As a consequence, at 29,841 lb (13536 kg) empty, it is appreciably heavier than the conventional takeoff and landing (CTOL) variant. Overall, however, it retains 70-80 percent commonality.

autumn of 1998, addressed a range of issues including supportable stealth technology, adverse weather and night capability, and mission planning. As each was issued, and as design studies yielded new technical answers, the contractors responded with a revised PWSC approach. Finally, a Joint Operational Requirements Document (JORD) was released in early 2000 and formed the basis for the EMD request for proposals issued later in the year. Boeing and Lockheed Martin submitted their proposals in early February 2001.

The Program Office used campaign-level simulations to evaluate how changes to the aircraft would affect the outcome of military operations. The Virtual Strike Warfare Environment (VSWE), a joint-service simulation, was extremely important in managing the trade-offs made through JIRD. Some of the key trades made using this process included resolution of the differences between the desire of the US Navy and USAF to carry a 2,000-lb (907-kg) bomb, and the Marine Corps' unwillingness to pay for that capability in other areas. The issue of whether and how the JSF should carry a gun was settled in the same way. However, these trades have not affected the three key concepts that have underpinned the JSF requirement from the beginning. The first is the assumption that other aircraft will

AIM-9X Sidewinder, but the AIM-120 AMRAAM — a weapon better suited to self-defense than 'dogfighting.' In Lockheed Martin's basic design, the missile locations are not even suitable for an AIM-9X, because the airframe blocks much of the seeker's field of view, although external wingtip AIM-9 stations are an option. The second principle of the requirement is first-day stealth, which allows the aircraft to perform its first missions as a stealth aircraft, with a limited weapon load, and then carry more ordnance as the campaign continues and defenses are beaten down. In this way, the JSF can be stealthy and yet deliver enough weapons to handle the expected number of targets. Both designs incorporate four large-capacity external hardpoints for extra fuel and weapons.

The third key concept is that the Pentagon expects to have retired its dumb bombs by the time the JSF enters service. The type's least accurate weapons will be standard Boeing GBU-31/32 Joint Direct Attack Munitions (JDAM) with an accuracy of 33 ft (10 m). By the time the aircraft enters service, a low-cost precision seeker (such as DAMASK, being developed at the US Navy's China Lake center and based on the same infrared/IR sensor now being fitted to Cadillacs) should also be available. As a result, a small JSF weapon load should

Superfighters

be as effective in terms of destruction as that caused by a much larger load of unguided weapons.

Lockheed Martin's design 'flew' the low-risk banner and, six months after the CDA source selection, both major partners in the defeated McDonnell Douglas team — Northrop Grumman (with its carrier experience) and British Aerospace (with its STOVL knowledge) — joined the X-35 program. While the project was run by Lockheed Martin Tactical Aircraft Systems (LMTAS) at Fort Worth, the prototypes were built by the Skunk Works at Palmdale. The X-35A CTOL prototype was the first to fly, on 24 October 2000. It completed its first series of flights in late November, and then returned to Palmdale where it was modified into the STOVL X-35B. The carrier-based X-35C is structurally identical apart from a 'picture-frame' structure that increases its wing area, and larger tail surfaces.

The X-35 is clearly a cousin to the F-22. The basic aerodynamics are similar and the two aircraft take the same approach to stealth, with a combination of flat and curved surfaces and a sharp chine around the perimeter of the airframe. The main differences between the two aircraft (apart from size and the single engine) are the X-35's new 'diverterless' inlet, with a bump on the inner wall rather than a splitter plate, and the axisymmetrical nozzle. The inlet was developed under a USAF program and tested in 1996 on an F-16. The bump works in conjunction with a swept-forward inlet lip, creating a local pressure rise that deflects the turbulent boundary layer upwards and downwards so that it spills past the inlet lips. Both the USAF and US Navy versions feature a low-observable axisymmetrical nozzle with a serrated aft edge, which is lighter and less expensive than the two-dimensional exhaust on the F-22. Unlike the latter, the X-35 does not use thrust vectoring in up-and-away flight. The JSF also lacks the Raptor's 'cheek' missile bays. Instead, it has two bays to the left and right of the keel, each with two doors. The inner door in each bay carries a launch rail for an AIM-120 AMRAAM. The outer door is slightly bulged on the Navy and USAF versions to accommodate a 2,000-lb (907-kg) weapon. The wing includes four hard-points rated at 5,000 lb (2268 kg) inboard and 2,500 lb (1134 kg) outboard.

The STOVL version is externally identifiable by a slight bulge in the spine and a shorter canopy, and both X-35s have these features because the X-35C can be converted to a STOVL aircraft if necessary. The lift fan, developed by Allison Advanced Development Company, is located behind the cockpit in a bay with upper and lower clamshell doors. It is driven by a composite driveshaft connected to the compressor face of the engine by a computer-controlled clutch using the same technology as carbon brakes. The shaft ends in a single gear that engages a facing pair of horizontal ring gears, each of which drives one of the two counter-rotating fan stages. The CDA system has a retractable D-section nozzle that deflects its thrust aft for transition and short takeoff whereas the production

aircraft will have an array of cascades, which weigh less. The lift fan supports almost half the aircraft's weight in hovering flight, producing 18,000 lb thrust (80.1 kN), and doubles the mass flow of the propulsion system — boosting its thrust by 44 percent.

Air from the engine fan feeds two roll-control ducts that extend out to the wing fold line. The core exhaust flows through a 'three-bearing' nozzle, developed by Rolls-Royce along the pattern of the Yak-141 exhaust. It has three oblique rotary joints that revolve in opposite directions to deflect the nozzle from the fully aft position to 15° ahead of the vertical. Another distinguishing feature of the STOVL version is an auxiliary inlet for the main engine, above the fuselage aft of the lift fan. This STOVL system has some inherently useful features. The drive shaft literally extracts energy from the rear of the aircraft and converts it into vertical thrust at the front, balancing the aircraft in hovering flight. Another advantage of this

system, compared to a direct-lift system such as that employed by the Harrier or Boeing X-32, is that pitch and roll control can be accomplished by modulating the thrust of the four lift 'posts' rather than by bleeding air (and power) from the engine to a dedicated control system. Valves in the roll ducts open and close differentially for roll control. In the pitch axis, energy can be switched between the engine exhaust nozzle and the fan by adjusting the main engine's exhaust nozzle and the inlet guide vanes on the fan. Total thrust and efficiency remain unchanged. Both STOVL systems have an impressive list of moving parts that must operate successfully in order to recover the aircraft in a vertical landing. However, Lockheed Martin took the lead with a mechanical transmission, four lift nozzles (two of which vector in hovering flight to provide control) and two large auxiliary inlets. All these apertures are covered by doors, most of which operate in a hot, noisy, high-vibration environment. All the doors must close with a near-perfect fit in order not to compromise the fighter's stealth characteristics and, if those characteristics are compromised, the pilot will not be aware of it. Problems with Lockheed Martin's clutch system, encountered early in 2000 and apparently solved by mid-summer, were hardly unexpected. The company made a change in the control system to provide smoother clutch engagements.

As the Lockheed Martin design evolved, the differences between the three variants were accentuated. In the original concept, the different service variants were to be externally identical, out to the edges of the fixed-wing structure. The Navy version would have larger leading-edge and trailing-edge flaps, longer outer wings and larger horizontal stabilizers. However, the CV version now has a different wing structure — its wing being larger than that of an F-15 and 34 percent bigger than the CTOL/STOVL wing. Lockheed Martin now feels that its choice of a tail-aft design has been vindicated because the designers have been able to provide the CV version with a much larger wing, while maintaining the same wing-body geometry. On a delta-wing (or the Boeing design's highly tapered trapezoidal shape) any attempt to increase span would have tended to lengthen or thicken the root, or driven the

Lockheed Martin's crowning glory was marked by the two 'Mission X' flights that mimicked typical operational sorties. Starting with a short takeoff in STOVL mode, the aircraft went supersonic before returning to make a vertical landing.

designer to a lower sweep angle. That would have changed the wing's lift characteristics and may not have matched the center of gravity of the body.

However, Lockheed Martin's decision has come with a cost. Its own figures show that the STOVL version of its JSF has an internal fuel capacity of just 13,316 lb (6040 kg) that yields a not-very-exciting internal fuel fraction of 0.30. This is on the low side for a supersonic fighter with an augmented low-bypass turbofan. Most aircraft with fuel fractions on that scale routinely operate with external fuel tanks. In a sense, this is of limited importance, however, as the variant's primary customer, the USMC, is mainly interested in close support and battlefield interdiction missions where LO is less important. The CTOL and CV versions, with a large fuel tank in place of the lift fan, have much higher fuel fractions.

To keep costs down the CDA aircraft employed many components and systems from other aircraft in their construction, and many systems do not reflect the considerably more advanced items planned for the PWSC. For instance, the cockpits of both aircraft have small multifunction displays rather than the giant screens planned for production, and have head-up displays (HUD) instead of the planned helmet-mounted displays (HMD). State-of-the-art 'power-by-wire' electric controls are not fitted, the CDAs retaining traditional hydraulic systems. No radars are fitted, and avionics are entirely unrepresentative of the PWSCs.

Besides a versatile airframe, the JSF program has an array of supporting programs working on technologies for needed systems. Both Pratt & Whitney and General Electric have been working on quite different designs for production engines. While the Boeing design called for a larger fan and mass flow,

Following initial trials at Edwards AFB, the X-35C spent a month at NAS Patuxent River, Maryland, where sea-level conditions more closely reflect those encountered in naval service. The tail graphic was designed to reflect the shape of the JSF's forward fuselage.

and a two-dimensional nozzle integrated into the fighter's afterbody structure, the engine for the Lockheed aircraft has a smaller fan. Its turbine is sized to drive the forward lift fan, and has to be integrated with two different final nozzles — a stealth nozzle for the CV and CTOL variants, and a vectoring nozzle for the STOVL aircraft.

The engine for the JSF has a prognostic feature built into its control system, intended to predict failures before they damage the engine or imperil the aircraft. This comprises sensors that monitor pressures, temperatures, vibration and stresses in the engine and sample the exhaust stream for metal particles. Combined with a computer model of the engine and with a detailed history of its use, this should allow signs of incipient failures to be identified. One respect in which the F-22's F119 engine will foreshadow the JSF's engine is in its attention to maintainability. The F119, for example, is designed so that no small items — filler caps, fasteners or clamps — separate from the engine during routine maintenance. Push-open ports are used to replenish and inspect fluids, and clamps are designed so they stay on the engine. Safety wires (which prevent threaded connectors from rotating) are banished in favor of

spider-shaped spring clips that do the same job.

GE has been heading the design of the alternate engine, the JSF120-FX, since 1996 but has not been allowed to say very much about it. The JSF120-FX core was tested in August 2000, and a full-scale prototype engine for the winning design should be completed and ground-tested in 2003. EMD should start in the same year and the alternate engine should be available for the fourth production lot of JSFs, for delivery in 2010. However, it appears that the new engine will only be loosely based on the original F120 (which was developed to power the F-22, but beaten by the F119) and will use the same core as an advanced version of the best-selling CFM56 commercial engine.

In 1998, the company and its French partner, Snecma, announced they were starting a program called TECH56, aimed at renewing the technology of the CFM56. This would include a new core (the hot section of the engine, comprising the compressor, combustor and high-pressure turbine) with fewer stages and blades. The GE-developed core uses some of the technology developed by GE and AADC under the Pentagon's Integrated High-Performance Turbine Engine

A particular challenge for the designers of the STOVL variant was to develop a platform that is stable and easily maneuvered at very slow speeds, without degrading the high-speed performance of the shape that is, by its very nature, an inherently unstable form.

It is no longer economically feasible for all three US armed services to acquire and maintain nine different 'tacair' platforms, along with all of the different models, blocks and up-grades that have created such huge supply deficits. The JSF addresses multi-service, multirole affordability.

Technology program. GE is also looking at advanced variable-cycle engines requiring no afterburning that could be used for later JSF variants. Pratt & Whitney's JSF engine will be the only engine available on the first 100 or so aircraft. After that the Pentagon's JSF engine buy will be split each year, with the size of each supplier's share determined by an annual competition. New export customers will be able to choose either engine.

A key difference between the two JSFs and the Harrier is the use of fly-by-wire control for the airframe and the propulsion system, with the entire powered lift and propulsion system controlled by computers. This should make the aircraft easier to fly. Both Lockheed Martin and Boeing adopted a similar control scheme. As the aircraft transitions from wing-borne to jet-borne flight, the throttle and stick functions change. The stick controls longitudinal and lateral acceleration while the throttle becomes a vertical speed commander. The transition is largely automated, and the pilot places an HMD cursor over the intended hover point and the aircraft flies to that point. Not surprisingly, propulsion tests have been exhaustive because of the potential for catastrophe if the control software so much as sneezes. Both propulsion systems were assembled in open-air rigs at Pratt & Whitney's West Palm Beach facility, and operated extensively with pilots in the loop — 'flying' system simulations.

While the JSF will not set any new records in weapon load, speed, agility and range, in many respects it is very unusual under the skin. Structures, subsystems and avionics have all been re-invented. The common factor in all these areas is to save money and although joint production will help reduce costs, the battle to meet the cost targets will be won or lost on the details. One of the biggest challenges is achieving low-cost stealth. Although details are veiled by national and competitive security concerns, the JSF is likely to follow the approach taken by the F-22's designers, who have attempted to reduce the very high maintenance costs associated with stealth on earlier aircraft. Gaps and openings in the skin are the biggest cause of high costs in stealth maintenance. Unless a gap is properly sealed, it will interrupt the flow of electromagnetic energy over the skin and cause unwanted and unpredictable radar reflections. Although there are ways to make it cheaper to test and repair breaks in the skin, the first key to affordable stealth is to minimize the number of openings and gaps. One important thrust in the JSF avionics system is to use shared electronic and optical sensor apertures. In the radio-frequency (RF) band, a total of just over 20 antennas should replace almost 60 antennas on the F-22, covering communications, navigation and identification functions with passive and active surveillance. A common set of IR sensors performs targeting, navigation and threat warning functions — eliminating 40 specially designed and treated antenna mountings. The use of large, integrated composite parts eliminates skin gaps and fasteners, and the JSF will make the greatest possible use of the weapon bays and landing gear bay doors to provide access to the most frequently maintained systems.

Where an access panel is needed, a stealth designer has a choice between two types. A conventional panel is light and inexpensive but has to be sealed with tape, caulk or putty after it is removed. Engineers call this 'breaking the LO bubble.' After the panel is re-installed, the seal has to be checked to make sure the aircraft is still stealthy. The alternative is a frequent-access panel, which can be opened and closed easily. However, it must be rigid and fitted with a secure latching system and a special gasket, so that it will not cause a physical or electromagnetic discontinuity in the surface when it is closed. Like the F-22, the JSF will use fewer different kinds of LO material than the B-2 and F-117, where LO goals were paramount and designers tended to select the material best suited to a particular location.

LO development for the JSF has been undertaken using models constructed to a standard of detail and fidelity unprecedented at such an early stage in a program before EMD. This has included testing at sophisticated facilities capable of

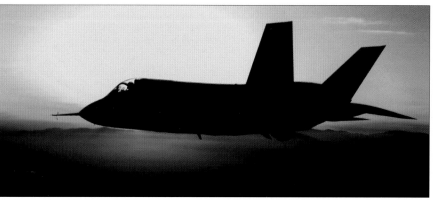

gathering and analyzing complex RCS information, including detailed modeling of small components and accurate assessments of the RCS-reduction performance of different types of radar-absorbent material (RAM). Lockheed Martin has aimed at LO systems that are damage-tolerant, and conducted tests that showed them to be combat-ready and repairable in a single shift. Some of these materials are likely to take the form of appliqué sheets rather than paints. Lockheed Martin and 3M have been working on this technology since the mid-1990s. The adhesive-backed polymer sheets — which can be colored with pigments or treated with IR or RAM — are pre-cut to fit the aircraft and can be removed and replaced easily.

Internally, the JSF is pioneering another major change in technology stemming indirectly from work under the Star Wars program in the 1980s that saw development of new ways to convert and control electrical power in lightweight, solid-state packages. This technology now makes it practical to use electrical power to replace hydraulic systems. Electrical wiring

Superfighters

requires less maintenance than hydraulic lines and is less vulnerable to combat damage. Lockheed Martin led the inflight demonstration of electric technology, and modified the hard-worked Advanced Fighter Technology Integration (AFTI) F-16 prototype as the first fighter to fly with all its primary flight controls both signaled and powered by electricity, and with no mechanical backup. These tests were completed in early 2001.

A team led by the company, and including Honeywell, Northrop Grumman, Hamilton Sundstrand and Pratt & Whitney has demonstrated the Thermal/Energy Management Module (T/EMM), the core of J/IST. The Honeywell T/EMM is an integrated turbine system, on a common shaft, which provides auxiliary and emergency electrical power, air for pressurization, and cooling for cockpit and avionics. Its unique feature is that it can operate in three modes. To start the aircraft or provide power on the ground, it operates as a gas turbine

Possessing stealth and precision bombing qualities, a large weapons bay, defensive missiles, advanced sensors and a datalink, the JSF should be an effective striker. While designed as a multirole aircraft, the emphasis is on air-to-ground capabilities.

APU using outside air. In flight, the T/EMM is driven by engine bypass air and provides electrical power and cool air. In the event of an engine flame-out or stall, the T/EMM is driven by compressed air stored in an onboard reservoir, maintaining essential power to the aircraft's controls until the pilot can get the JSF pointed downhill and perform an air-start. The T/EMM replaces the air-conditioning system, auxiliary generator, APU and emergency power unit (on the F-16, the last-named uses hydrazine and is a logistical nuisance) with a single system.

Potentially, the T/EMM and the more-electric systems can simplify the propulsion system. A modern fighter engine has a 'tower shaft' which links the engine shaft to an airframe-mounted accessory drive — a compact package of gears, clutches and constant-speed drives that, in turn, drives the hydraulic pumps, electrical generators and the environmental control system (ECS) compressor. The only JSF system mechanically connected to the engine may be the primary starter-generator.

The JSF uses new structural technology to reduce both weight and cost — a radical change from earlier advanced composite materials, which saved some weight but cost the earth to produce. Lockheed Martin uses fiber-placement technology to build the inlet duct, building the complex component directly from carbon-fiber tape, wound around a mandrel and simultaneously impregnated with epoxy matrix material by a robotic tool. Components which would usually have been made from many sheet metal parts and innumerable fasteners are produced by high-speed machining, instead.

The tools and materials that are used to build an aircraft are

only half the cost battle, though. The cost of manufacturing and assembling an aircraft is built into every part, and the way in which it is designed. Lockheed Martin has worked with IBM and Dassault to expand Dassault's CATIA computer-aided design system into a 'virtual development environment'. The goal is 100 percent digital prototyping. As the designer works on a component, the effects of a design decision on part manufacture, assembly and support are simulated on the computer before any physical work is done. By simulating all these effects, it is possible to calculate the impact of a design decision on life-cycle cost. Advanced CAD techniques are key to building three distinct JSF versions on the same production line. The designer's dilemma is that each version encounters different structural loads. If the airframes are identical, and all parts are strong enough to take the load imposed by the heaviest version, the other variants will be too heavy. On the other hand, if the aircraft are different the benefits of commonality are lost.

By the middle of August 2001, all test data and final bids were submitted to the Program Office. The decision as to which contractor would proceed to EMD with its design in the 'winner take all' contest was announced on 26 October, in favor of Lockheed Martin. The so-called 'down select' was based on a host of factors — cost, maintainability, manufacturing proposals, growth potential and through-life supportability being as important as flight characteristics. It is not even the case, necessarily, that the winner is the best-performing aircraft. Win or lose, what both companies have achieved in the competition is nothing less than remarkable. Supersonic STOVL is now a reality and the project has done a great deal to focus attention on how to build combat aircraft at lower cost, without sacrificing efficiency. Key technologies such as simpler composite structures, integrated power subsystems and commercially based avionics are being brought to maturity much faster in the JSF program than otherwise might have been the case. That said, it is imperative the program now stays on track.

The USAF requires its JSFs to have a range of at least 590 nm (1093 km; 679 miles) and desires a range of 690 nm (1278 km; 794 miles), while the USMC will settle for a lesser range. However, the US Navy will require an equal or greater range than the USAF for its version. Maximum level flight speed must be at least Mach 1.5 and maneuverability must be comparable to that of current aircraft. The Navy was initially the most demanding customer in terms of stealth because its JSFs will be the only stealthy aircraft it will have to penetrate tough defenses with minimal support. In contrast, the USAF expects to have B-2s, F-117s and strike-configured F-22s for this mission. As the program has evolved, however, USAF and Navy requirements have become more closely aligned, and the USMC's primary mission is visual close air support (CAS) with external weapons, so stealth is less important. Still, the primary features of the design that make stealth attainable — such as shape and internal stores — are inherent to the basic structure of the aircraft, and have to be included for all versions.

By the time the first EMD aircraft flies in mid-2005, the Pentagon will be committed to the type. If the JSF's date for entry into service slips, the Marine Corps could run out of fighters and the USAF's fighter force will dwindle. Thus, the technical risks involved in the program must be under control before EMD starts. JSF is inventing breakthroughs across the board in cost/performance relationships, including dramatic reductions for avionics and LO systems. However, unlike any previous military aircraft, the JSF cannot achieve its goals at twice the advertised cost and be considered a success.

FLIGHT-TESTING

Boeing was the first of the competitors to fly, when the company's chief test pilot took the aircraft aloft from Palmdale on 18 September 2000, getting air under the wheels for the first time at 7:53 PDT. The second flight was undertaken five days later, and the third flight was made on the same day the rival X-35A made its first flight. Despite being beaten out of the start-gate by

Some have jokingly referred to the STOVL as a 'collection of doors flying in close formation.' While the forward spine doors allow air to the lift fan, the aft set covers the auxiliary intake for the engine.

Boeing by over a month, the Lockheed Martin team pursued an aggressive flight-test schedule from the outset, setting an incredible pace which reached up to six flights a day in the latter stages, and culminated in a total of 110 flights for the CV/CTOL phases. The company claimed many records for new aircraft testing.

Following a series of engine tests with the aircraft held back by cables, Chief Test Pilot Tom Morgenfeld began taxi trials in the X-35A (CTOL version) on 13 October 2000. Such trials would normally occupy several weeks or months, but were completed on 21 October. On 24 October, an incredible 11 days after taxiing began, Morgenfeld positioned the X-35A at the end of Palmdale's runway at the start of its first flight. The time was 9:06 PDT. After about 30 minutes in the air, the aircraft landed at Edwards AFB, California, home of the Air Force Flight Test Center and also the site of the initial JSF test effort. The flight was far from just a positioning cycle, however. During the sortie many test points were accomplished, the aircraft flying a series of figure-eights at 10,000 ft and 250 kts to assess basic handling.

Morgenfeld is a veteran of the Lockheed Skunk Works, having been a member of the F-117 and YF-22 test teams. He flew the X-35A during its next three flights, opening up the flight envelope and testing basic systems — being joined in this work by the US Air Force's Lt. Col. Paul Smith, who took the X-35A aloft on 3 November. As well as basic handling and systems tests, the early flights tested aspects of the propulsive system, with throttle movements and afterburner light-ups being a regular feature. Meanwhile, the envelope was expanded to Mach 0.85 and an altitude of 25,000 ft.

As the handling, control and basic performance were checked out, formation flying began, enabling instrumentation to be verified and precise handling to be measured. With confidence in the handling established, Smith performed a series of inflight-refuelings on the 10th flight, clocking up a 2-hour 50-minute sortie in the process. Morgenfeld was particularly impressed by the refueling characteristics of the X-35A, indicating it was far and away the easiest tanking he had done. He indicated the X-35 is very stable in position. Refueling (using the 412th Test Wing's test flight-rated NKC-135 tankers), envelope expansion, further flight handling tests and systems tests occupied the next flights,

Test pilots were impressed with the X-35's 'carefree' handling qualities and docile performance 'in the circuit.' Good behavior around the boat was of particular concern to the US Marine Corps and US Navy, which demanded stringent requirements, as was ease of air-to-air refueling. While Lockheed Martin's demonstrator took to the air for the first time almost a month after Boeing's first flight, the LM team undertook an incredibly intensive program that validated the X-35's performance over an amazingly short period of time.

Superfighters

so that by 14 November all the test points required to demonstrate the JSF in the CTOL configuration had been completed. This had been achieved in just over 14 hours of flying, accumulated in 16 flights spread over just 22 days. During this period the first Marine Corps pilot, Maj. Art Tomasetti, flew the aircraft on the 225th anniversary of the USMC's establishment.

With the main objectives accomplished, a further 10 flights were scheduled to expand the flight envelope and continue the technical risk-reduction program. More refuelings were completed, and the aircraft was taken up to 34,000 ft. The maximum angle of attack achieved was 20°, while the airframe was loaded with 5g during maneuvers. 18 November was 'Brit' day. Two British pilots, RAF Sqn. Ldr. Justin Paines and BAE Systems' Simon Hargreaves, took their first flights in the X-35A on that date. Capping a successful program, Morgenfeld flew the X-35A to Mach 1.05 on 21 November to prove the supersonic handling, and on the next flight undertook some field carrier landing practices (FCLP) to prepare for the X-35C test program. With these objectives achieved, Morgenfeld flew the X-35A back to Palmdale on 22 November, on its 27th and last flight in CTOL configuration.

On arrival, the aircraft was whisked back into the Skunk Works workshop where engineers prepared to fit the lift fan assembly and thrust-

While the F-35 will be a single-engine fighter, unlike its 'sister' platform the twin-engine F-22, design similarities are striking. Radar-defeating lessons learned from the Raptor program have clearly influenced the look of the JSF. Given that the JSF will not be a particularly fast jet, stealth will be crucial to its attack mission.

vectoring nozzle for the STOVL tests. This was undertaken during 28-29 December, after which the aircraft was redesignated the X-35B. On 22 February 2001, the aircraft was back outside and strapped to the hover pit to begin testing the STOVL propulsion system. By 10 March it was running at full vectored power.

Having been without an aircraft in the air for nearly three weeks, Lockheed Martin rejoined the flight-test fray on 16 December 2000, when X-35C project test pilot, Joe Sweeney, lifted off from Palmdale at 9:23 PST in the CV demonstrator. Almost half an hour later he touched down at Edwards AFB to initiate the CV test phase. Sweeney was a Navy A-7 flier before becoming a seasoned test pilot. After leaving the Navy he joined General Dynamics and flew many of the F-16 test programs. Had the A-12 stealth attack project gone ahead, Sweeney was the pilot nominated to perform the first flight.

The X-35C flew again three days later, with Sweeney at the helm once more. During this flight he flew a number of approaches in preparation for the coming FCLP work. The first flights from Edwards were aimed at proving the handling and systems of the aircraft before carrier approaches could begin in earnest. The early flights were undertaken not just by Sweeney

but the US Navy's Lt. Cdr. Brian Goszkowicz, as well. FCLPs began on 3 January 2001, and like the Boeing team, the X-35C team initially used a Fresnel lens system set up at the side of the runway at Edwards. Many of the subsequent missions from there ended with FCLPs being flown. On 23 January two more pilots took their first flights in the Navy version: Tom Morgenfeld and Paul Smith, who between them had performed the bulk of the X-35A test work. During their flights the X-35C's compatibility with the KC-10 tanker was checked out. A week later, Tomasetti of the USMC flew the aircraft, and two days after that he took the aircraft for its longest flight to date. This was a three-hour, cross-country to prepare it for its forthcoming two-leg trip to NAS Patuxent River in Maryland, where it would conduct simulated carrier landings. On 2 February, the RAF's Justin Paines flew a 1-hour 30-minute sortie.

At around 2,000 ft elevation, Edwards AFB is not an ideal place to conduct carrier evaluations. At 'Pax,' also home to the US Navy's flight-test organization, it could operate at sea level. Over a period of two days the aircraft was flown there from Edwards, night-stopping at Lockheed Martin's Fort Worth plant. It was the first transcontinental crossing by an 'X-plane' and was accomplished smoothly, with all test systems up and running one working day after the aircraft arrived. However, initial trials there were hampered by poor weather and, later, the schedule encountered a shortage of tankers. However, during the month the X-35C spent at 'Pax' it flew 33 times and introduced two more pilots to the aircraft, including Lt. Cdr. Greg Fenton, who recorded the type's 100th FCLP on 1 March. During a hectic final week, the FCLP total was pushed to 250 with the aircraft flying up to six times a day.

Although envelope expansion continued, carrier suitability was the backbone of the 'Pax' trial program, with Navy landing signals officers (LSO) controlling and monitoring the FCLP approaches. The aircraft was deliberately flown outside the standard approach parameters to monitor its behavior under corrective control inputs. Importantly, the X-35C proved that it could approach with full control inside the US Navy's specified approach speed limits. Pilots and LSOs alike were impressed with the aircraft's characteristics, citing in particular the precision, smoothness and predictability of control inputs. Sweeney commented that he was not sure he had flown an airplane on the ball that was so precise or required less workload of the pilot — and that he would have no hesitation 'taking it to the ship tomorrow.' On 11 March the Lockheed Martin X-35C completed its test schedule at 'Pax,' bringing to an end the CTOL/CV portion of the Joint Strike Fighter flight-test program.

The flights by both the Lockheed Martin and Boeing CTOL and CV prototypes were, in themselves, of moderate technological significance. The crucial tests came when the companies had to demonstrate the short takeoff and vertical landing (STOVL)

features of their designs. In 40 years of design and demonstration, no company had previously shown a practical supersonic STOVL fighter. The nearest attempt was the Yakovlev Yak-141 fighter demonstrator that used a STOVL system the JSF program rejected in 1996.

Before STOVL flight trials began, both Boeing and Lockheed Martin had run their STOVL demonstrators (Boeing X-32B and Lockheed Martin X-35B) to full power in vertical flight mode, but only when fully tethered over a hover pit. Flight-testing required the demonstration of safe and predictable vertical flight, and the ability to transition between wing-borne and jet-borne flight. One should not dismiss the enormity of the task facing the two teams. Despite the experience gained by the US and its UK partner in STOVL operations with the Harrier family, the JSF competitors were breaking new ground in many technological areas. Furthermore, the STOVL capability had to be achieved with no discernible penalty to the supersonic performance of the CTOL/CV versions.

The three-bearing main engine nozzle rotates downwards for hovering — the angle being changeable from the horizontal to forward of the vertical. Subtle changes in the thrust angle and the lift fan, further forward, allow the aircraft to maneuver fore and aft during the hover, while differential thrust settings of the fan and nozzle provide pitch attitude control.

STOVL tests carry an added element of risk. Unlike traditional flight-testing, in which speeds and altitudes gradually increase and envelope expansion takes place at high altitude, STOVL testing involves deceleration — and consequently shrinking aerodynamic control authority — at decreasing altitudes. The aircraft is flying more slowly and lower as it enters

Edwards AFB was the initial destination for both the Boeing X-32 and Lockheed Martin X-35, when they made their maiden flights from Palmdale. Preliminary flight-testing was carried out at the base — home to the Air Force Flight-Test Center (AFFTC) and its 412th Test Wing.

— the lift fan. This offers two major advantages over the direct-lift concept employed by Boeing. Firstly, it greatly improves the thrust recovery from the engine, and secondly it avoids many of the problems caused by hot exhaust gases re-entering the engine.

Both of Boeing's X-32s were built in the former Rockwell facility at Palmdale in California, and it was from this airfield that Dennis O'Donoghue made the first, conventional rolling takeoff in the X-32B on 29 March 2001. After 50 minutes, he landed at Edwards AFB, where a few test flights took place

the flight regime where the aerodynamic environment is influenced by the interaction between the ambient air and the exhaust flow — some 400 to 660 lb (180-300 kg) of heated and energized air per second. This is a little-understood area where computer projections are not definitive. Moreover, as Harrier experience has shown, loss of control at low altitude can rapidly place the aircraft in an attitude where safe ejection is impossible. In jet-borne flight at 100 ft (30 m) altitude, the pilot is unwise to wait too long to see whether an anomaly will resolve itself.

It is interesting to note that the three pre-1996 JSF competitors had chosen three different propulsion concepts for their STOVL aircraft. As stated, Boeing employed the direct-lift concept, as proven in the Harrier family, while the rejected Northrop/McDonnell Douglas design employed the LPLC concept used by the Yak-38 and VAK 191. Lockheed Martin opted for a completely different tack, and one which had not hitherto been employed

thereafter. On 16 April the aircraft completed the first transitions from conventional to STOVL mode, and back again, albeit at altitude. Lockheed Martin moved cautiously to a first flight. Unlike Boeing, which chose a fly-then-hover approach, it elected to begin flight-tests with vertical takeoffs.

As previously indicated, tests first got underway over a hover pit, which consists of a metal grate beneath which is a chamber. The latter draws off exhaust gases and cold fan air, allowing an aircraft to mimic hovering without leaving the ground. The hover pit outlet doors can be opened or closed to simulate hovering in and out of ground effect. Initial trials began with the X-35B firmly rooted to the grate by means of special undercarriage boots, which not only restrained the aircraft, but also measured the lift forces.

Further hover pit testing without the wheel restraints, but employing weight restraints instead, culminated in the first full hover in July. At the controls was Simon Hargreaves of BAE Systems. After more such flights, the X-35B took off conventionally for the trip to Edwards, the site for the remainder of the flight-test program. It should be noted that both Edwards and Palmdale are in the California desert, about 2,500 ft (760 m) above sea level, and some tests took place in air temperatures as high as 96°F. Even in these hot-and-high conditions, the X-35B hovered easily on less than full throttle. Furthermore, during these tests the aircraft was successfully hover-landed at 34,000 lb (15422 kg), twice the weight of a 'legacy' STOVL like the AV-8B.

While hovering and wing-borne flight had been mastered, the big test came on 9 July when the first airborne transition from STOVL to CTOL mode was undertaken. Then, on 16 July, Hargreaves brought the aircraft in from wing-borne flight to a vertical landing, something that was repeated three days later by Paines.

On 20 July the Lockheed Martin team achieved its primary goal — 'Mission X'. This demonstrated the standard modus operandi of the aircraft, beginning with a STOVL-mode, short running takeoff; transition to CTOL mode for a supersonic dash; and then transition to STOVL for a vertical landing. Tomasetti flew the mission. Another 'Mission X' was flown on 26 July by Hargreaves, who also added a refueling cycle to the mission. On 30 July the X-35B completed its flight program with all goals completed.

The first aerial refueling hook-ups were undertaken by the USAF's Lt. Col. Paul Smith during the X-35's 10th flight on 7 November 2000, with tanking provided by a 412th Test Wing test-flight-rated NKC-135E. In all, four hook-ups were made at an altitude of 23,000 ft (7010 m). This represented an important element in the early envelope-expansion program for the CTOL variant, which was completed on 22 November 2000 with the aircraft's 27th flight.

AVIONICS

Avionics account for as much as one-third the cost of a fighter, so JSF cost goals give the contractors no option but to find ways to make electronic systems less costly. Broadly speaking, the JSF goal is to take the capabilities of the F-22, add air-to-surface and subtract a lot of weight and a lot of money. Like the F-22, the JSF will have a centralized system in which most avionics functions, such as mission management and signal processing, reside in an integrated core processor (ICP), a powerful battery

The JSF will be fitted with a centralized avionics system built around a powerful battery of computers known as an integrated core processor, or ICP. It will handle most mission management and signal processing functions, and is likely to take the form of 'plug and play' modules that will have built-in redundancy and offer ease of maintenance.

of computers. As with the F-22, the ICP is likely to comprise a backplane that provides power, cooling and data connections for easily changed snap-in modules.

The main difference will be the emphasis on open architecture and the use of commercial standards. The goal is to design the ICP so the modules can use whatever processors the commercial market can supply, as JSFs are built and upgraded. Not only are these commercial chips likely to be cheaper and higher-performing than a custom chip, but a chip developed today for the JSF may not even be available in 2008. The switch to an open systems architecture (OSA) thus will change the way the system is designed and acquired, and how it will be supported and upgraded in service. An OSA is intended to be similar in concept to a Windows-based PC — both hardware and software are defined by unclassified specifications, and any subsystem which meets those specifications should work. This will give avionics developers wide latitude in adding new functions to the JSF system, or in developing new and better substitutes for existing components. One of the main aims of OSA, in fact, is to make it easy to introduce new computer technology into the system, reducing the risk the JSF's avionics will be obsolete before they enter service

As on the F-22, JSF sensors are apertures that act as peripherals to the ICP, which will fuse sensor information and off-board data with database information, before feeding it to the displays. One example of this new technology is the JSF sensor and processing suite. Raytheon, which led this effort on the Boeing CDAs, unveiled some of its JSF avionics work in

mid-2000, including a previously undisclosed link between the JSF and the F/A-18E/F Super Hornet program.

From its El Segundo facility in California, Raytheon produces the Multi-Function Integrated Radio-Frequency System (MIRFS) — the forward-looking active, electronically scanned array (AESA) radar. Teamed with BAE Systems (the former Lockheed Sanders), the company was developing electronic warfare systems for the Boeing entry and working with the primary contractor and Harris on its ICP. Raytheon was also the supplier for two elements of the IR system — the distributed infrared system (DIRS) and the targeting FLIR (TFLIR).

The MIRFS is designed to both detect and jam enemy radars, blurring the boundaries between EW and radar. The unit is reported to be just one-quarter as heavy as an AESA using 1995 technology, and uses advanced transmit/receive modules which cover four radar channels. As well as offering radar modes such as synthetic aperture radar (SAR) and ground-moving target indication (GMTI), it functions as a sensitive passive receiver and a very powerful jammer.

The DIRS comprises six fixed, staring focal plane array (FPA) sensors, each with a 60° x 60° field of view, located around the aircraft behind flush windows and covering a complete spherical field of view. The DIRS has three simultaneous functions. It provides all-round imagery to the pilot's HMD, even enabling a 'through the floor' view that is useful in a vertical landing. It also acts as a missile-warning system (MWS), detecting missile exhaust plumes; and as an IR search and

track (IRST) system, detecting and tracking high-contrast IR targets like aircraft.

The TFLIR is a long-range, high-performance, mid-wave IR staring array with a boresighted laser designator. It is carried in a retractable belly turret and is mechanically steerable throughout the lower hemisphere, so that it can be rotated aft for bomb damage assessment. The ICS, which manages sensor, CNI and display functions, is based on commercial PowerPC chips and uses a commercial software architecture.

Raytheon indicates it has changed the way it develops avionics to avoid systems becoming obsolete by the time EMD is completed. The new approach is based on what was described by a spokesman as 'decoupling technology development from EMD.' The company's intention is to establish a continuous

Superfighters

stream of technological development. When the customer needs a new or improved product, it can be developed quickly using the latest mature technology. As improvements emerge from the technology stream, they are incorporated into upgraded products. Again, the key to this approach is open architecture and compatibility, so that a new technology like a new AESA module can be used on any radar system in the family, for both new and retrofit applications. The first program in this new 'family' concept was that for Boeing's proposed JSF and the F/A-18E/F. The radar for the former and the AESA radar for the latter (due to be installed in aircraft delivered in 2005-06) are the same apart from the array size, having identical transmit/receive (T/R) and processor modules. The TFLIR on Boeing's JSF was a repackaged version of the ATFLIR hardware under development for the Super Hornet. The EW receiver hardware is designed so that it can be

Despite the cutting-edge systems being employed for the F-22 Raptor, in many respects the JSF represents the next generation in avionics — particularly with the new emphasis on open architecture and use of commercially available components designed to help mitigate obsolescence.

Despite the complexity of the STOVL system, during the flight-test program the X-35B demonstrated flawless operation and the ability to generate ample thrust for vertical lift, even in very high ambient temperature conditions. The hot desert climate and thin air that is a feature of Edwards AFB forced both contenders to demonstrate their 'vertical' capabilities under circumstances far more testing than are likely to be faced during carrier-borne operations.

fitted into the Super Hornet's ALR-73(V)3 RWR.

Northrop Grumman, supplying the MIRFS and EO sensors for the Lockheed Martin JSF, has been flying its MIRFS demonstrator since late 1998 — proving technology for simpler T/R modules that can be assembled automatically. It is likely that the AESA and EO suite bear a resemblance to the integrated AESA and IR system Northrop Grumman is developing for the F-16 Block 60, in the same way Raytheon's systems developed

for the Boeing JSF were related to those for the Super Hornet. Lockheed Martin chose Litton Advanced Systems Division to team with BAE Systems on its JSF's passive EW system. The Litton radar warning system uses its long-baseline interferometry processing technology, and is claimed to be comparable in performance to the latest Improved Capability III (ICAP-III) version of the EA-6B Prowler — at half the size, weight and cost. Unlike current fighters, the JSF will be able to identify emitters and locate them quickly and accurately enough to launch a GPS-guided weapon against them, or pass on their locations to another weapon system. From the outset, the JSF program aimed to deliver a multirole AESA for the aircraft at a fraction of the weight and cost of the F-22's radar. According to the Pentagon's Defense Science Board that goal will be achieved.

The Lockheed Martin JSF cockpit will make use of very large-format, flat-panel displays and a binocular, full-color HMD. The latter will provide the pilot with all-round night vision — even 'through the floor' using the distributed IR system. In an environment with several laser threats, it will even make it possible for the pilot to fly with a blacked-out cockpit. Lockheed Martin is working with Vision Systems International on the development.

While Boeing designed its cockpit displays around ruggedized commercial off-the-shelf (COTS) liquid-crystal direct-view displays, Lockheed Martin teamed with Rockwell Collins (the former Kaiser Electronics) to use an 8 x 20-in (20 x 50-cm) projection display. These displays use the same technology as current commercial LCD projectors, with the image generated on a small reflective LCD, manufactured on a single chip, rather than on the screen itself. A light source illuminates the LCD and the display image is projected on to the front screen. Projection displays can be built in a wide range of shapes and sizes using a common 'optical engine,' and improved technology — such as better LCDs — can be shared across a range of different products.

The Lockheed Martin/Rockwell Collins prototype display, combined with the binocular HMD adopted for the JSF, represents the realization of the 'big picture' concept envisioned by McDonnell Douglas cockpit-design expert Gene Adam in the early 1980s. It is a measure of Adam's vision that he predicted, in the mid-1980s, that high-definition TV would drive the development of large-format display technology capable of being integrated into a fighter cockpit.

WEAPON SYSTEMS

While the Boeing X-32 and Lockheed Martin X-35 were very different from each other, both were designed to meet the same basic set of requirements. All three services require an internal load of two JDAMs and two AMRAAMs. The Navy and USAF want to carry the 2,000-lb (907-kg) GBU-31 and the USMC is content with the 1,000-lb (454-kg) GBU-32. In 1998, the three services resolved the vexed question of a gun. The outcome

of vertical thrust, which in turn is limited by the power of a derivative F119 — and that drives the designer to the smallest, lightest possible aircraft. The Navy, however, needs its JSF to carry a heavy load of weapons and fuel, and have a big wing for carrier approaches plus extra structural strength to withstand catapult launches and arrested landings.

Both Boeing and Lockheed Martin have used their airborne avionics test beds to demonstrate the use of both onboard and offboard sensors to acquire and attack targets. In Lockheed Martin's demonstration, at Aberdeen Proving Grounds in

was that the USAF version will have an internal gun, while the USMC and Navy aircraft can be fitted with a gun pack that will fit into the weapon bay, displacing one of the JDAMs.

The JSF is expected to be able to perform precision attacks at night, under the weather and, to some extent, against targets that are obscured by fog, rain or cloud. Due to the fact one of the most serious emerging threats to tactical aircraft are new surface-to-air missiles, the JSF is also expected to provide its pilot with much better awareness of radar-guided threats and missile launches than systems on current aircraft can support. Stealth rules out external pods, so the necessary electronic and optical sensors must be carried internally.

With the same 'basic' aircraft required to meet the operational needs of all three services, factors like stealth, speed, range and weapon loads have to play one against the other, due to the fact that respective missions will differ. The most basic conflict in the JSF design has always been typified by the Marine Corps/Royal Navy STOVL requirement, and the Navy's weapon load and mission radius. The STOVL version needs to land vertically at the end of its mission, with reserve fuel and unused weapons. This limits its empty weight to a proportion

Whereas most modern fighters, like the F-16, carry Sidewinders or other short-range air-to-air missiles for self defense, the JSF is not designed for close-in air combat. Its primary defensive weapon will be the AIM-120 AMRAAM, which its advanced identification and targeting system will allow it to field at longer range. Despite this, plans call for most to be equipped with a gun.

Maryland, a Northrop Grumman Joint STARS detected a set of simulated targets and transmitted their locations to the BAC One-Eleven Cooperative Avionics Test Bed (CATB). This data was used to cue the CATB's electro-optical system on to the target. In a second test, the CATB used its radar in SAR/GMTI mode to acquire and locate the targets.

The X-35B's tail was given smart markings that featured this 'Hat Trick' emblem to signify three successful 'goals' — the X-35A, -35b and -35C. The HATRIK call-sign was also used for the LM test flights. While Boeing chose a 'stop, then down' approach to its STOVL flight-test program, Lockheed Martin adopted the opposite with an 'up, then away' display for its X-35B.

Superfighters

PRODUCTION ORDERS

During the JAST phase, US armed forces' requirements were assessed at close to 3,000 aircraft. At that time, the USAF estimated it would need almost 2,000 of the fighters, while the US Navy was looking for 300 examples. Procurement of the STOVL version is currently stated at 609 for the US Marine Corps, and probably another 150 for the RAF and Royal Navy as Harrier/Sea Harrier replacements. Some of the latter may be

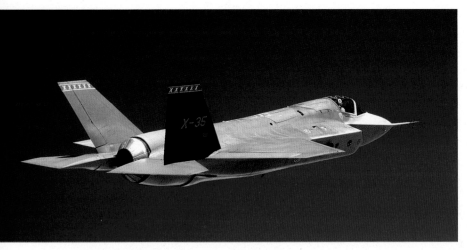

procured as CV aircraft if the UK decides to follow a STOBAR (Short Take-Off But Arrested Recovery) approach for its new large-deck carriers. Current AV-8B operators Italy and Spain are seen, among others, as likely candidates for STOVL JSF acquisitions. No doubt, some of these numbers will change over time, as production is still some years away.

From the outset, the JSF program was envisaged with a sizable export component, which raises a difficult and unresolved issue — technology transfer. Stealth technology was developed under the utmost secrecy in the US and is still subject to tight and specific export restrictions. A secretive committee, the Low Observables/Counter Low Observables Executive Committee (Excom), rules on the export of stealth-related technologies and ensures that no Pentagon agency accidentally permits the export of technology that could compromise another agency's secret program.

There are, in theory, three ways to deal with the LO export issue. One is to deliver the same configuration to all customers. The second is to develop an export version with a lower, but known level of LO, and the third is to delete sensitive materials from export copies altogether. The latter is an unacceptable solution, however. One of the earliest lessons learned about

stealth was that stealth which cannot be measured and maintained in fine detail cannot be exploited tactically. A sanitized JSF would be a non-stealthy aircraft and would have to operate with the same protection, like onboard countermeasures and escort jammers, as today's aircraft.

Early in the JSF program, managers talked about modular stealth technology whereby export JSFs could be delivered without the most sensitive materials but would still be stealthy. However, there are problems with this approach too. Developing a JSF variant with a fully modeled radar cross-section level higher than that of the standard US aircraft would be expensive. It would involve a complete new test program and might result in many components, like antennas, being different. Moreover, it would require different software for the onboard systems that compute the detection range of radar threats against the JSF and display the information to the pilot. Such software would have to be separately supported throughout the fighter's service life. The debate also raises questions as to whether the export version would need an active electronic jammer, unlike the standard model, and whether it was worth giving up maneuverability and AIM-9 capability for a reduced level of stealth.

By late 1998, according to some JSF program officials, the commanders-in-chief (CINC) in charge of US forces around the world had weighed into the debate. Coalition operations, they argued, would be extremely complicated if different partners in the force had JSFs with different stealth characteristics. This would not only complicate tactical planning but the fact that an ally's JSFs were more vulnerable than those belonging to US forces would be politically sensitive. In early 1999, there were indications that the single-configuration option had been chosen. However, this still raises serious security issues. LO treatments require maintenance at the flightline level and will be physically accessible to a large number of people. Furthermore, threat-warning software in every JSF relies on a database that models the fighter's detectability to all known threat radars. An adversary who obtained that software would be able to optimize its defenses against the fighter.

This thorny question remains unresolved. The JSF Program Office says that it does not have the authority to take a decision, and the LO/CLO Excom has not ruled on the issue, with one exception. The UK has full access to JSF stealth technology but with tight firewall restrictions limiting that country's ability to participate in European LO programs. Technology sensitivities aside, several countries have indicated an interest in taking part in the JSF program. The UK is a full partner, and has announced its intention to contribute as much as $2 billion to EMD. By May 2002 Canada and Turkey had joined the project as 'associate partners', while the Dutch government had taken a decision in favor of participation in principle, although this awaited parliamentary ratification, a process delayed by the mass resignation of the Dutch cabinet in March 2002. On 24 May 2002, Denmark announced it would sign on as a Level 3 partner, while other countries, including Australia, Belgium, Italy, Israel, Norway and Singapore, have indicated their interest.

The current schedule calls for the first flight of an engineering and manufacturing development (EMD) aircraft in 2005, with initial production-model deliveries to the USAF and US Marine Corps beginning in 2008. The UK is looking to the JSF as a replacement for its Sea Harriers beginning in 2012 and Harrier GR.7/9s three years later.

Lockheed Martin JSF
(Proposed STOVL Version)
The bulged area aft of the cockpit will house the lift fan, resulting in a reduction in the extent of the canopy.

Superfighters

SPECIFICATIONS / VARIANT PROPOSALS

As of May 2002, no detailed specifications for the Lockheed Martin Joint Strike Fighter had been released.

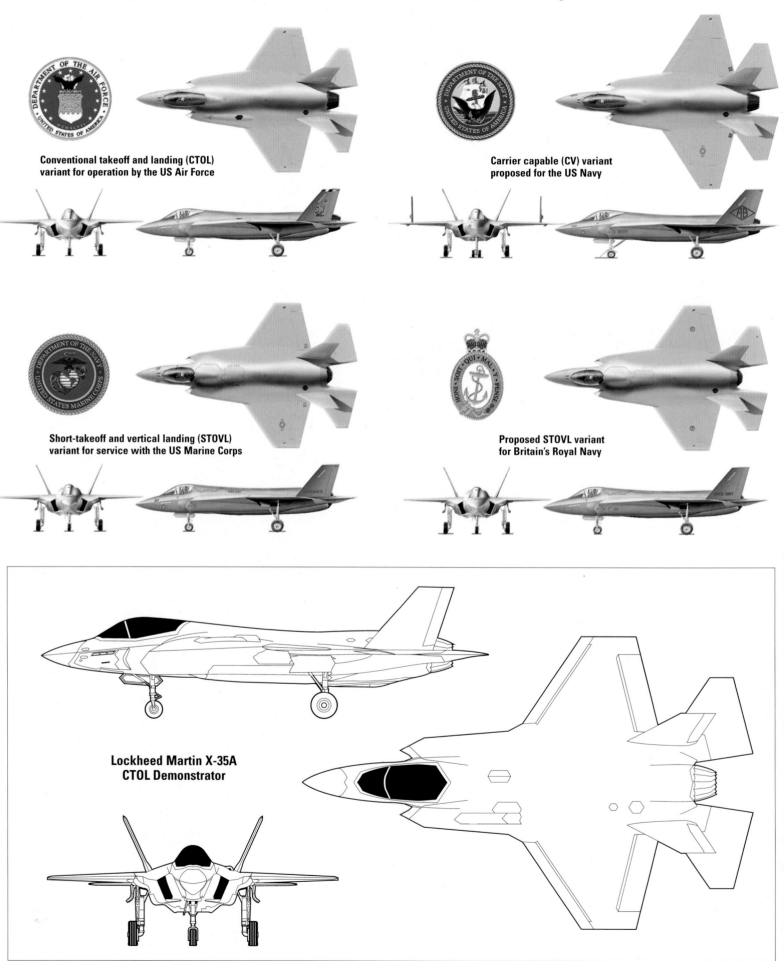

Conventional takeoff and landing (CTOL) variant for operation by the US Air Force

Carrier capable (CV) variant proposed for the US Navy

Short-takeoff and vertical landing (STOVL) variant for service with the US Marine Corps

Proposed STOVL variant for Britain's Royal Navy

**Lockheed Martin X-35A
CTOL Demonstrator**

CHAPTER 3

Eurofighter Typhoon

DEVELOPMENT & FLIGHT-TESTING

When US analysts first studied the new generation of West European advanced fighters — the so-called 'Gray Threat' — the Eurofighter was rated more highly than its competitors and was viewed as being a lethal opponent to any US fighter short of the F-22. However, such comments were viewed by some in the USA as an attempt at scaremongering intended to justify the need for the F-22. Their inference was that the Eurofighter, Rafale and Gripen represented no real threat to late mark F-15s or F-16s. The Eurofighter's credibility was further dented as the program experienced minor technical problems and very major delays, most of them caused by German 'politicking.' It became customary for journalists to use the prefix 'troubled' when describing the Eurofighter program, and in the absence of evidence to the contrary, it became too easy to underrate the aircraft.

Some critics claimed the aircraft's origins in Cold War requirements automatically meant it was somehow conceptually obsolete and irrelevant in the post-Cold War world. Superficially, this may have seemed a compelling argument, though all it really meant was that the aircraft was designed to meet the very worst-case threats, and was thus perhaps over specified for some low-intensity conflicts. RAF demands ensured the Eurofighter was well suited for out-of-area and deployed operations, and will be able to cope with any future threat. Yet perceptions about the Eurofighter's lack of performance and agility did not serve the project well. Early appear-

ances by the aircraft, flying with its flight control system in the reversionary 'emergency' mode, were relatively unimpressive — at the very time successive Farnborough and Paris air shows were dominated by dazzling displays of slow-speed agility by new Russian 'superfighters.' Ultimately, that all changed. The German government came fully on board and, today, the Eurofighter convincingly demonstrates its extraordinary capabilities. Most impartial observers find it hard to argue with the assessment that it is currently the world's most advanced multirole fighter.

While the idea of a multinational fourth-generation European fighter dates back to the 1970s, the program, in its current form, began with Anglo-Italian-German cooperation on an advanced fighter in the early 1980s. A five-nation Outline Staff Target was issued in 1984 that included Spain and France, but France dropped out in 1985 to develop the Rafale. The other nations issued a European Staff Requirement in December 1985 and launched full-scale development in 1988. The industrial partners — BAe (now BAE Systems), DASA (now EADS-Deutschland), Alenia and CASA (now EADS-CASA) — formed Eurofighter GmbH to manage the development program in 1986, and a separate consortium, called Eurojet, was set up to coordinate and manage the engine program. The first flight was expected in 1990 but it was a difficult and troubled time, marked by squabbles over price, technology, workshare and European politics. The first flight date slipped, first by months and then by years. In 1995 a Revised European Staff Requirement was issued, by which time the first three prototypes had begun flying, and workshare arguments were finally

The Eurofighter's sleek delta canard design features a constant leading-edge sweep and drag-reducing swept foreplanes that increase lift. For its construction, full advantage has been taken of new-generation composite materials, titanium and advanced alloys that have resulted in an aircraft remarkably light for its size. Production of the first batch is well under way and entry into service is approaching. Meanwhile, the four main partners are already actively discussing major enhancements to the platform.

resolved in 1996. Britain committed to the production investment phase in September of that year, followed by Spain two months later and by Italy and Germany in late 1997.

Survivability, reliability, availability and low-life-cycle cost have been development priorities, as was a high degree of growth potential. In fact, many of these aspects are contractual obligations. Eurofighter GmbH will be forced to pay compensation if certain maintenance-man-hour per flying hour (MMH/FH) and mean-time-between-failure (MTBF) criteria are not achieved in service. In addition, 15 percent growth potential is built into the engines, the mission computer and other key systems with the intention of avoiding a midlife upgrade in favor of a continuous technology insertion program (CTIP).

Seven development Eurofighters have been flying in support of the flight-test program and the use of so many aircraft, as well as four separate flight-test centers (one in each of the four partner countries), has inevitably led to some duplication of effort. However, it has also allowed very rapid test progress to be made. By the end of 2000 some 94 percent of initial operating capability (IOC) requirements had been examined by these aircraft.

The initial prototype, DA1 (98+29), first took to the air on 27 March 1994. The intention had been for it to fly in 1992, which was then reset for October 1993. Again that timing was missed because of a need for additional

work with the critical flight control system (FCS) software. This followed earlier losses of a YF-22 and JAS 39 Gripen because of FCS software problems. DA1 was assigned to aircraft handling and engine development and flew from Manching in Germany with Peter Weger at the controls. The aircraft was painted in three-tone gray with the palest shade on the undersides and the darkest shade on its topsides (from midway along the fuselage sides and including the fin and the topsides of the wings). A quartered, quadrinational roundel was designed consisting of black (outer ring), red and gold (inner ring) for Germany in the top-left segment; and (clockwise): blue, white and red for the UK; red, yellow and red for Spain; and red, white and green for Italy. This multinational roundel was applied to the forward fuselage, aft of the canard foreplane and above and below each wing. German iron crosses, with the code, were applied further aft on the fuselage and above the port and below the starboard wingtips.

At one time, it was intended that DA1 would be transferred to Warton, and a British military serial (ZH586) was reserved for it. This was not utilized when DA1 was briefly detached to Warton in England for supersonic trials in 1987, however. This prototype was scheduled to fly 635 sorties in support of the flight-test program. By February 2001, it had flown 232 times and had recorded 184 hours and 25 minutes of flight time. The aircraft also had been re-engined with EJ200 power plants by early 1999.

The maiden flight of DA2 (ZH588) was delayed until 6 April 1994 by poor weather, and Chris Yeo was its pilot for the highly successful, 50-minute flight from Warton. The aircraft was used for envelope expansion and 'carefree' handling trials, and was given the same basic color scheme as DA1 but with toned-down RAF roundels instead of iron crosses placed above and below each wing, outboard of the quadrinational roundels. For the third phase of its flight-test program, DA2 was fitted with a spin recovery parachute on a gantry anchored to the bottom of the rear fuselage, between the engines, and to the upper fuselage alongside the fin root. Scheduling called for 635 test sorties to be flown.

A low-level refueling sortie? In a somewhat unusual view, DA2 is seen with its probe connected to the drogue system of an RAF Tristar parked ahead of it. It was the first Eurofighter to be fitted with an inflight refueling probe, which retracts into the starboard side fuselage ahead of the pilot, and is seen below undertaking a trial 'dry prod' with a DERA-operated VC10.

This was the first Eurofighter to exceed Mach 2, in the hands of Paul Hopkins during flight number 203 on 23 December 1997, and the same aircraft deployed to Leeming five months before for HAS compatibility trials.

DA2 was also the first aircraft to fly with an inflight refueling probe fitted and made a number of 'dry prods' with an RAF VC10 K.Mk 3, in January 1998. The aircraft was re-engined with EJ200 power plants and made its first flight thereafter (number 217) on 26 August 1998. Decorated with the same lion, crown and rose badge originally applied to DA4, it also received a similar red, white and blue tail chevron. DA2 entered a scheduled lay-up for fuel system modifications, having last flown on 18 December 2000. To that point it had accumulated 303 hours and 3 minutes of flight time — more than any other Eurofighter — making it 'fleet leader' also having flown 345 times. Suitably modified, it returned to the test fleet to resume handling trials, retaining its all-black color scheme (applied to cover 'unsightly' black air pressure pads) but with a No. 43 Squadron 'Fighting Cock' badge on the fin. In May 2002 it was flying with the spin-recovery gantry fitted.

DA3 (MMX602), the first Italian-built Eurofighter, made its maiden flight on 4 June 1995 and was the first aircraft to operate with EJ200-1A engines. Before the decision was made to reduce from eight to seven the number of prototypes that would be built, this aircraft was to have been designated DA4, and the DA3 designator was to have been allocated to Warton's two-seater, which became DA4 instead. That aircraft was assigned to EJ200 engine integration, stores release and gunfiring trials, while increased-thrust EJ200-1C engines were fitted to the real DA3 after the first 40 flights. Production-standard EJ200-3A engines were fitted in May 1997. DA3 wore an overall, single-tone, light-gray scheme with multinational insignia in the same positions as on the RAF aircraft — but with Italian roundels carried only on the fuselage. The aircraft also had a red, white and green chevron on each side of the fin and later gained a *Reparto Sperimentale di Volo* (RSV) fin badge. The RSV is Italy's evaluation and acceptance/clearance unit.

DA3 was not fitted with radar and so, like DA1 and DA2, carried a test instrumentation boom above the nose. The aircraft was given hardpoints for underwing pylons and has flown with fuel tanks fitted. The schedule called for DA3 to fly 430 sorties in support of the flight-test program but early utilization was lower than planned due to fuel tank leaks. By February 2001, when the aircraft was on lay-up prior to receiving a gun and certain other modifications, it had accumulated 191 hours and 51 minutes in the air and had flown 246 sorties.

The second Warton-built prototype (ZH590) was originally to have been designated DA3 but was redesignated DA4, following a reduction in the number of flying prototypes. The aircraft was rolled out in an overall single-tone, gray color scheme similar to that applied to the Italian prototypes. However, national insignia were painted in the same positions as on DA2. The aircraft was entirely stripped of paint before its first flight, which was made in primer finish, then repainted in an overall gray shade slightly darker than the radome. The aircraft also received a red, white and blue chevron on the tail fin similar to that applied to the Italian aircraft but the fin flash was posi-

DA2 made its maiden flight from Warton in England on 6 April 1994. The aircraft has been involved in envelope expansion trials and in verifying 'carefree' handling qualities. It resumed envelope expansion duties fitted with production-standard EJ200-03Z engines in June 2001, following a six-month lay-up. DA2 flew at Mach 2 on 23 December 1997, and above 50,000 ft (15,240 m) in April 1999.

tioned closer to the fin cap and a new badge comprising a crown, red Lancashire rose and golden lion on a black shield was applied. With 420 sorties planned, DA4 was tasked with two-seat handling trials, radar development plus avionics integration and development. Although it was the first two-seater built, it was the last of the prototypes to fly — making its maiden flight on 14 March 1997, with Derek Reeh at the controls. Like DA6 (the other two-seater) it has not been retrofitted with an inflight refueling probe.

The aircraft was temporarily grounded in the late 1990s because of unspecified equipment shortages and so the opportunity was taken to incorporate modifications while the aircraft was laid up. By 13 April 2000, when it flew last before lay-up, it had recorded 98 hours and 57 minutes of flight time, amassed during 97 flights. Following the long lay-up, during which it received upgrades to its avionics and power-generating systems and completed ground trials for the defensive aids subsystem (DASS), DA4 re-entered the development program in late 2001. Its first flight to follow was used to verify a variety of systems, including the engines, radar, AMRAAM integration and ground-proximity warning system (GPWS). Subsequent flights will support the fighter's initial clearance into service with preliminary testing concentrating on weapon system integration between the AMRAAM and ASRAAM, radar and GPWS. A fully guided AMRAAM test launch against an airborne target (a Mirach) was undertaken by Craig Penrice in April 2002 over the Benbecula sea range off the Scottish Hebrides.

The original DA5 (98+30) was cut from the flight-test program and was to have been a Warton-built prototype. Those duties were transferred to DA4 and the eventual DA5, Germany's second Eurofighter, which should have been DA6. DA5 initially flew in primer apart from the radome, which was fully painted, with codes and national insignia in the usual positions and with a quadrinational roundel below the cockpit. Code JP005 was stenciled on the tail fin and the aircraft was assigned to radar development and weapons systems integration. It was subsequently painted in a two-tone disruptive camouflage with a darker shade of gray covering most of the upper fuselage, the lower part of the tail fin and inboard parts of the upper surfaces of the wing. It also received a Bavarian flag emblem and 'BAVARIAN AIR FORCE' logo on both sides of the tail fin, together with the title 'DA5 - EJ200.' This was the first Eurofighter to fly with radar, which was fully functional for its first flight on 24 February 1997. It was powered by EJ200-3A engines. In October 1995, DA5 clocked up the type's 500th flight and, in 1998, was used as the display aircraft at the air shows in Berlin and Farnborough. The schedule calls for this prototype to fly 385 sorties and, by February 2001, it had made 176 of those flights and spent 136 hours and 17 minutes in the air. In March 2001, it completed Captor radar trials at Laage, including multibogey scenarios in which the radar successfully tracked up to 20 targets simultaneously (comprising *Luftwaffe* F-4Fs and MiG-29s).

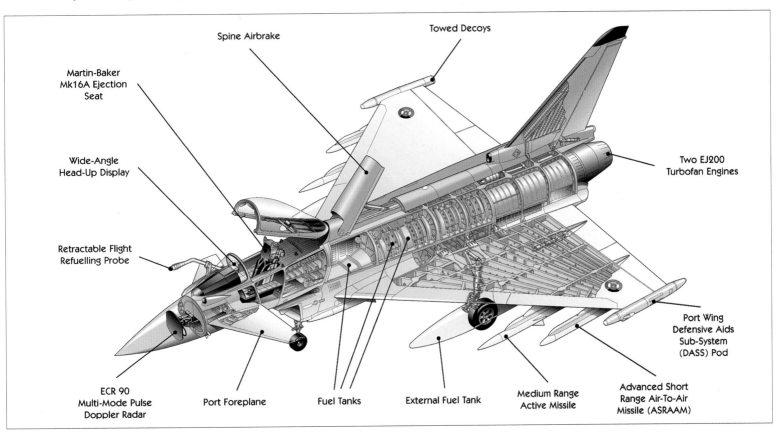

Superfighters

DA6 (XCE-16-01) originally was to have been DA7, and was the first two-seat Eurofighter to fly. It beat DA4 into the air, making its maiden flight on 31 August 1996. The pilot was Alfonso de Miguel and the aircraft flew with Phase 2A FCS software and was tasked with two-seat handling as well as developing and testing two-seat avionics and systems in a 315-sortie flight-test program. DA6 wore the same basic over-all-gray color scheme as the Italian aircraft. Quadrinational roundels but no national insignia were applied above and

Advanced weapons like the Storm Shadow and Meteor, shown here fitted to DA7, will not be available until much later in the decade. The ASRAAM is part of the FDC armament fit.

below each wing and the aircraft received a stylized bull badge on each side of its tail fin. Currently flying, the aircraft had amassed 191 hours and 50 minutes in the air by February 2001, during 199 flights.

The second Italian prototype (MMX603), which was to have been DA8 originally, became DA7 and made its maiden flight on 27 January 1997. This example is tasked with performance testing and weapons integration in a planned 290-sortie flight program. It undertook the Eurofighter's first missile launch, firing an AIM-9 on 15 December 1997, and was given the same color scheme as the first Italian prototype, DA3. Through February 2001, it had flown 177 times and had recorded 94 hours and 21 minutes in the air.

Production-standard EJ200-03Z engines began flight-tests in October 1999, fitted to Italy's DA3 prototype at Caselle. By that time, development EJ200 engines already had accumulated more than 3,600 hours in the seven prototypes, of which 1,170 were flight hours. In December the first inflight re-light was accomplished and, in late March 2001, NETMA awarded the Eurojet consortium a technical certificate for the production-standard EJ200-03Z engine. This signified the end of long-running trials and bench tests for the power plant, although BAE Systems DA2 resumed flight-testing in June 2001 fitted with -03Z engines in place of the final development engine, the -03Y.

The Eurofighter is designed to operate with 220-Imp gal (1000-lit) and 330-Imp gal (1500-lit) drop tanks. The small tanks were first carried by DA3 in December 1997, and in June 1998 DA7 successfully jettisoned a tank. In February 1999, DA3 (the primary external stores trials airframe) flew with the big tanks fully fuelled and, in March, exceeded Mach 1 while carrying the smaller units. By the end of that month it had taken two of them to Mach 1.6, a speed that was repeated in December with three tanks installed.

With air defense the priority for all four core nations, the first Eurofighters are being delivered to IOC standard with AIM-9L and AIM-120B missiles, and a limited air-to-ground capability. Full operating capability (FOC) is slated for March 2005, followed by a declaration to NATO intended for January 2006. Beyond that, the Batch 2 production configuration has yet to be defined but will be essentially similar to FOC, with additional software/avionics changes. More radical are the improvements being studied for the Batch 3 production aircraft under the Eurofighter Enhancement Program, driven currently by the UK and Germany, although Italy and Spain may join later.

As well as integration of new 'smart' weapons, and adoption of the Storm Shadow, Taurus and Meteor, Batch 3 aircraft may also feature conformal fuel tanks (CFT) and terrain-referenced navigation (TRN), and it is believed advances in helmet displays will allow removal of the head-up display (HUD). Furthermore, ITP, the Spanish engine partner, has studied thrust-vectoring for the EJ200 engine. The power plant has a 30 percent thrust growth potential in its current form. Already under review (but not yet funded) are staged thrust increases to 23,155 lb st (103 kN) as the EJ230, and 26,300 lb st (117 kN). By around 2010 Eurofighters could be fielding electronically-scanned (e-scan) active array radars, as well. The Airborne Multirole, Multifunction, Solid-state Active-array Radar (AMSAR) program is a technology demonstration being conducted by BAE Systems (UK), Thales (France) and EADS (Germany) to produce a radar with a fixed, electronically-steered antenna array that uses similar technology to the AESA radar being fitted to USAF F-15s and that which is planned for the F/A-18E/F, F-22 and JSF. An AMSAR prototype scanner is expected to fly in the BAC One-Eleven test bed in 2003 but its first application is expected to be in the Dassault Rafale, primarily to enhance the French fighter's exportability. Integration into the Captor radar (described later) is not expected before 2010, although it is possible the timing could be brought forward.

Further technologies, like those that will be part of the Future Offensive Aircraft System (FOAS) study, may be injected into the Eurofighter as they become available because the type is a central part of FOAS studies, in its own right. Potentially, it could form the basis for the new aircraft, although FOAS has a wide-ranging brief that includes unmanned combat air vehicles (UCAV)

First taking to the air on 24 February 1997, DA5's primary test role has been avionics and weapons integration. The aircraft was the first to be fitted with the 'C' model of the Captor radar, which it flew during February 1997.

and other types, present or planned. BAE Systems has also conducted a 'Sea Typhoon' study for a carrierborne version. This was mooted as a potential aircraft for the UK's two planned aircraft carriers, although the MoD is now committed to the Lockheed Martin F-35 (assuming the program survives) as its Future Joint Combat Aircraft (FJCA).

On the training front, Eurofighter GmbH announced on 1 May 2001 that it had been awarded a $949-million contract to supply combat simulators for the four nations developing the aircraft. Under the overall program, dubbed the Aircrew Synthetic Training Aid (ASTA), 18 full-mission simulators (FMS) and nine Cockpit Trainer/Interactive Pilot Stations – Enhanced (CT/IPS-E) systems will be produced. The principal contractors are BAE Systems and Thales, and the system will offer full mission simulation, including 'dogfighting,' weapons and electronic warfare.

In mid-2001, reports suggested the Eurofighter project was running behind schedule again and that the price tag for development had risen to nearly $5.43 billion — up from a budgeted $4.09 billion. If this is the case, it means the Eurofighter no longer falls into the category of relatively cheap new-generation fighter. Before the Batch 1 production contract was signed, the UK's National Audit Office indicated the aircraft the RAF would acquire would cost £40.2 million ($66 million) each — or £61 million ($100 million) each, inclusive of research and development. It now appears the latter is closer to £81 million ($117 million) each.

Purchase price is not the only factor to be considered, however, since through-life costs (the actual costs of ownership) are paramount. Such costs for the Eurofighter are contractually guaranteed to be significantly lower than those of any rival, yet the aircraft will have a superior radar, greater combat persistence (more missiles) and better performance where it counts (supersonic acceleration, agility and 'carefree' handling at high-Alpha and lower speeds) than alternative platforms. Even in its Block 50N or Block 60 form, the Fighting Falcon cannot match the Eurofighter as a long-range, all-weather BVR fighter. Fine aircraft as they are, neither the F-16 nor the Gripen can compete in terms of capabilities.

Yet even if the Eurofighter's full capabilities are not available with the first aircraft off the line, even a degraded aircraft would mark an improvement over all of today's best fighters. In any case, it is anticipated that any deficiencies or delays affecting the initial operational standard Eurofighter will relate to its air-to-ground, not its air-to-air capabilities. With its advanced helmet-mounted sighting and display system, and direct voice input (DVI), the full-standard Eurofighter promises to have a better environment and a better man-machine interface for its pilot than the F-22 Raptor when it enters service. It may be that the F-22 will 'supercruise' faster and will almost certainly be stealthier but head-on the Eurofighter enjoys a very low radar cross-section (RCS) signature. While important, a low RCS is only one aspect of the stealth equation. Low-emission sensors and targeting devices are also very important. Even if an F-22 is invisible to radar, as soon as it starts transmitting with its own radar it will become detectable, not having a passive (emission-free) target detection sensor unlike the Eurofighter. The latter is fitted with a highly sophisticated IRSTS. Crucially, the F-22 also lacks DVI, which makes multiple-target sorting and allocation faster for the Eurofighter. The Eurofighter has been designed to take down large numbers of MiG-29s, Su-27s, Mirage 2000s — maybe even Rafales as the French have a history of being less pernickety about to whom they sell advanced weapons.

While production gears up, over 90 percent of the interim operating capability flight trials have been completed, and much of the production-standard equipment has been cleared. Trials continue, and are ramping up with the arrival of the five Instrumented Production Aircraft (IPA) into the test fleet. By mid-June 2001 the DA fleet had accumulated 1,298 hours during 1,586 flights. The total development program calls for 4,000 hours in the air.

Eurofighter Typhoon

1. Glass-fiber-reinforced plastic (GFRP) radome, hinged to starboard for access
2. Euroradar Captor multimode pulse-Doppler radar scanner
3. Scanner tracking mechanism
4. Retractable inflight refueling probe
5. Instrument panel shroud
6. Eurofirst PIRATE forward-looking, infrared search and track sensor
7. Radar equipment bay
8. Air data sensor
9. Port canard foreplane
10. Foreplane diffusion-bonded titanium structure
11. Foreplane pivot mounting
12. Hydraulic actuator
13. Rudder pedals
14. Instrument panel with Smiths Industries full-color, multifunction head-down-displays (MHDD)
15. BAE Systems Avionics head-up display (HUD)
16. Rear view mirrors
17. Upward hinging cockpit canopy
18. Pilot's Martin Baker Mk 16A 'zero-zero' ejection seat
19. Control, column handgrip, full-authority digital active control technology (ACT) fly-by-wire control system
20. Engine throttle levers, HOTAS controls
21. Side console panel
22. Boarding steps extended
23. Boundary layer splitter plate
24. Air conditioning pack beneath avionics equipment bay
25. Cockpit rear-sloping pressure bulkhead
26. Cockpit pressurization valves
27. Canopy latch actuators
28. Canopy rear decking
29. Avionics equipment bay, port and starboard
30. Low-voltage electro-luminescent formation lighting strip
31. Forward-fuselage strake
32. Air conditioning system heat exchanger exhaust
33. Port engine air intake
34. Intake ramp bleed-air spill duct
35. Port engine air intake
36. 'Varicowl' hydraulic actuators
37. Canopy external release
38. Lower UHF antenna
39. Aft retracting nosewheel
40. Forward-fuselage, semi-recessed missile carriage
41. Pressure refueling connection
42. Fixed wing inboard leading-edge segment
43. Missile launch and approach warning antennas
44. Missile launch and approach warning receivers
45. Leading-edge slat drive shaft from central actuating motor
46. Intake ducting
47. Forward-fuselage fuel tank, port and starboard
48. Gravity fuel fillers
49. Airbrake hinge mounting
50. Canopy hinge point
51. Center- and forward-fuselage section of two-seat combat capable training variant

52. Student pilot's station
53. Instructor's station
54. Dorsal fuel tank
55. Repositioned avionics equipment bays, port and starboard
56. Dorsal airbrake
57. Airbrake hydraulic jack
58. Center fuselage internal fuel tankage
59. Tank access panel
60. Auxiliary power unit (APU), cannon bay on starboard side
61. APU exhaust
62. Cannon ammunition magazine
63. Titanium wing panel attachment fittings
64. Main undercarriage wheel bay

65. Carbon-fiber composite (CFC) center-fuselage skin paneling
66. Machined wing panel attaching fuselage main frames
67. Anti-collision strobe light

68. TACAN antenna
69. Dorsal spine fairing, air and cable ducting
70. Center section internal fuel tankage
71. Secondary power system (SPS) equipment bay, engine-driven airframe-mounted accessory equipment gearboxes
72. Eurojet EJ200 afterburning low-bypass turbofan engine
73. Forward engine mounting
74. Hydraulic reservoirs, port and starboard, dual system

75. Engine bleed-air primary heat exchanger
76. Heat exchanger ram air intake
77. Starboard wing panel integral fuel tankage
78. Starboard leading-edge slat segments
79. Wing CFC skin panels
80. Starboard wingtip electronic warfare (EW) equipment
81. Starboard navigation light
82. BAE Systems Avionics towed radar decoy (TRD)
83. Dual TRD housings
84. Starboard outboard elevon

104. Variable-area afterburner nozzles
105. Nozzle hydraulic actuator
106. Runway emergency arrestor hook
107. Rear fuselage semi-recessed missile carriage
108. Port CFC inboard elevon
109. Inboard pylon-mounted chaff/flare launcher
110. Elevon honeycomb core
111. Outboard elevon all-titanium structure
112. Outboard pylon-mounted chaff/flare launcher
113. Rear ECM/ESM antenna fairing

114. Port wingtip electronic countermeasures/ electronic surveillance pod
115. Wingtip formation lighting strip
116. Port wingtip electronic countermeasures/electronic surveillance pod
117. Wingtip formation lighting strip
118. Port navigation light
119. Electronics cooling ram air intake
120. Outboard missile pylon
121. Titanium leading-edge slat structure
122. Pylon mounting hardpoints
123. Titanium leading-edge slat structure
124. Cable conduits
125. Elevon hinge fairing-mounted chaff/flare launcher and controller
126. Port mainwheel leg strut
127. Hydraulic retraction jack
128. Undercarriage mounting stub spars
129. Wing panel multi-spar structure
130. Cable conduits
131. Elevon hinge fairing-mounted chaff/flare launcher and controller
132. Port mainwheel
133. Mainwheel leg strut
134. Hydraulic retraction jack
135. Undercarriage mounting stub spars
136. External fuel tank on inboard 'wet' pylon
137. Port two-segment leading-edge slat, extended
138. Mauser 27-mm cannon in starboard wing root
139. Ammunition feed chute
140. Transverse ammunition magazine
141. AIM-120 AMRAAM advanced medium-range air-to-air missile
142. Euromissile Meteor advanced BVR missile
143. BL.755 cluster bomb
144. AIM-9L Sidewinder, short-range air-to-air missile
145. MBDA ASRAAM advanced short-range missile
146. Three-round missile carrier/launcher pylon adapter
147. GBU-24/B Paveway III 2000-lb (907-kg) laser-guided bomb
148. MBDA Storm Shadow stand-off precision-attack weapon
149. MBDA ALARM anti-radar missile
150. Type 117 1000-lb (454-kg) retarded bomb

© Mike Badrocke

85. Starboard outboard elevon
86. HF antenna
87. Upper UHF/IFF antenna
88. Rear position antenna
89. Fuel jettison
90. Rudder
91. Honeycomb core structure
92. Fin and rudder CFC skin panels
93. Formation lighting strip
94. Fin CFC 'sine-wave' spar structure
95. Heat exchanger joints
96. Fin attachment joints
97. Rear engine mounting
98. Engine bay lining heat shroud
99. Afterburner ducting
100. Tailpipe sealing plates
101. Brake parachute housing
102. Rudder hydraulic actuator
103. Brake parachute door

AVIONICS

The Eurofighter was always specified as a single-seater that demanded a state-of-the-art, electronic 'glass' cockpit and a human-machine interface superior to that of any fighter before — with high-tech avionics systems linked via an integrated network of digital databuses. There is no doubt that one of the most impressive features of the Eurofighter is its cockpit. No first-generation data is presented to the pilot. Instead, all information is processed and fused by the system to present an overall 'big picture' that is based on inputs from various sensors, including those offboard via the multiple information distribution system (MIDS).

The system can be controlled with minimum pilot workload thanks to the voice, throttle and stick (VTAS) system, which combines hands-on throttle and stick (HOTAS) inputs with direct voice input/output (DVI/O). The DVI/O can theoretically handle 600 words but initial capability has been capped at 80 to avoid potential phonetic difficulties. When combined with the MIDS and datalink, DVI/O allows pilots to sort targets and allocate them to other members of the formation by voice

keep it abreast of projected air threats for at least the first 25 years of the Eurofighter's operational career. As previously mentioned, in early 2001 the radar underwent a seven-sortie evaluation, including a mission flown by Germany's DA5 during which it flew against 16 F-4Fs and four MiG-29s from JG 73 at Laage, Germany. A series of head-on and tail-chase engagements were undertaken, in a clutter-rich environment. Operating mostly in track-while-scan mode, the radar is reported to have performed extremely well.

A total of 147 Captors is currently on order to equip the 148 aircraft in Batch 1 production, of which one is to be a static test airframe. The radars are completed at BAE Systems' Crewe Toll facility, which has the capacity to produce up to 10 sets a month. Like the Batch 1 aircraft, initial production sets are optimized for air-to-air work, although they possess considerable air-to-surface capability, including moving target and sea search modes. This capability is expected to be enhanced with a series of upgrades planned for the first two years of Eurofighter operations.

DA4 has been designated for the ground-based Defensive Aids Sub-System (DASS) trials. This system is fully automated with an optional pilot override and encompasses missile

All information is presented on the head-up display (HUD), helmet and three multifunction head-down displays (MHDD), although the current Eurofighter cockpit retains hidden standby instruments. In batch 3 Eurofighters the HUD is expected to disappear in favor of a full helmet visor display. Below is a mock-up of the anticipated production-standard cockpit.

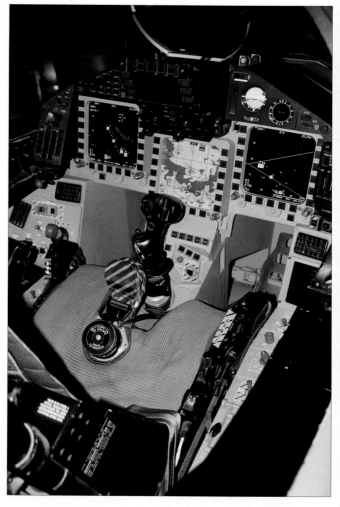

alone. For obvious reasons, safety-critical actions, such as weapons firing or undercarriage deployment remain manual actions. As well as providing aural warnings, the aircraft's system can also be interrogated by voice, and will provide voice answers. Fuel state and 'how far to X?' are obvious issues to which the system can respond without the pilot having to change the display set-up.

In February 2001, the first two production-standard Captor (previously ECR90) radars were delivered to Eurofighter — one to BAE Systems and one to Alenia. Eurofighter had received 16 pre-production radars, dubbed the 'C' model, which were tested in DA4, DA5 and DA6. Another Captor is flying in a test BAC One-Eleven that had accumulated some 400 hours of inflight testing in the course of more than 200 flights, by mid-2001. The 'C' model radar first flew in the One-Eleven in 1996, and in the Eurofighter on 25 February 1997 (aboard DA5). From the outset the radar has shown excellent air-to-air performance, while retaining plenty of scope for incremental modification to

The Captor radar, originally the ECR90, first flew in its 'A' model form in this BAC One-Eleven test bed — which has played an important role in the radar's development. At a future point the test bed will be fitted with the AMSAR 'e-scan' antenna that may be incorporated into Batch 3 aircraft. Ahead of the One-Eleven is DA4, which flew the ECR90 from the outset.

At right, the starboard wing pylon of DA2 houses two towed radar decoys (TRD) for the Defensive Aids Sub-System (DASS). Each is trailed on a cable to lure radar-guided missiles away from the aircraft. Another key element of the DASS — the chaff dispenser — can be seen in the rear of the outboard pylon. Flares are housed in the undersides of the flap tracks.

warning and laser warning receivers; ECM/ESM in the port wingtip pod; towed radar decoys, of which two are in the starboard wingtip pod; chaff in the rear of the permanently fixed outer wing pylons; and flares in the flap tracks. Germany and Spain initially stayed out of the EuroDASS consortium, which has developed the suite but both have subsequently joined. There are some differences depending on the customer. Germany and Italy have not specified their laser warning receivers, while Italy is studying an alternative to the TRD in the form of the Cross Eye electronic countermeasures system.

Mounted on the port-side forward fuselage, at right, is the Eurofirst (a consortium led by FIAR) PIRATE (Passive Infrared Airborne Tracking Equipment), which functions as a FLIR for low-level flight and as an IRST in the air-to-air role.

Superfighters

WEAPON SYSTEMS

The Eurofighter is an extremely agile air dominance fighter designed to meet perceived needs for the first half of the 21st century. It will be optimized for all-weather, BVR and close-in combat and ultimately offer significant ground attack capability. The aircraft will be able to fly close air support (CAS), suppression of enemy air defenses (SEAD) and maritime attack missions, in addition to interdiction sorties.

In its initial guise, the Eurofighter will be equipped for air defense only — employing a traditional AIM-9L Sidewinder and AIM-120B AMRAAM combination. Alternatives to the AIM-9L, to be fielded by FOC aircraft, will be the ASRAAM and IRIS-T. The AMRAAM will give way to the Meteor in the late 2000s. Initially, air-to-surface stores will be restricted largely to free-fall weapons but this will change over time, and should grow to include the Brimstone anti-armor weapons for the RAF, ALARM Storm Shadow and Taurus. Anti-ship missiles like the Kongsberg Penguin may also be integrated.

Weapons testing has been undertaken primarily by Italy's DA7, which undertook the first live firing of an AIM-9 Sidewinder on 15 December 1997. Two days later an AIM-120 AMRAAM was jettisoned when trials of the Eurofighter's primary BVR weapon in its initial configuration commenced. Since then, Sidewinder and AMRAAM trials have continued to clear the weapons for IOC and, because of the longer lead times associated with guided weapons, trials have focused on these two systems. Meanwhile, testing of air-to-ground weaponry as

DA7 is seen firing an AIM-9L on 15 December 1997 (top) and during the first AIM-120 jettison trial two days later. Missile tests are conducted over the Decimomannu range in Sardinia.

All 13 hardpoints are occupied by a mixed loadout of two Storm Shadows, two ALARMs, four Meteors, two Paveway LGBs, two ASRAAMs and a single 1000-lit tank.

This configuration represents the RAF's intended air dominance loadout — with four Meteors, two ASRAAMs and three 1000-lit supersonic tanks

of mid-2001 had been restricted to pit drops. While air tests will be conducted as IOC approaches, as previously indicated this will be limited to free-fall weapons like iron and cluster munitions, as well as LGBs.

On 16 May 2000, the UK's defense minister announced the country would purchase the European consortium Meteor BVR air-to-air missile (AAM), ending a long and hotly fought contest with Raytheon. The Meteor uses ramjet power to achieve long range, yet retains maximum end-game maneuvering energy. Developing the seeker head and guidance system builds on work performed for the MBD MICA missile, used by the Mirage 2000-5 and Rafale. Following the decision to release an RAF Eurofighter for test and integration work, the six-nation Meteor BVRAAM group hopes to bring forward the missile's in-service timing to 2007/8. The UK is leading the team, which also includes France, Germany, Italy, Spain and Sweden. As well as being adopted as the primary BVR armament for the Eurofighter, the Meteor is also planned for the Gripen and Rafale and development testing is proceeding using a BAe 125 equipped to represent the missile, and a BAC One-Eleven fitted with the Captor radar. As of May 2002, Germany had yet to fully commit to the Meteor, casting doubt on the program's future. To cover the gap between Eurofighter and Meteor service entry dates, Britain's MoD is procuring up to 400 AIM-120B AMRAAMs commercially, which will comprise the initial missile equipment for the RAF's aircraft alongside MBD ASRAAMs. Germany will employ the IRIS-T short-range weapon, but will initially use AIM-9L Sidewinders, as will the other nations.

In late December 2000, MATRA BAE Dynamics conducted the first full flight-test of the Storm Shadow/SCALP EG long-range standoff missile, from a Mirage 2000. Two of these weapons are to be flown by Eurofighters in the standoff precision strike role. Both the RAF and Italy have specified the missile for their aircraft, while Greece has ordered the weapon for its Mirage 2000-5 Mk 2 fighters, and probably will carry it on its Eurofighters if that nation's buy comes to fruition. However, Germany has opted for the KEPD-350 Taurus standoff missile.

While reconnaissance is a stated role of the Eurofighter, none of the partner nations has yet outlined a formal requirement for this capability. However, pod-mounted sensors will be integrated later in the program when such requirements materialize. Another potential role is SEAD, for which Germany is developing its Armiger missile. An anti-radiation weapon is also planned around the Meteor.

The Meteor consortium pools the missile expertise of France, Germany, Italy, Spain, Sweden and the UK. The ramjet-powered weapon has a very fast flyout to extreme range and has been designed to fit the AMRAAM recesses.

Paveway laser-guided bombs will be included in the initial batch of air-to-ground weapons. On the wing an AMRAAM also can be seen.

A free-fall option for the Eurofighter is the BL755 cluster bomb, of which six can be carried (including twin racks on the inboard pylons). This aircraft is also fitted with 1500-lit external fuel tanks.

Impacting the Eurofighter's weapon load for a particular mission will be the number of fuel tanks fitted. The aircraft can carry three (a 1000-lit on the centerline and one 1,000-lit or one 1,500-lit under each wing). DA7 undertook the first jettison test on 17 June 1998, when it released a supersonic 1,000-lit tank covered with photo-calibration marks. The larger tank can be deployed only for subsonic flights.

Below, the brimstone is an anti-armor weapon based on the AGM-114 Hellfire. Up to 18 can be carried on triple-launchers.

Superfighters

FLIGHT CHARACTERISTICS

While maximum performance and agility have been enhanced through the use of powerful new engines, the Eurofighter's structure has been designed to deliver low weight and an advanced, unstable configuration. The aircraft is exceptionally unstable in pitch and, without constant inputs from the full-authority, quadruplex, digital flight control computers, would rapidly diverge in pitch and break up within seconds. However, this characteristic allows the highest possible pitch rates for deliberate maneuvers. In addition, the digital FCS has allowed the size of the control surfaces to be kept to a minimum, thereby helping to reduce airframe weight and drag. At supersonic speeds, the aircraft is also unstable in yaw.

At Farnborough in 1998, the aircraft demonstrated a level of agility that no other fighter present could match, including maneuvers that graphically illustrated the benefits and degree of 'carefree' handling endowed by the aircraft's sophisticated fly-by-wire FCS. It should be remembered, too, that while the Eurofighter was no longer flying in 'worst-case failure mode,' it was only operating at the show with FCS Phase 2A, which limited operations to $7.25g$ and a $28°$ angle of attack (AoA). It was still without the autopilot and autothrottle that are part of the Phase 2B1 software package. Increased g, a higher AoA and an expanded 'carefree' handling envelope became a reality with Phase 2B2 and, at IOC, the aircraft will be capable of flying at $9g$ — at higher than $30°$ AoA.

Judging a fighter on the basis of air show performances is unwise, though extremely tempting. Such routines have, however, highlighted the ability of the Eurofighter to maintain an aggressive display sequence without the need to 'unload' and restore lost energy between maneuvers, something that other fighter manufacturers have yet to display convincingly. When the Russian MiG-29 and Su-27 demonstrated very high AoA and post-stall capabilities in the late 1980s and early 1990s, people were quick to point out that the tactical application of tail-slides, 'cobras' and the like was very limited. This was fair comment but the real significance of the Russian performances lay in the fact that they demonstrated an extraordinary degree of confidence in high-AoA handling at air show altitudes. They also demonstrated a useful ability to point the nose 'off axis' for a snap missile release or gunshot.

Similarly, the Eurofighter's high-Alpha velocity vector (HAV) roll would have relatively limited combat applications because any low-speed, decelerative maneuver needs to be used with care. Further, the sensible fighter pilot will always 'bug out' rather than engage in a slow-speed, close-in turning fight because of the latter's unpredictable outcome. The HAV roll

did demonstrate an ability to change direction quickly and unpredictably, however, and more significantly it gave an impressive demonstration of the pilot's confidence in the aircraft's handling. In other words, a Eurofighter pilot can make maximum control inputs in any situation and still be confident the flight control computers will sort it out.

Independent analysis suggests the fighter enjoys the same degree of superiority over its rivals in a slow-speed turning fight as it does in BVR combat. This is because of many factors that include not only high-Alpha and high-g capabilities but high rates of roll, the sophisticated helmet-mounted sighting and display system, and its comprehensive array of short-range weapons and aiming systems. Furthermore, as well as being extremely maneuverable in a close-in turning fight, the type's subsonic performance is matched by superb supersonic agility, with impressive instantaneous and sustained turn rates, and very rapid acceleration. From 'brakes off' on takeoff, loaded with internal fuel, four AIM-120s and two AIM-9s or ASRAAMs, the Eurofighter lifts off in seven seconds using just 1,400 ft (427 m) of runway. Two and one-half minutes from commencing its ground roll, the aircraft can be at 35,000 ft (10668 m) — scorching along at Mach 1.5.

At low weights, the Eurofighter has a thrust-to-weight ratio of unity (1:1) with maximum dry power, and can accelerate from 200 kts (370 km/h) to Mach 1 in just 30 seconds without recourse to the afterburner — and with one engine at idle! Furthermore, it can maintain supersonic flight without reheat, carrying a load of six air-to-air missiles. Even with interim RB.199 turbofan engines, the Eurofighter has demonstrated an ability to exceed Mach 2. It should not be forgotten, too, that the fighter is not a modern-day Lightning that had to sacrifice range and payload for outright performance. In air-to-air configuration, the Eurofighter has about the same range as a Panavia Tornado F.Mk 3.

In the air-to-surface role, the Eurofighter can carry a SEPECAT Jaguar-size payload twice as far as that aircraft can and, in payload/range terms, is broadly similar to the Tornado IDS. Minor modifications already being considered, including provision for conformal tanks, could give the Eurofighter an equivalent payload and range capability to that enjoyed by the F-111 Aardvark formerly in US service. Yet it would still remain more agile than the new F-35.

PRODUCTION ORDERS

Production and support Memorandums of Understanding (MoU) were signed on 22 December 1997, and contracts followed on 30 January 1998 between Eurofighter GmbH and the NATO Eurofighter and Tornado Management Agency (NETMA), which represents the military customers. These contracts confirmed production for the *Aeronautica Militare Italiana* (AMI), *Ejército del Aire* (EdA), *Luftwaffe* and Royal Air Force at 620 aircraft.

design/manufacture) will allow other assembly lines to be established easily, should export customers require this. Subassembly of components for the first production aircraft began in December 1998.

To provide economy and streamlining of the production process, a complex delivery schedule has been formulated to provide maximum efficiency in transporting components between sources and assembly lines. The just-in-time concept has been applied, whereby components arrive at the assembly lines as they are needed and the special trucks which ferry components will rarely travel empty. For instance, a truck

In September 1998, shortly after the name 'Typhoon' was adopted for export aircraft, the Supplement 2 production order was signed. This covered the initial 148 fixed-price aircraft that comprise Batch 1, to be completed in the basic configuration optimized for air defense and with only limited air-to-surface capabilities. Also included were 363 EJ200 engines. Construction of major assemblies had already begun at the four production plants set up in the partner countries, each of which has different responsibilities because all manufacturing is single sourced. BAE Systems produces the forward fuselage, canards, windscreen, canopy, dorsal spine, vertical fin, inboard flaperons and part of the rear fuselage. DASA builds the center fuselage, while Alenia handles the left wing and outboard flaperons, and CASA the right wing and leading edge flaps. In terms of workshare, Britain will get 37 percent for its 232-aircraft order (37.5 percent

Arranged on the Manching flightline is Eurofighter DA1 and the three types it will replace in *Luftwaffe* service — MiG-29, Tornado IDS and F-4. However, the Phantom shown here is actually a Greek example being upgraded by EADS-Deutchland.

The second Warton-built Eurofighter's contribution to the flight program has been two-seater handling and radar integration. DA4 first flew on 14 March 1997.

of the projected production count). Germany will get 30 percent of the work against its order for 180 aircraft (29 percent of planned production), while Italy's order for 121 aircraft (19.5 percent of production) will earn it a 19 percent workshare. Spain's 87-aircraft order represents 14 percent of the projected production figure and will earn it an equivalent workshare.

The fighter is being manufactured and assembled in some of the most modern manufacturing facilities in the world, taking advantage of the latest 'lean manufacturing' techniques. The assembly lines are located at Warton in the UK (BAE Systems), Manching in Germany (EADS-Deutschland), Caselle in Italy (Alenia) and Getafe in Spain (EADS-CASA). The multi-facility approach has been designed for maximum flexibility and efficiency, and the highly flexible CAD/CAM (computer-aided

delivering a forward fuselage from BAE to EADS-D Manching will return from Germany with a center fuselage for Warton. In late 2000, the first production components began arriving at the assembly lines — each of which is a state-of-the-art facility. Warton's Hangar 302 (the former Tornado assembly line), for example, has a sophisticated automated laser alignment facility (as does the EADS-CASA assembly line). For mating, the three main fuselage sections are each mounted on three computer-controlled jacks. A laser tracks optical marks on each component and supplies inputs to a computer, which then moves the jacks in order to maneuver the components into the correct marry-up position. Following such mating, the assembled section moves to a second team which installs systems and equipment, while a third team handles customer acceptance,

Superfighters

painting and attends to any problems that surface during the three-flight (average) acceptance procedure. Warton's facility can handle 15 aircraft at a time. The first production aircraft, IPA1, spent over a year in final assembly, acting as the 'guinea pig' while working practices were established, and the line hopes to be turning an aircraft from components to finished product in 16 weeks by aircraft number 20. Output from Warton is expected to peak at 4.5 a month, with some excess capability built-in for possible export work.

The Eurofighter's order book puts it well ahead of the other

Batch 1 deliveries comprise 55 Eurofighters for the RAF, 44 for the *Luftwaffe*, 29 for the AMI and 20 for the EdA, of which one will be used for static testing. Within the total, the first five aircraft from the production line are designated IPAs and will join the seven-aircraft trials fleet for test purposes. While the IPAs represent the interim operating capability configuration and are being assembled on the production lines, they also feature additional test equipment. Some months behind schedule, the first three IPAs took to the air in 2002 on the following dates in April:

Visually the most stunning of the development aircraft, DA2 was painted black to cover the black patches liberally applied (mainly on the starboard side) for air pressure trials.

'superfighters' that have made it to the production phase — including the F-22 (339 aircraft on order). This is, perhaps, a first for a European aircraft program. Arguably its closest rival, the French Rafale, is being built slowly and in relatively small batches. Furthermore, the four assembly lines will ensure there is sufficient flexibility to expand production for export, should that become necessary.

Hitherto, US manufacturers have been able to take advantage of massive domestic orders to guarantee economies of scale and, thereby, low unit prices for export customers — and the certainty of 'top-up' and attrition buys have allowed production lines to stay open longer than could otherwise be justified. Today, only the Lockheed Martin F-35 looks set to be procured in really large numbers, with over 3,000 required by the US and UK, and more orders expected from other customers/partners. With interest from countries outside the four-nation consortium, coupled with a reasonably competitive price tag, the Eurofighter Typhoon's prospects look quite good. Certainly, it appears to have largely emerged from its turbulent and troubled development days.

Of the first batch of 148 aircraft, 52 will be delivered as two-seaters to allow training to begin in earnest within the air forces of the four partners. Two further batches, each comprising 236 aircraft (and 519 and 500 engines, respectively) will include expanded air-to-surface capabilities. These have yet to be fully defined but Batch 3 examples should reflect full multirole capabilities and will incorporate several additional planned technologies. On top of the 620 production aircraft and 1,382 engines thus far committed to, an optional batch of 90 aircraft is included within the overall deal.

No.	Company	Configuration	First Flight
IPA1	BAE Systems	Two-seat	15 April
IPA2	Alenia	Two-seat	5 April
IPA3	EADS-Deutschland	Two-seat	8 April
IPA4	EADS-CASA	Single-seat	due mid-2002
IPA5	BAE Systems	Single-seat	due mid-2002

In order to make 10 aircraft available for initial production configuration verification, five of the original aircraft (DA3 through DA7) progressively are being modified to IOC standard.

From all three planned batches, the RAF will receive a total of 232 Eurofighters (plus 65 options), of which 55 are included in the first production batch (37 single-seaters and 18 two-seaters). In all, single-seaters will number 195 and two-seaters 37, most of which will serve as trainers. The service is giving priority to replacing the 80 or so Tornado F.Mk 3s that currently undertake the air defense mission, and initial deliveries to the RAF were expected in June 2002. However, under the Case White program, the initial aircraft will remain at the Warton facility where No. 17 Squadron, an operational evaluation unit (OEU), is being established. Up to 12 aircraft will be based there.

An operational conversion unit (OCU), scheduled to be No. 29 Squadron, will be formed at Coningsby in 2004, and the OEU will move into the Lincolnshire base, where the first front-line unit will form in January 2005. The Tornado F.3 OCU, currently at Coningsby, will move to Leuchars to make room for the incoming OCU, while Leeming is scheduled to receive Eurofighters from 2005/6, and Leuchars from 2008. At that point, retirement of the Tornado F.Mk 3 is expected. Further

DA1 streams its brake chute while its nose is kept high for aerodynamic braking. The Eurofighter's FCS has evolved through a number of iterations, the latest of which is Phase 3 (IOC). Phase 4 will allow the use of air-to-ground stores. The aircraft is inherently stable in yaw, neutral in roll and unstable in pitch.

Eurofighters, with expanded multirole capabilities, will replace the Jaguar force at Coltishall, although no base has yet been specified.

The German *Luftwaffe* currently has a requirement for 180 Eurofighters — 147 single-seaters and 33 two-seaters, with no options planned. The type will enter service first with JG 73 *'Steinhoff'* at Laage in January 2003, which currently operates one squadron of F-4Fs and one squadron of MiG-29s. Displaced F-4F ICE aircraft will be distributed to the other Phantom wings, as Eurofighter conversion is

undergone in the following order: JG 74 in late 2005 at Neuberg, JG 71 in early 2007 at Wittmund and JG 72 in mid-2010 at Wittmund (the latter having already disbanded in early 2002).

Plans called for deliveries of the 140 air defense-optimized versions to be complete by around 2010, and for the remaining 40 aircraft to come from the third production batch. These would feature full multirole capabilities and be earmarked to replace the oldest of the *Luftwaffe's* Tornados. However, the

service has decided to reassess its plan to have only 40 examples equipped for ground-attack as well as air defense roles — and possibly double the number of multirole-capable aircraft within its order. Germany is currently scheduled to receive 28 single-seaters and 16 two-seaters from the first production batch. The split is 58 and 10 for Batch 2, and 61 and 7 for Batch 3. Software for the main air-to-surface roles is planned for Batch 2 (2005/10), with an expanded version offering full swing-role capabilities to be fielded with Batch 3 between 2011 and 2014.

The AMI is to receive 121 aircraft (105 single-seat and 16 two-seat) into Italian service, of which the first (a two-seater) should be deliv-

DA1 and DA2 head out in tandem. Of the seven development aircraft, five are single-seat models. Britain and Spain built the two-seaters.

The fighter's very large intakes are clearly evident in this head-on view. Radar-absorbent materials (RAM) are utilized around the intakes to help maintain the Eurofighter's extremely small frontal radar cross-section (RCS). It is a particularly stealthy warplane at this angle.

ered in July 2002. Options are being held on a further nine aircraft. The AMI plans to equip five fighter groups and an operational conversion unit, within three wings, and each of the six *gruppi* (squadrons) is expected to be allocated 15 aircraft. The remainder will be held in reserve and the service has yet to release official confirmation of the units that will operate the type. However, it is widely assumed that the first unit to form (from February 2004) will be a squadron from the 4° *Stormo* (4th Wing) at Grosseto. The other two wings expected to gain Eurofighters are the 36° *Stormo* at Gioia del Colle and the 37° *Stormo* at Trapani.

Spain's *Ejército del Aire*, in whose service the aircraft will be designated the C.16 Tifón (CE.16 if a two-seater), is to receive 87 Eurofighters with an option for a further 16. The EADS-CASA prototype, DA6, is designated XCE.16 and operates from the air force's *Centro Logístico de Armamento y Experimentación* (CLAEX) test center at Torrejón. In late 2002, the first series production aircraft will be delivered to serve the training unit being formed at Getafe, the EADS-CASA factory airfield near Madrid, which will provide a cadre of six instructors for the OCU. First-batch deliveries will comprise two aircraft in 2002, four in 2003, eight in 2004 and six in 2005 — for a total of 20. From the second production batch Spain will receive seven aircraft per year beginning in 2006 through 2009, and five in 2010, making that batch total 33. The third batch will comprise 34 aircraft for delivery between 2010 and 2015, and will complete Spain's order for 87 examples (which includes 16 two-seaters).

The first Spanish unit to form will be the OCU at Morón – nominated as 113 *Escuadrón* of *Ala* 11 (113 Squadron of 11 Wing) — which will stand up in January 2004. It will have seven two-seaters and eight single-seaters on strength. The first frontline unit will be *Ala* 11's 111 *Escuadrón*, which is expected to be declared operational in 2007 with 18 aircraft. In 2010, the wing's third squadron, 112 *Escuadrón*, will be declared operational,

also with 18 aircraft. Until recently a Mirage F1 operator, *Ala* 11 thus will have 51 C.16/CE.16s assigned, while the remaining 36 examples will be divided equally between 141 and 142 *Escuadrones* of *Ala* 14. They currently fly Mirage F1s from Los Llanos and will start receiving the new jet in 2008/9. Re-equipment should be complete by 2015.

The RAF has been studying how best to gear up its pilot training for the Eurofighter and other new-generation combat aircraft that will follow. At the moment, 70 percent of the service's fast-jet pilots fly in two-seat aircraft, yet the future firmly lies with single-seaters — at least insofar as the Eurofighter is concerned. In order to prepare a cadre for the new aircraft, a number of F.Mk 3 pilots are undergoing retraining that includes tours in the Jaguar or Harrier to gain relevant single-seat and offensive support role experience. Similarly, some Jaguar and Harrier pilots will be sent to the F.Mk 3 force to gain experience in air defense flying, the techniques and tactics of BVR air combat and the use of related systems like radar and JTIDS. With the shortage of fast-jet pilots likely to worsen, there is even a possibility the service might have to retrain Tornado F.Mk 3 navigators as pilots.

Eurofighter GmbH's first serious attempt to find a customer outside the four-nation consortium was unsuccessful but, in truth, the United Arab Emirates was never likely to be a serious possibility. The disappointment was short-lived. In terms of competitiveness, the European aircraft has an important edge because of the timing of the F-22 project, that program's huge price tag and the issue of export sensitivity. Even those nations that might be cleared to receive F-22s may not be able to wait that long or may not be able to afford the type. What is more, the Raptor is still far from being ready for service. Many have recognized the price obstacle and have suggested that the F-35 might be a suitable alternative to the Eurofighter but, given the roles the European aircraft will fulfill, it does not represent a direct alternative. However, the all-round capabilities and promised low prices make it a highly attractive proposition for nations seeking a one-type air force. On the other hand, it does not match the Eurofighter's sophistication, especially in the air defense role.

While the Eurofighter has been developed with the interests of Germany, Italy, Spain and the UK uppermost, the type has

Eurofighter Typhoon

Initial Typhoon operations will focus on the air superiority role and the type is eagerly awaited by the four partner nations. Over the years, these countries have lagged further behind in terms of a state-of-the-art defense capability as the Eurofighter's in-service date has slipped. Of the four, Spain (with its upgraded Hornets) is in the most favorable position, while Germany (F-4 and MiG-29), Italy (F-104 and leased F-16) and the UK (Tornado F.Mk 3) have glaring requirements for a new fighter. Once the fighter commitment is fulfilled, limited air-to-ground capabilities will be added, although full multirole potential may not be realized until Batch 3 Typhoons appear around 2010.

Superfighters

The Italian DA3 leads the two German aircraft (DA1 and DA5) in formation during trials at Decimomannu, Sardinia. DA3 was the first aircraft to fly with EJ200 engines and has been used for various stores tests, including pit-drops of free-fall weapons during 1999. Italy plans to equip five fighter groups and an operational conversion unit with the type, and has 121 of the aircraft on order.

obvious potential elsewhere, although it faces stiff competition from the Rafale and advanced variants of the F-15, F-16, F-18 and Su-35. For nations seeking to acquire new fighters after 2010, the F-35 undoubtedly could impact export sales as could a potential export version of the F-22. Given the timings of those projects, the Eurofighter should enjoy a good window of opportunity over the next few years, and the partner countries naturally are seeking to exploit this. Initial marketing arrangements between the four reflect traditional ties and previous sales campaigns, so that BAE Systems is pursuing Australia, Singapore and the Middle East, while EADS-Deutschland leads the sales effort in Europe. EADS-CASA's main marketing responsibilities lie with South Korea, South America and Turkey, while Alenia is pursuing Brazil.

In November 1999, Eurofighter International (EFI) was formed to undertake all Typhoon sales — the four partners holding similar stakes in the new company to their overall shares in the program. While the individual partners pursue sales interest to the 'Request For Information' level, EFI takes over at the 'Request For Proposal' level and subsequent transactions, providing a channel for contractual purposes. In effect, the original Eurofighter partner company's sales team will continue whatever deal is under way, under secondment to EFI. Principal Eurofighter sales efforts are currently aimed at the following markets.

Australia: Faced with a considerable rise in the technological capabilities of nations to its north, Australia has outlined plans for a new fighter to replace the F/A-18

Hornets currently in service and being upgraded with ASRAAM and AMRAAM missiles. A Request For Information was issued in 1998, and in December 2000 Project Air 6000 was outlined. This foresees a need for up to 75 new fighters for its air force from 2012 onwards, for the purpose of defending its northern approaches. Another 25 strike aircraft will be needed to replace its F-111s from 2020, and a single type to meet both requirements makes sense. The Typhoon is one of the leading contenders, alongside the Rafale, Super Hornet and advanced Strike Eagle.

Brazil: Alenia's connections with Embraer because of the AMX program means the company is leading the sales effort in Brazil as the *Força Aérea Brasileira* searches for a new fighter.

Greece: Reflecting Eurofighter's first sales success, the Greek government announced in February 1999 that it would purchase at least 60 Typhoons in a deal worth a reported $10.2 billion, with options for another 30. Under the initial deal, Greece would have made annual payments from 2001 onwards to ensure a delivery time scale of 2006/10. The acquisition was confirmed on 8 March 2000 but, in January 2001, Greece sought to postpone payments. On 29 March that country announced the deal would be postponed until after 2004, to allow the funding of various social programs and the hosting of the Olympic games that same year. Despite the postponement, Greece remains officially committed to an eventual Typhoon purchase, but several commentators have noted it is increasingly unlikely.

Netherlands: The *Koninklijke Luchtmacht* (KLu) has identified a 100+-aircraft requirement to replace its F-16AM/BM fighter force at around the end of the decade. A Request For Information was sent to Eurofighter in June 1999, and in April

Spain's single prototype, DA6, has been involved in two-seat handling trials, including 'carefree' handling. It has also participated in hot-climate testing at Morón as well as verification of the environmental control system, for which EADS-CASA is the lead company.

At first glance the Eurofighter's intake could be mistaken for being highly radar-reflective. However, the shape shows a clear upward snaking so the engine fan faces are hidden from direct view by opposing radars. A prominent splitter plate is positioned above to remove the sluggish boundary layer near to the fuselage, while a lower flap ('varicowl') beneath is designed to improve airflow capture at high AoA and low speeds.

2000 the KLu chief of staff was treated to a flight in DA4. In early 2001, NETMA sent an invitation to the Dutch government to become a participant in the Eurofighter program, in an attempt to woo the country away from the JSF. Any Dutch participation in the Typhoon program would involve Batch 3 Enhanced Eurofighter production machines that are expected to enter service around 2010. However, in February 2002 the Dutch cabinet announced that the Netherlands would join the F-35 SDD program as a partner, subject to parliamentary ratification. The consequent resignation of the cabinet and general election have delayed the F-35 debate, and may again allow Eurofighter back into the bidding. Even if the KLu does not purchase Typhoons, Dutch companies like Philips, Signaal and Stork could become part of the Eurofighter production team.

Norway: This country was one of those actively courted by EADS-Deutschland. Faced with a need to replace its F-5 and F-16A/B fleet, the Royal Norwegian Air Force looked at the Typhoon, Rafale and an updated version of the F-16 (Block 50N) for service entry quoted as 'no later than 2006.' The Rafale was later dropped from the competition. The initial plan calls for acquisition of 20 aircraft to replace Northrop F-5s, with another 10 as a follow-on option. Norwegian evaluation of the Typhoon included a visit by DA5 to Rygge Air Base in June 1998, during which compatibility with local hardened shelters was validated. A liaison officer to NETMA was assigned in October, and flights by a Norwegian pilot were made in December 1998 and August 1999. By May 2000, a decision was immi-

nent but the incoming Labor government then announced the competition would be shelved.

In February 2001, a major round of cuts was announced aimed at reducing the air force's combat force to 48 F-16s, despite protests from the service that a minimum of 62 fighters was required. At the same time, it was announced the fighter replacement program would be reinstated but that it would not provide aircraft in time for the 2006 deadline set by the air force. By March 2001 the choice appeared to be between industrial participation in either the JSF or Typhoon Batch 2/3 programs, or an off-the-shelf approach that would allow the F-16, Rafale, Gripen and others to be re-evaluated, as well as the JSF and Typhoon. The revised requirement is for 48 aircraft for delivery from 2008 onwards and, to spread costs, this possibly could be divided into two 24-aircraft batches — one in 2008/10 and the second in 2015/18. A further batch of 12, which would bring the overall buy much closer to the air force's requirement, is being discussed subject to funding becoming available.

As the Norwegian requirement was pushed back, so the specter of the F-35 has risen again, and Lockheed Martin is pushing Norway hard to join the program. While Denmark announced in late May 2002 it would become a Level 3 partner in the JSF program, similar courting of Belgium and the Netherlands is being pursued. The US manufacturer is hoping to put together a deal similar to the one in which all four countries were sold F-16s in the so-called 'Sale of the Century'. If, however, the Eurofighter is selected, Norwegian industry can expect to participate strongly as a member of the manufacturing team. Kongsberg Defence and Aerospace (KDA) already builds composite rudders and flaperons for the Eurofighter, under contract to BAE Systems.

Poland: The former east-bloc nation issued an RFI for a long-term 60-fighter purchase in June 1999, responded to by EADS-Deutschland. The less expensive Gripen or F-16 is the most likely outcome, however.

Saudi Arabia: BAE Systems leads Eurofighter's efforts in the this country but no specific requirement or time scale regarding a new air superiority fighter has been stated officially. Any deal remains very much up in the air.

Singapore: Eurofighter was one of a number of companies which responded to an RFI issued by the Republic of Singapore Air Force in late 1999, covering 20-40 air superiority fighters. BAE Systems leads the sales effort. One element in which Singapore is reportedly interested is the ability of pilots and ground personnel to be trained at Warton under a similar program to the RAF's Case White.

Superfighters

SPECIFICATIONS

Wing span	35 ft 11 in (10.95 m)
Length	52 ft 04 in (15.96 m)
Height	17 ft 04 in (5.28 m)
Wing area	538.21 sq ft (50.00 m2)
Wings aspect ratio	2.205
Canard area	25.83 sq ft (2.40 m2)
Empty weight	21,495 lb (9750 kg)
Max. takeoff weight	46,297 lb (21000 kg)
Max. speed ('clean' at 36,090ft)	1,321 mph (1,147 knots)
Max. climb rate	CLASSIFIED
Service ceiling	CLASSIFIED
Combat radius	288-345 miles (463-556 km)
g limits	+9 /-3
Accommodation	Single pilot on Martin-Baker zero-zero ejection seat
Power plant	Two Eurojet EJ200 afterburning turbofans, each rated at 13,490 lb st (60.0 kN) dry and 20,250 lb st (90.0 kN) with afterburner
Armament	One 27-mm Mauser BK27 cannon

Short-range air-to-air missiles
Medium-range air-to-air missiles
Air-to-surface missiles
Antiradar missile
Guided and unguided bombs
Cannon is fitted in starboard-side fuselage
Other weapons accommodated on nine hardpoints and four under-
fuselage missile stations. Total ordnance load 14,000+ lb (approx. 6500 kg)

Germany's *Luftwaffe* is reassessing its original plan to have only 40 of its 180 Eurofighters equipped for ground attack as well as air defense roles, and may double the number of multirole examples within the overall count. As matters stand now, the service is due to receive 28 single-seaters and 16 twin-seaters from the first production batch. The follow-on numbers are 58 and 10, respectively, within Batch 2; and 61 and 7, respectively, within Batch 3. JG 73 has been designated the first operational unit and should begin the process of replacing its F-4s and MiG-29s in 2003. JG 74 will follow, but it will not be until 2007 when JBG 31 (the ground attack wing at Nörvenich) begins to receive replacements for its Tornado IDS models. The aircraft on the opposite page has a dummy cockpit painted on its fuselage underside, designed to confuse an enemy pilot during close-in air combat.

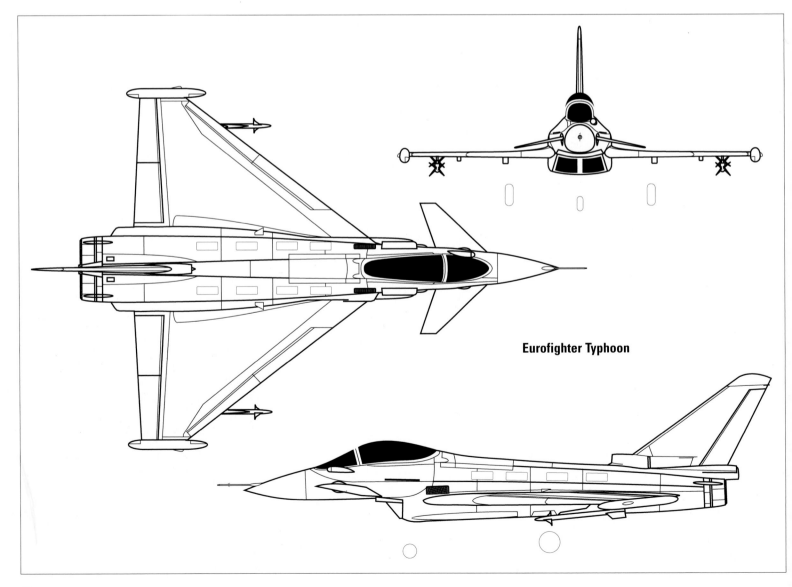

Eurofighter Typhoon

CHAPTER 4

Saab JAS39 Gripen

DEVELOPMENT & FLIGHT-TESTING

First taking to the air in 1988, the Saab JAS39 Gripen has since become the backbone of Sweden's air defense. Originally developed to fill *Flygvapnet* (Swedish Air Force) requirements for a fourth-generation fighter, the Gripen has evolved into a functional 'swing-role' combat aircraft — a concept that involves employing a multirole platform for multiple purposes during the same mission. As it has demonstrated in operational service, the type is well equipped to meet the requirement. During training sorties it is routine for a Gripen four-ship, for instance, to launch for a low-level ground attack, conduct reconnaissance and, perhaps, undertake air-to-air 'targeting' thereafter before returning to base.

The program that led to development of the Gripen got under way during the depths of the Cold War when non-aligned Sweden was exploring a fighter replacement for its Drakens and Viggens. Initially, a number of foreign types were studied that included the (then) General Dynamics F-16 Fighting Falcon and McDonnell Douglas F/A-18 Hornet. However, the government decided Sweden should develop its own platform, thereby enabling the Linköping-based Swedish Aviation Company (Svenska Aeroplan Aktiebolage or Saab) to continue its long tradition of building fighters. It was a major technical and financial challenge for a nation of just eight million people but the project survived many setbacks throughout the 1980s and 1990s.

Since being founded on 2 April 1937, Saab has developed 13 different types and built more than 4,000 aircraft, most of which were specifically tailored to *Flygvapnet* requirements. Sweden's long-standing policy of armed neutrality probably contributed significantly to the development of its highly capable aviation industry — one that does not rely primarily on foreign technology. For more than 50 years the company has manufactured all major aircraft and missile systems used by the

The JAS39B is the two-seat model of the Gripen and currently serves as a trainer. Although it carries no gun, this version is fully combat capable and additional missions are likely to be developed for it as air-to-ground capabilities are expanded. Suppression of enemy air defenses (SEAD) is an obvious choice if an anti-radar missile is adopted. The Swedish Air Force has expressed a desire to have such a weapon operational on the Gripen by 2006/7.

Swedish Air Force — fighters like the Saab 29 Tunnan, Saab 32 Lansen, Saab 35 Draken and Saab 37 Viggen. Today, Sweden is probably the world's smallest country with the know-how to develop modern combat aircraft comparable to advanced designs fielded by much larger nations.

In late 1979, Sweden's government (Riksdag) initiated development of a *Jakt/Attack/Spaning* (meaning fighter/ attack/reconnaissance) or 'JAS' combat aircraft. With the goal of having one platform fill all three roles, a number of Saab designs were reviewed. However, it was Project 2105 (which subsequently became Project 2108 and then Project 2110) that the Defense Materiel Administration (*Försvarets Materielverk* or

FMV) recommended to the government. The project called for an unstable, lightweight, single-seat, single-engine, fly-by-wire, delta-winged aircraft with all-moving canards. It was to be powered by an RM12 afterburning turbofan in the 18,000-lb (80-kN) class — a modified and upgraded version of the General Electric F404-400 power plant built by Volvo Flygmotor. On 30 June 1982, the FMV contracted for five prototypes and an initial production run of 30 airframes.

On 9 December 1988, the first prototype (serial 39-1) undertook its maiden flight with test pilot Stig Holmström at the controls. He had previously logged more than 1,000 hours in the JAS39 simulator. However, during the comprehensive flight-test program serious problems were experienced with both the advanced fly-by-wire flight control system (FCS) and unstable design configuration. During the sixth flight, on 2 February 1989, 39-1 crashed while landing at Linköping. Fortunately, test pilot Lars Rådeström was able to walk away from the accident suffering only a broken arm — but a serious delay in the program's development ensued.

Detailed analysis traced the cause of the accident to pilot-induced oscillation (PIO) that resulted from flaws in the pitch control routine of the FCS. Major software improvements were undertaken in cooperation with Calspan in the United States, using a modified Lockheed NT-33A to explore FCS performance. The Gripen flight-test program resumed 15 months later and proceeded largely to schedule until 18 August 1993, when production aircraft 39102 was lost in a dramatic crash during an air display over Stockholm. On exiting a roll, Rådeström lost control of the aircraft and, within six seconds, the Gripen had stalled at a dangerously low altitude. It left him with no option but to abandon the aircraft. He ejected safely and, miraculously, no one was hurt on the ground when the Gripen crashed onto a small island in the center of the city, in front of thousands of spectators.

Saab later announced the accident had been caused by high amplification of stick commands by the FCS, in combination

company had previously faced. After the first crash the company was able to recreate the incident using Calspan's test bed aircraft. Saab rewrote the FCS and, soon after the second crash, had correctly identified a unique set of problems. While the accidents were attributed to PIO, the situations were unusual inasmuch that control of the aircraft was lost very quickly. By adding an intelligent, rate-limiting filter to the FCS and making certain other changes, the difficulties were finally overcome.

By 1996 more than 2,000 test flights and air-to-surface and air-to-air weapons separation tests had been completed successfully. Spin recovery and high-Alpha (angle of attack) testing explored the Gripen's flying envelope, and trials at 28° Alpha were concluded using early-standard FCS software, even though that set had a preliminary limit of only 20°. Extreme high-Alpha testing, using the specially equipped all-black prototype 39-2, was successfully completed as well. Since 1997, operational Alpha limits have been increased significantly in response to customer requirements and expectations are that an operational FCS limit in the region of 50° will be achievable.

The original flight-test program called for five single-seat prototypes (39-1 through 39-5) but when the first production aircraft (serial 39101) took to the air on 10 September 1992, it replaced 39-1 as a test bed. Later, a two-seat Gripen prototype (serial 39800) also became a flight-test platform, completing its first flight on 29 March 1996. Prototypes 39-2 and 39-4 were retired in 1999 and dispatched to the air museum in Malmslätt. Meanwhile, Saab continues to operate its own test fleet for basic systems development, and borrows additional Gripens from the air force as required.

Despite its small size, Sweden has built an aerospace industry that is at the cutting-edge in terms of of latest-generation avionics, weapon development and advanced airframe design. As a key player, Saab has gained an enviable reputation as the designer of a distinctive line of fighters. In formation with the JAS39A in the foreground is a Saab J35 Draken (leading) and a Saab JA37 Viggen. Unlike its predecessors, the Gripen is a true multirole aircraft — one that continues to evolve and is said to be meeting fully the expectations of Sweden's *Flygvapnet* (Air Force).

with rapid and significant stick movements by the pilot. Again test flying was suspended and it was not until December 1993 that FCS shortcomings were finally resolved. Not having the benefit of outside experience to draw on, Saab had to take the lead in identifying and solving problems no other aerospace

AVIONICS

'Air supremacy gained through information superiority' is at the heart of Sweden's FV 2000 military doctrine. In the case of the Gripen, acquired information comes from three main sources — on-board sensors, communications and the datalink. The Ericsson PS-05/A multi-mode, pulse-Doppler X-band radar is the main avionics sensor and provides the jet with its ability to perform in air-to-air and air-to-surface roles. The radar's planar array is a small, conventional and mechanically driven unit utilizing FM pulse-compression for long-range detection. Many details about the PS-05/A are still classified but the Gripen is reported to be capable of detecting typical fighter-size targets at a distance of 74 miles (120 km). The pilot has three selectable search patterns: 2 x 120°, 2 x 60° and 4 x 30° with a scan rate of 60° per second. Surface mapping and search covers an area that is expandable from 3.1 x 3.1 miles (5 x 5 km) to 25 x 25 miles (40 x 40 km).

Four main tracking modes are available to the pilot in combat. Track-while-scan allows enhanced situational awareness and multiple targets to be monitored, while priority-target tracking enables high-quality, multiple-target tracking to be accomplished during missile engagements. Single-target tracking can be employed when highest quality monitoring is required, like gun aiming, and air combat mode is available for automatic target acquisition during short-range, air-to-air engagements.

Central to the Gripen's warfighting capability is its unique Communication and Datalink 39 (CDL39), which is probably the best in the world. *Flygvapnet* has plenty of experience with datalink systems, having explored this technology since 1965 with its J35F Drakens and JA37 Viggens, thereafter. In beyond-visual-range (BVR) combat, where information and situational awareness are key, a datalink system gives the user unrivaled battlespace awareness. The advantages of datalink systems are well recognized in other quarters, too. The Joint Tactical Information Distribution System (JTIDS) used by US armed forces and Britain's RAF, and NATO's Link 16 are other examples. However, JTIDS and Link 16 are fitted to just a few aircraft and are generally command-driven systems used to guide other aircraft. They do not allow a free flow of information between platforms and tend to be limited in the type of data they can handle. Furthermore, compared to the CDL39, their basic data exchange rates are painfully slow. Such aircraft as the Super Hornet and Eurofighter Typhoon will be the first operational types outside Sweden to have datalink capabilities that come close to the system fielded by the Gripen.

The CDL39 consists of two Fr41 analog radios, one Fr90 digital radio, an audio management unit (AMU), a ground telecommunication amplifier (GTA), an audio control panel (ACP) and a communication control display unit (CCDU). The latter two are located in the cockpit and serve as interfaces for the pilot. The most advanced component of the CDL39 is the Rockwell-Collins-supplied Fr90 that operates in the 960-1215 MHz bandwidth and uses electronic warfare (EW) resistant technologies like frequency hopping, encryption and advanced coding. The CDL39 is fully integrated with Sweden's new Tactical Radio System (TARAS) — a secure radio network for JAS39 and JA37D fighters, S100B Argus AEW&C platforms, S102B Korpen SIGINT aircraft and ground-based units of the Stridlednings Central Command and Control Center (StriC). The FMV is currently determining how best to make the CDL39

The JAS39 demonstrates excellent short-field capabilities. The combination of a delta-wing and canards enables a Gripen in air defense configuration to complete its landing roll in just 1,650 feet (500 m). The large canards tilt almost 90° forward after the aircraft touches down, to act as enormous air brakes that also help keep the nosewheel firmly on the runway and maximize wheel-braking efficiency. The fighter is also fitted with a pair of conventional air brakes. Under harsh field conditions, the Gripen is capable of operating from snow-covered runways as short as 2,650 feet (800 m).

A Gripen pilot is able to acquire external data from on-board sensors, the communications suite and an extremely effective datalink. Without a doubt, the JAS39 is the most datalink-intensive fighter in service today, fielding capabilities that far exceed those of other fast jets. Coupled with the aircraft's low radar cross-section (RCS), the datalink helps makes a the Gripen a particularly stealthy adversary.

was based around an Ericsson EP-17 fully electronic display system. It consists of a Hughes wide-angle, holographic head-up display (HUD) and three monochrome 5 x 6 inch (12 x 15 cm) head-down displays (HDD) run by separate Ericsson PP1 and PP2 display processors. The latter company also developed the SDS80 central computer, consisting of a number of D80 computers running the major systems. This avionics standard is referred to as Mk 1.

Several changes have impacted Batch Two, including the fact that Lockheed Martin replaced Lear as the FCS vendor. Saab is still responsible for writing the FCS software but Lockheed Martin now supplies the computer hardware. Another supplier change was made with respect to the HUD when Kaiser Electronics took over from Hughes. Finally, Ericsson switched to avionics standard Mk 2 with a new PP12 display processor that combines the functions of the earlier PP1/2 boxes into a single, smaller and more powerful unit. In addition, D80E computers have been introduced, which have five times the memory and 10 times the speed of the D80. Such improvements are gradually being retrofitted to Mk 1 Gripens, to bring about a common JAS39A/B standard.

Additional modifications and improvements are still being introduced to production Batch Two aircraft. As a consequence,

communicate with JTIDS to facilitate international Gripen operations.

Up to four aircraft can be transmitting (active) on the datalink at any one time and an unlimited number can be receiving (passive). According to one *Flygvapnet* source, the CDL39 has a range of 300+ miles (500 km) in the air, which can be extended using intermediate aircraft as relay platforms. Its most basic function allows the CDL39 to transmit radar/sensor pictures and aircraft/weaponry status data anywhere on the TARAS network. To send data on the link, all the pilot has to do is select the appropriate radio channel (pre-set by the mission planning system) and begin transmitting. Extensive testing has shown it to be unjammable.

The Gripen's datalink offers enormous flexibility. For example, in the air-to-surface role one aircraft 'package' can attack a target, obtain a radar picture of the target area and relay it to the cockpits of the next wave of aircraft. Those crews thus have the benefit of an accurate image of the target area, enabling them to know which have been successfully hit already. Furthermore, that same information can be relayed back to the StriC for informed decision making on the ground. In the air-to-air role it is possible for one Gripen to transmit its radar picture of an airborne target to the radar screen of another aircraft. The second aircraft can then leave its radar switched off, approach the target and engage it without ever betraying its presence. Furthermore, any weapons launched can be guided to the target using the first aircraft's radar, and use of the AEW&C radar allows an even larger 'air picture' to be datalinked to a formation of Gripens, effectively increasing their combat reach.

As proof of the capabilities bestowed on the Gripen by its datalink system, the air force has run air defense exercises deploying just six JAS39s to defend half the country. Using the CDL39, three pairs flying combat air patrol (CAP) can monitor Sweden's entire east coast — from the northern edge of the island of Gotland in the Baltic, to Ronneby Air Base and beyond to the southern tip of the country. Gripen pilots each know where every other is at all times, what they are seeing and what they are doing. One senior *Flygvapnet* pilot with considerable Draken and Viggen experience likened his first encounter with the Gripen to having been cured of 25 years of blindness.

Swedish Gripen orders are being fulfilled in three batches. With avionics development ongoing, it is not surprising that aircraft thus have been and will be delivered with different systems and capabilities. All Batch One aircraft were fitted with a Lear Astronics triplex, digital fly-by-wire FCS, and the cockpit

avionics standard Mk 3 is being incorporated into the last 20 Batch Two examples (serial 39207 onwards). The new standard incorporates a completely new super computer developed by Ericsson. Called the D96, it replaces the D80E. Also known as the Modular Airborne Computer System (MACS), it offers more program memory and processing power utilizing PowerPC chips on a VME bus structure, and facilitates the introduction of advanced color HDD cockpit displays. As a result, Batch Two aircraft include Mk 2 and Mk 3 examples.

All Batch Three aircraft will have Mk 4 avionics, comprising a new and much larger 6 x 8-inch (16 x 21-cm) MFID 68 active-matrix, LCD color HDD, and Ericsson Saab MPEG-2-based DiRECT digital mass memory in place of the current High-8 analog 8-mm cockpit video recorder. The two-seater will be used for advanced tactical training as well as operational missions, having either a second pilot or a system operator in

the back seat. Unlike the JAS39B, the JAS39D will have a separate radio and display processor in the rear cockpit so tasks can be accomplished independently. This will allow special missions to be performed by the aircraft, like acting as 'strike package' leader or scenario commander, suppression of enemy air defenses (SEAD) or employment of electronic counter-measures (ECM).

According to current *Flygvapnet* plans only Mk 3 Gripens will be retrofitted with Mk 4 avionics because baseline Mk 1 and Mk 2 aircraft do not have sufficient computing power to handle the upgrade. While the FMV has expressed a desire to see all Gripens brought up to full Mk 4 standard, no formal funding is in place for this. As a result, the air force will have two Gripen variants in service, fielding noticeably different avionics standards that offer different capabilities. Within *Flygvapnet*, the latest variant is often referred to as '208-status' since serial 39208 will be the first Mk 3/4 Gripen to go into operational service. Serial 39207 will be retained by Saab for use as a JAS39C prototype and re-serialed 39-6, while the two-seat test bed, serial 39800, will become the JAS39D prototype. Thus, the last 20 Batch Two Gripens will be brought up to full Batch Three standard. Whether these JAS39A/Bs will be re-designated JAS39C/Ds is an open question.

A second-generation electronic warfare fit will be introduced with Batch Three models (Batches One and Two aircraft having an interim EW fit only). This is being developed by Ericsson Saab Avionics and is known as Electronic Warfare System 39 (EWS39). Capabilities will include full emitter detection, identification and location; dynamic threat analysis and countermeasures deployment. In addition to the existing self-defense measures (a radar warning receiver or RWR in the wing tips, ECM modules in the fin and nose, and BOP 403 chaff/flare dispensers in the wing root), EWS39 will add two pylon-mounted BOP 402 countermeasures dispensers, a laser warning system, a missile approach warning system and one BOL 500 towed RF decoy. The latter will be carried in a housing under the port wing. EWS39 will give the JAS39C/D full self-defense and escort jammer capabilities for all missions.

Batch Three Gripens will be fully NATO-interoperable to ensure *Flygvapnet* JAS39C/Ds are capable of participating in multinational operations worldwide. Improvements will include night vision goggle (NVG) compatibility and a new IFF system. Further Gripen upgrades under consideration by the

air force (but not yet contracted for) either include or included passive search-and-track systems (Saab Dynamics IR-OTIS, featuring a Russian-style infrared ball sensor mounted in front of the canopy), a helmet-mounted display from one of two competing sources — the Oden display from Celsius or a joint Ericsson Saab/Pilkington proposal, and a phased-array radar with an Ericsson active electronically scanned antenna (AESA).

The Gripen is cleared for an impressive array of ordnance that help bring true multirole capabilities to the type. Air-to-air ordnance can include AIM-9L Sidewinders (Rb 74), AIM-120 AMRAAMs (Rb 99) and the IRIS-T. The single-seater is also fitted with a single 27-mm Mauser BK27 cannon. Air-to-surface options include the AGM-65 Maverick (Rb 75) seen below and on the outboard wing pylons of the aircraft top left, and the Rb 15F anti-ship missile visible on the inboard wing pylons top left. In addition, the JAS39 can field the DWS 39 anti-armor dispensing weapon, as well as the KEPD 150 Taurus — a standoff weapon equipped with GPS/INS guidance, terrain-referenced navigation and an imaging infrared terminal seeker. While the fighter was developed to meet *Flygvapnet* specifications, NATO weapon systems have been integrated to facilitate possible joint operations with other nations and to enhance the Gripen's export prospects. Now under development in Europe is the Meteor missile, a highly advanced air-to-air weapon that will far exceed the capabilities of the AIM-120. The Gripen will field the missile when it enters service in a few years time.

Weapon Systems

Gripen weapons carriage trials began shortly after the type's first flight in 1988. From the outset several representative external store combinations were used to ascertain their impact on aircraft performance, handling qualities and 'flutter,' as well as for load and stress testing. Actual weapons firing qualifications began in 1991 and Gripens in service with

use against wide-area, non-armored targets. It weighs 1,450 lb (650 kg) and has 24 laterally firing launch tubes. Typical submunition loads include the MJ1, which is an 8.8-lb (4-kg) airburst weapon used against soft targets, and the larger 39.2-lb (18-kg) MJ2 fitted with a proximity-fused, anti-armor warhead. The Bk90 is an unpowered launch-and-forget weapon with a glide range of about 3-6 miles (5-10 km) depending on the launch speed, launch height and attack profile selected. Equipped with its own inertial navigation system (INS), radar

Separation tests for the AGM-65 Maverick (Rb75) began in 1993 and the weapon became operational on the Gripen in 1997.

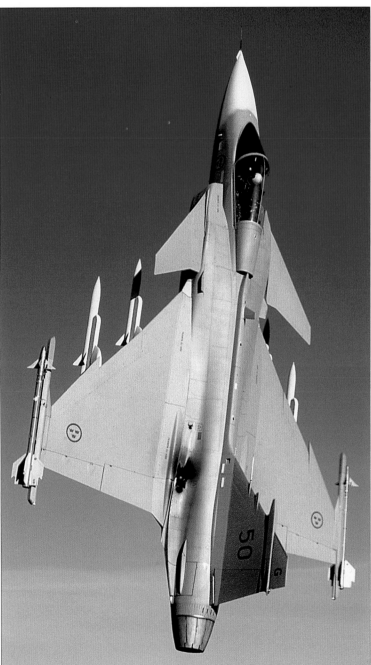

Fitted with a lethal air-to-air load, this example has AIM-9L Sidewinders on the wingtip stations and four AIM-120 AMRAAMs under its wings.

Flygvapnet (plus the export model) are now cleared for a wide range of air-to-ground and air-to-air ordnance fitted to eight hard points. Meanwhile, several new systems are under development for the Gripen's future arsenal.

Basic armament consists of a built-in 27-mm Mauser BK27 cannon, recessed under the port center-fuselage in the single-seater, which is capable of firing 120 rounds. Saab has developed a unique auto-gun aiming function integrated with the radar and autopilot, which is operational on both the JA37 and JAS39. The auto-aimer tracks a target and calculates the correct engagement range and deflection angles. Once the pilot opens fire, the radar tracks the course of the outgoing shells and the autopilot controls the aircraft to steer the gunfire onto the target. The system is extremely reliable and accurate and allows hands-off gun attacks to be made against targets at very long distances, day or night and in bad weather.

Initially, the Gripen began replacing the oldest Viggen variants in *Flygvapnet* service — attack AJ/AJS37s. The Gripen's all-round weapon for attack purposes is the short-range, air-to-surface Rb75 missile — the Hughes AGM-65A/B Maverick. 'Rb' is an abbreviation of Robot. Sweden uses the original TV-guided versions of the Maverick, the AGM-65A and the AGM-65B with a zoom function allowing targets to be acquired at twice the range of the AGM-65A. The Maverick has a declared range of 1.8 miles (3 km) but *Flygvapnet* sources claim the Rb75 has an effective range against a tank-size target of at least twice that. Another system from the attack Viggen employed by the JAS39 is the Bofors M70 135-mm unguided rocket system. The missiles are carried in pods of six.

More specialized attack weapons include the Bk90 (DWS39 Mjölner) standoff sub-munitions dispenser, which was cleared for operational use on the Gripen in 1997. 'Bk' is short for *Bombkapsel*, meaning bomb dispenser. It is a Swedish-developed version of the German DASA DWS24 dispenser designed for

Superfighters

altimeter and on-board computer, it navigates to its pre-programmed target using four tail-mounted control fins.

For sea strikes, the Gripen's primary weapon is the Rbs15F medium-range, anti-ship missile developed by Saab Dynamics. It is an air-launched version of the Rbs15M originally used by fast naval patrol boats. It weighs 1,320 lb (600 kg), including a 440-lb (200-kg) armor-piercing, HE warhead. It is powered by a Microturbo TRI-60-3 turbofan that extends the missile's maximum range to an impressive 15 miles (24 km). The Rbs15F variant is an extremely smart and agile anti-ship missile, specially designed for coastal defense in the narrow waters of the Swedish archipelago. After launch, the subsonic missile flies a step-down, sea-skimming attack profile using INS data

for mid-course corrections and an active radar seeker for terminal guidance. In a typical four-aircraft attack, the flight leader can acquire targets with his aircraft's radar and then datalink his target solution to the rest of the flight. The other crews are then free to make independent attacks to the same plan. Individual pilots can set up multiple attacks by selecting a desired time-on-target and launching their Rbs15Fs, leaving the missiles to sort out the correct attack profiles.

For air defense, the Gripen carries Rb74 (AIM-9L Sidewinder) infrared-seeking missiles as standard, and for BVR combat the Rb99 (AIM-120B AMRAAM) has been cleared for operational use since mid-1999. From the outset, the Gripen was designed to be AMRAAM-compatible and contracts between Sweden and the US government have ensured all essential systems like the PS-05/A radar function with the active-radar homing AMRAAM. The JAS39 is capable of conducting multiple Rb99 engagements against four targets — the maximum number of missiles the aircraft is currently cleared to carry. Its radar can perform priority track-while-scan functions on all four, while simultaneously maintaining track-while-scan locks on another 10. In the future, a twin Rb99 launcher may be installed on the centerline weapon station.

With the ordnance described both integrated and operational, the Gripen is fully capable of fulfilling its current roles. Meanwhile, *Flygvapnet* is seeking to expand its weapon options. The service has indicated acquisition of laser-guided bombs (LGB) is a fast-track, high-priority objective. The Rafael/Zeiss Optronic Litening pod has been chosen for integration on the type and will be carried on the starboard-side, under-fuselage station. The Litening is a combined FLIR/laser navigation and targeting system usually paired with various Paveway LGBs. Gripen integration and qualification was initiated in 2001.

The air force will also acquire a new precision standoff

On the inboard wing stations are DWS39 (Bk90) anti-armor dispensing weapons. Initial Gripen jettison testing of the ordnance was undertaken in 1992 and operational use began five years later.

Fitted to the inboard wing pylon of this partly concealed JAS39A is a radar-seeking Rb 15F ship-killing munition that has a straight-line range of 125 miles (200 km) and offers far greater area coverage than either the Block 1C Harpoon or MM40 Excocet.

mounted sights and be effective against cruise missiles. Gripen flight-testing for the Rb98 was initiated in 1999, and initial operational capability (IOC) is expected in 2004.

The air force recently put forward a requirement for adoption of an anti-radar missile system to give the Gripen 'Wild Weasel' (suppression of enemy air defenses or SEAD) capabilities. So far no commitments have been made public but the idea is likely to be addressed soon, given the importance of the role in connection with international peace-keeping missions. The advanced JAS39D two-seat Gripen would be a key element of any SEAD weapon system but funding is the primary issue. Still, the service hopes to field such a system by 2006/7.

With 'downsizing' a fact of life for most of the world's air forces, *Flygvapnet* has been no exception. Recently announced plans to reorganize the force will impact both the number of operational units and bases. Under the latest plan, there will be just eight Gripen squadrons flying from four bases. The multirole capabilities of the type will go a long way to mitigating operational reductions, particularly when later batch (more capable) versions join the fleet.

weapon for its Gripens, in the shape of the German-Swedish Taurus KEPD-350. The KEPD (an abbreviation for Kinetic Energy Penetration and Destruction) family is a series of turbojet-powered, standoff weapons fitted with GPS/INS guidance, terrain-referenced navigation (TER NAV) and an imaging infrared terminal seeker. There are two versions. With a range of 93 miles (150 km), the KEPD-150 carries a 2,336-lb (1060-kg) warhead, whereas the KEPD-350 has a 3,086-lb (1400-kg) warhead and has a range 217 miles (350 km). The KEPD-350 was developed for *Luftwaffe* Tornados and Eurofighters, whereas the smaller KEDP-150 was always earmarked for the Gripen. However, recent improvements in the -350's load-carrying capacity have allowed the larger weapon to be integrated in preference to the -150.

As a replacement for the aging Rb74, the Rb98 infrared imaging system tail control (IRIS-T) is being developed for

Flygvapnet also wants to have a reconnaissance management system (RMS) operational by 2004, particularly as current plans call for Sweden's remaining reconnaissance-capable AJSF/AJSH37 Viggens to be retired by then. Now under development by Ericsson Saab Avionics, the new Gripen RMS recce pod will employ electro-optical sensors and image storage on digital media instead of traditional film cameras. The system, destined for use by single-seat Gripens, will also include a fully digitized image processor, a datalink option and near real-time cockpit presentation. No other details have yet been released. In the meantime, Saab has integrated the British-built Vinten Vicon 70 Series 72C tactical EO/IR recce pod into export models for low- and medium-altitude reconnaissance. While the Vinten has been adopted as an affordable export option, *Flygvapnet* awaits a decision regarding the more capable RMS solution it proposes.

Another important weapon system destined for the Gripen is the Meteor, the advanced long-range BVR air-to-air missile currently under development by a consortium led by Matra and BAE Systems. The 'launch and leave' Meteor is being designed to penetrate dense and highly sophisticated EW environments, and offers performance several times better than existing AMRAAMs. The ramjet-powered missile features an active radar seeker with mid-course update capabilities and, after being fired, will be capable of receiving targeting data from the launch aircraft or a number of other platforms. These will include another fighter, an AWACS or the Saab Erieye, allowing the launch aircraft to escape to relative safety immediately after releasing the weapon.

Flygvapnet Gripens. It is a next-generation, agile dogfight missile. IRIS-T is a pan-European missile program led by Germany's BGT and with participation from Sweden, Spain, Norway, Italy, Greece and Canada. It uses a combination of wings and thrust-vectoring to provide range and maneuverability, and has an IIR seeker of the focal-plane array type. The weapon is powered by a new solid-propellant rocket motor and has an effective range of approximately 7.5 miles (12 km). Furthermore, the warhead can be adapted from existing Sidewinder missiles. It will be fully integrated with helmet-

SAAB JAS39 Gripen

1. Pitot head
2. Vortex-generating strakes
3. Glass-fiber radome
4. Planar radar scanner
5. Scanner tracking mechanism
6. Radar mounting bulkhead
7. ADF antenna
8. Ericsson PS-05A multi-mode pulse-Doppler radar equipment racks
9. Yaw vane
10. Cockpit front pressure bulkhead
11. Lower UHF antenna
12. Incidence vane
13. Electro-luminescent formation lighting strips
14. Rudder pedals, digital flight control system
15. Instrument panel, with triple Ericsson EP-17 CRT MFDs
16. Instrument panel shroud
17. Single-piece, frameless windscreen panel
18. Hughes wide-angle head-up-display (HUD)
19. Ericsson ECM pod
20. Starboard intake stores pylon
21. Cockpit canopy, electrically actuated, hinged to port
22. Canopy breaker miniature detonating cord (MDC)
23. Starboard air intake
24. Martin-Baker S10LS 'zero-zero' ejection seat
25. Sloping cockpit rear pressure bulkhead
26. Side mounted engine throttle lever, hands on throttle and stick (HOTAS) controls
27. Port side console panel
28. Cockpit section honeycomb skin panel
29. Door-mounted taxiing light
30. Nosewheel leg door
31. Twin-wheel nose undercarriage, aft retracting
32. Hydraulic steering unit
33. Cannon muzzle blast suppressor
34. Port engine air intake
35. Boundary layer splitter plate
36. Air conditioning system heat exchanger intake duct
37. Avionics equipment compartment, access via nosewheel bay
38. Boundary layer spill duct
39. Cockpit rear avionics equipment shelf
40. Starboard canard foreplane
41. UHF antenna
42. Heat exchanger exhaust ducts
43. Environmental control system equipment for cabin conditioning, pressurization and equipment cooling
44. Self-sealing fuel tank between intake ducts
45. Canard foreplane hydraulic actuator
46. Foreplane hinge mounting trunnion
47. Port intake ducting
48. 27-mm mauser BK27 cannon barrel, single gun offset to port
49. Temperature probe
50. Port navigation light

51. Centerline external fuel tank
52. Ammunition loading door
53. Ground test panels
54. Formation lighting strips
55. Port canard foreplane, carbon-fiber composite structure
56. Ammunition magazine
57. Center fuselage aluminium alloy structure and skin paneling
58. Upper fuselage aerodynamic strakes
59. VHF antenna
60. Dorsal spine fairing
61. TACAN antenna
62. Bleed air and cable ducting
63. Fuselage integral fuel tankage
64. Hydraulic reservoir, dual system port and starboard
65. Forged and machined wing attachment fuselage main frames
66. Engine compressor intake
67. IFF antenna
68. Wing attachment carbon-fiber composite cover panel
69. Starboard wing integral fuel tank
70. Pylon hardpoints
71. Starboard stores pylons
72. Leading-edge dogtooth
73. Two-segment leading-edge maneuvering flap
74. Carbon-fiber composite wing skin panelling
75. Combined wingtip RWR and missile launch rail
76. Wingtip missile installation
77. Rear position light, port and starboard
78. Starboard outboard elevon
79. Inboard elevon

80. Inboard elevon actuator housing fairing
81. Bleed air spill duct
82. Formation lighting strips
83. Automatic flight control system equipment
84. Fin root attachment joints
85. Rudder hydraulic actuator
86. Carbon-fiber composite skin panelling with honeycomb substrate

87. Flight control system dynamic pressure sensor head
88. Forward RWR antenna
89. ECM transmitting antenna
90. UHF antenna
91. Glass-fiber fin-tip antenna fairing
92. Strobe light/anti-collision beacon
93. Carbon-fiber composite rudder
94. Variable-area afterburner nozzle
95. Nozzle control actuators (three)
96. Port airbrake panel, open
97. Airbrake hinge fairings
98. Airbrake hydraulic jack
99. Afterburner ducting
100. Volvo Aero RM12 afterburning turbofan engine
101. Rear equipment bays, port and starboard
102. Microturbo Auxiliary Power Unit (APU)
103. Airframe-mounted accessory equipment gearbox bay
104. Titanium wing root attachment fittings
105. Port wing integral fuel tank
106. Multi-spar wing panel primary structure with carbon-fiber skin panelling
107. Inboard elevon actuator

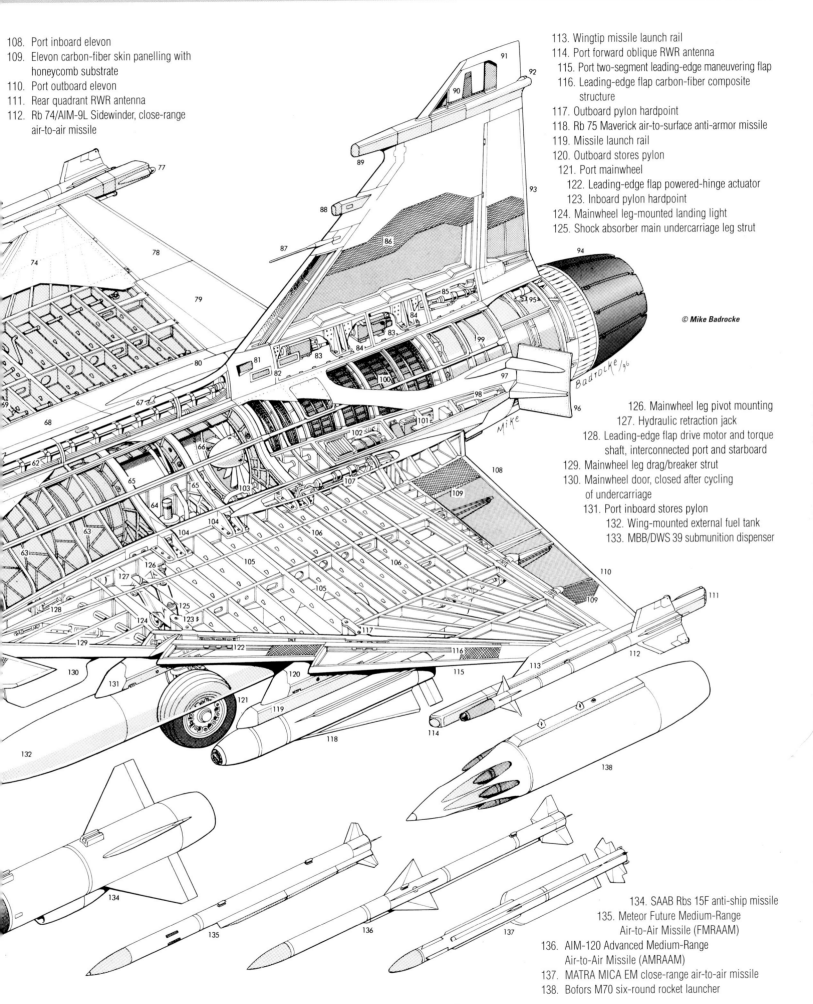

108. Port inboard elevon
109. Elevon carbon-fiber skin panelling with honeycomb substrate
110. Port outboard elevon
111. Rear quadrant RWR antenna
112. Rb 74/AIM-9L Sidewinder, close-range air-to-air missile

113. Wingtip missile launch rail
114. Port forward oblique RWR antenna
115. Port two-segment leading-edge maneuvering flap
116. Leading-edge flap carbon-fiber composite structure
117. Outboard pylon hardpoint
118. Rb 75 Maverick air-to-surface anti-armor missile
119. Missile launch rail
120. Outboard stores pylon
121. Port mainwheel
122. Leading-edge flap powered-hinge actuator
123. Inboard pylon hardpoint
124. Mainwheel leg-mounted landing light
125. Shock absorber main undercarriage leg strut

© Mike Badrocke

126. Mainwheel leg pivot mounting
127. Hydraulic retraction jack
128. Leading-edge flap drive motor and torque shaft, interconnected port and starboard
129. Mainwheel leg drag/breaker strut
130. Mainwheel door, closed after cycling of undercarriage
131. Port inboard stores pylon
132. Wing-mounted external fuel tank
133. MBB/DWS 39 submunition dispenser

134. SAAB Rbs 15F anti-ship missile
135. Meteor Future Medium-Range Air-to-Air Missile (FMRAAM)
136. AIM-120 Advanced Medium-Range Air-to-Air Missile (AMRAAM)
137. MATRA MICA EM close-range air-to-air missile
138. Bofors M70 six-round rocket launcher

OPERATIONAL & FLIGHT CHARACTERISTICS

Having been tailored to meet *Flygvapnet* operational requirements, the Gripen can operate from 2,650-ft (800-m) snow-covered runways, and meet a ground turnaround time between sorties (for refueling, re-arming, essential servicing and inspection) of just 10 minutes. These capabilities are key elements of Sweden's BAS90 system that provides for wartime operations from dispersed road strips. Furthermore, the type has been designed to allow major maintenance to be easily performed under field conditions. During one *Flygvapnet* demonstration, a Gripen returned from a mission and a team of three completely removed its hot RM12 engine, then reinstalled it and the aircraft took off again, all within a period of 45 minutes.

is in the range of 1,150-1,300 ft (350-400 m).

Flying characteristics are optimized for fighter missions that make high demands on speed. The Gripen is fully 'supercruise' capable, meaning it can cruise at supersonic speeds without using the afterburner, even when carrying external loads. This is due partly to the extremely low induced drag of the design. Pilots have described the Gripen as turning and holding its speed like no other aircraft they have previously flown — cutting through the air in a way that is often unusual for a delta-wing.

While the Gripen's 9g-capability is similar to other modern fighters in service today, its 6g-per-second onset rate and carefree handling make g-lock a serious concern. The latter refers to the situation in which a lot of g is pulled quickly and the early effects of high g, like tunnel-vision and a tingling sensation, are not felt long enough to warn a pilot of his impending blackout. To help combat this, flight clothing for Gripen pilots includes an all-over G-suit that completely covers

Fitted with one engine, the JAS39 is powered by a Volvo Aero RM-12 turbofan. The power plant is based on the General Electric F404 and rated at 12,140 lb st (54 kN) dry and 18,100 lb st (80.51 kN) with afterburner. Originally designed for use in twin-engine jets, its output had to be increased and certain other changes were incorporated when the power plant was adapted for single-engine operation.

The combination of a delta-wing and canards not only gives the Gripen excellent flying characteristics but very good takeoff and landing performance as well. Less than 1,650 ft (500 m) of runway is needed for an aircraft in air defense configuration. During the landing roll the large canards are tilted almost 90° forward, making them act as air brakes that generate enormous amounts of drag and force down the nose gear so the nose-wheel brakes quickly becomes effective. In addition, the Gripen has conventional air brakes positioned on the rear fuselage sides. The takeoff technique reportedly used to maximize time-till-airborne is to apply full dry power (12,000 lb st/53.4 kN) against the brakes, then release them at the same time the afterburner (18,100 lb st/80.5 kN) is selected. Carrying a full internal fuel load but with no stores fitted, the Gripen lifts off after some 18 seconds at a speed of just over 200 mph (330 km/h), after rotating at about 150 mph (240 km/h). Adopting a climb speed of 340 mph (550 km/h) results in an impressive climb rate according to one crewman not previously familiar with the type. He also commented on the Gripen's excellent flying qualities and ease of handling, and described making a tactical ILS landing at an approach speed (finals) of 175-185 mph (280-300 km/h), and touching down at approximately 168 mph (270 km/h) flying a 12° angle-of-attack. On a separate approach made at a 14° angle-of-attack, the touchdown speed was reported to be 146 mph (235 km/h).

One particularly interesting feature is the braking logic, which allows the pilot to apply full brakes while still airborne. The braking system only activates after the nose-wheel has touched the ground and it is at this point that all of the control surfaces, including the canards, immediately move to maximum-drag positions — resulting in tremendous deceleration. The stopping distance from a 14° Alpha approach

the legs, a G-jacket that inflates in a similar fashion to the leg G-suit, and pressure breathing that acts against the jacket to force air to the pilot. The claim is that this additional protection equates to an overall reduction of 3-4g. In simple terms, when a pilot is pulling 9g it feels more like 5-6g if the clothing is worn.

The Gripen's real-world performance is impressive. On a combat air patrol 240 miles (385 km) from base, carrying two Rb99 AMRAAMs, two Rb74 Sidewinders and two fuel tanks, the aircraft can stay on station for two hours. Needless to say, imminent introduction of air-to-air refueling capabilities to the JAS39 will stretch this further. With three 1,000-lb GBU-16 laser-guided bombs loaded for a LO-LO-LO strike profile, the Gripen has a radius of 350 nm (403 miles/648 km). Carrying two GBU-16s and extra fuel tanks, the radius extends to 450 nm (517 miles/833 km). Furthermore, on a typical HI-LO-HI anti-shipping mission the Gripen's maximum range is 270 nm (310 miles/500 km) with two Rbs15Fs carried, while its maximum point-to-point (ferry) range is 1,500 nm (1,725 miles/2778 km).

According to reports from those operationally familiar with the Gripen, it is widely outperforming original specifications and yielding lower than expected aerodynamic drag and fuel-burn, and greater range and rate of climb than anticipated. It is also reported to be setting new standards for reliability, maintainability and availability, achieving 7.6 flight hours between failures. This translates to less than 10 maintenance man-hours per flight hour, which is just about the lowest of any frontline fighter. While its flyaway price is comparable to that of a new F-16C/D, the Gripen's operating costs are reported to be less than US $2,500 per flying hour, inclusive of fuel and all maintenance. This means the Gripen is already meeting 'swing-role' operational goals the air force has set for the period 2001-2020.

Saab JAS39 Gripen
This artwork depicts the fighter armed with the Meteor air-to-air missile. This European-developed, advanced BVR weapon promises far superior performance over existing AMRAAMs and will begin equipping a number of combat types later in the decade.

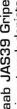

Saab/BAE Systems

FLIGHT OPERATIONS

Preparations for JAS39 operations started in December 1987 when the air force commander-in-chief decided F7 *Skaraborgs Flygflottilj* at Såtenäs should become the first operational Gripen wing. A few months later, it was announced that conversion training for all future JAS39 pilots should be centralized at F7 as well. A planning directive from *Flygvapnet's* headquarters in Stockholm itemized F7's future tasks as including centralized flight training, recurrent simulator training, operational test and evaluation and the setup of local combat-ready divisions (squadrons). The main arguments for selecting F7 Såtenäs were its relatively remote and isolated location, lack of physical obstacles and good prevailing conditions for flight training and exercises. For similar reasons the AJ37 Viggen entered *Flygvapnet* frontline service there back in 1973. However, early deployment planning pointed up the need for the facilities at Såtenäs to be upgraded not only to

The JAS39 Gripen is rapidly assuming the mantle of the Saab 37 Viggen — long the backbone of Swedish air defense, and flown in a number of variant forms (including reconnaissance, like the second aircraft from the left). The Gripen will be capable of more efficiently filling all of the roles flown by the Viggen, particularly when later batch aircraft start entering service.

accommodate the two local operational divisions, but a full division of 16-20 experienced pilots converting from Drakens or Viggens and each class of 5-12 new pilots coming directly from the Central Flying School (*Flygskolan*). F7 is also the designated site for export Gripen training.

A dedicated center for Gripen conversion training (Gripen Centrum) was constructed at Såtenäs and officially opened in June 1996. To optimize training efficiency all functions related to flight training have been concentrated at this one facility. These including class rooms, simulators, a meteorological office, flight operations plus a gymnasium. The facility is located close to the aprons and hangars so pilots can walk directly to and from their aircraft. With strong emphasis given to simulator training, Gripen Centrum houses two full-mission units (highly advanced dome-type simulators) and four multi-mission trainers (MMT). The latter are simpler systems having cockpit instruments and a screen to display an external environment. The simulators can be linked in such a way that

pilots can 'fly' missions either together or against one another. Plans call for all bases at which Gripens are to be stationed to be equipped with an MMT for local use.

The so-called FUS39 (*Flyg Utbildnings System* 39 or Flight Conversion System 39) has been established at Gripen Centrum. It comprises two fundamentally different training cycles. The first converts pilots with Viggen or Draken fighter experience while the other instructs new pilot graduates coming either straight from basic flying training (*Grundläggande Flyg Utbildning* or GFU) or basic tactical flying training (*Grundläggande Taktisk Utbildning* or GTU) courses with only 200 hours flying experience on SK60 trainers. Gripen conversion courses performed at F7 are designated TIS39:A and TIS39:Y. The first element of the designation stands for *Typinskolning* 39, meaning Type Conversion 39. The 'A' suffix denotes experienced pilots (*Äldre*, meaning older) while the 'Y' suffix denotes new pilots (*Yngre*, meaning younger). TIS39 is made up of four phases that take students through flying

Sweden's policy of abandoning permanent airfields and dispersing its aircraft to temporary locations in the country in the event of war, means the Gripen had to be designed with primitive field operations in mind and be capable of operating from roadstrips. Given the fighter's advanced avionics and other sophisticated systems, meeting these requirements was an added challenge for the designers.

training, avionics systems, weapon systems and basic combat training.

To date only pilots with fighter experience have converted to the Gripen, each having received some 60 flying hours and 40 simulator hours during the six-month TIS39:A. As extensive use is made of the advanced FMS and MMT simulators, TIS39:A does not require JAS39B (two-seater) flight training, and experienced pilots fly their first mission in the JAS39A after just 15 'flights' in the simulator. In November 2001, the first TIS39:Y course commenced at F7. Under the program Gripen conversion lasts 12 months and flying is split roughly 70 percent/30 percent between the single- and two-seat versions. Pilots then transfer to an operational *flygflottilj* for 12 months of advanced operational Gripen training. This course is called the *Grundläggande Flygslags Utbildning* JAS39 (GFSU JAS39), following which crews achieve full operational status.

The first Gripens delivered to the air force were taken on charge in 1994 by *Taktisk Utprovning* JAS39 or TU JAS39 (Operational Test and Evaluation JAS39). The unit was initially based at Malmslätt, to maximize cooperation with the Swedish Defense Materiel Administration's testing unit (FMV:PROV) also based there, and because of its close proximity to Saab's Linköping facility. Today, TU JAS39 is based at F7 Såtenäs, tasked with developing Gripen mission tactics and operational guidelines primarily. It also participates in Gripen systems development that encompasses integration of new weapons and sensors; command, control and information systems; mission planning and analysis equipment; and simulators. In addition, it is responsible for verification of tactical system functions.

Initial *Flygvapnet* operational units completing conversion to the JAS39 Gripen were F7's own divisions, which previously operated AJS37 Viggens. First to achieve operational status on 31 October 1997 was 2nd div./F7 (radio callsign 'Gustav Blå'). One year later, 1st div./F7

('*Gustav Röd*') followed. The second wing to undertake Gripen conversion was F10 at Ängelholm. Its two squadrons — 2nd div./F10 ('*Johan Blå*') and 1st Div/F10 ('*Johan Röd*') — initiated TIS39:A training at F7 Såtenäs in January 2000 and January 2001, respectively. Following that, F7 instructors assisted with GFSU:A training of F10 pilots with the entire process taking about a year for each division. '*Johan Blå*' has the distinction of being first to convert directly from the 1950s-vintage J35J Draken to the JAS39.

Original plans called for Sweden's 204 Gripens to equip 12 divisions by 2006, organized within six *flygflottiljer*. However, in March 2000 the Riksdag decided on a new defense plan that reduced the number of proposed Gripen divisions from 12 to eight. This was largely cost-driven. Two wings were earmarked for closure: F10 Ängelholm and F16 Uppsala. F10 was already heavily involved in the Gripen conversion process and F16 was to have been *Flygvapnet's* third Gripen wing. The decision came as a shock to many and although it seemed a strange development, the government considers this to be the best overall solution. It means *Flygvapnet's* eight Gripen divisions will be organized within four *flygflottiljer* — F4 Östersund, F7 Såtenäs, F17 Ronneby and F21 Luleå, and all will complete the conversion process by 2004. It was also decided at the time to increase the number of Gripens per division from 16 to 24 aircraft so the active inventory count would be unchanged. However, that decision was later reversed. Consequently, the air force will not fund further upgrades to its first 40 Gripens and these aircraft are to be leased or sold elsewhere.

Superfighters

The first operational unit to fly the Gripen was F7 *Skaraborgs Flygflottilj*. The wing has two JAS39 squadrons and is also the center for type training.

Despite the new developments, *Flygvapnet* decided to complete the conversion and build-up of F10's two Gripen divisions at Ängelholm before transferring them to F17 Ronneby. They will equip 1st div./F17 ('*Qvintus Röd*') and 2nd div./F17 ('*Qvintus Blå*') there before December 2002. Meanwhile, the pilots of 2nd div./F21 ('*Urban Blå*') have completed their TIS39:A at F7 Såtenäs and GFSU:A JAS39 at F10 Ängelholm, and began operational Gripen flying back at F21 Luleå in January 2002. 1st div./F21 ('*Urban Röd*') will continue to fly the AJSF37 Viggen in the recce role until the JAS39 is able to assume tactical recce missions, possibly in 2004. *Flygvapnet's* fourth and last wing to receive the Gripen will be F4 Östersund and 1st div./F4 ('*David Röd*') is expected to achieve operational status by July 2002. It will be followed by 2nd div./F4 ('*David Blå*') in April 2003.

As of February 2002 more than 100 JAS39As and 10 JAS39Bs had been delivered to Sweden's air force, and more than 20,000 flight hours had been logged at the end of 2001. Four aircraft in particular have flown more than their fair share of this total, being part of the PRI39 (Priority 39) program aimed at gaining early experience of airframe wear and tear. Two Batch One aircraft (serials 39121 and 39122) and two Batch Two models (serials 39131 and 39142) have each accumulated 800 hours. They have since undergone thorough structure and systems examinations. PRI39 will continue until both airframes have been subjected to 1,600 flying hours. Furthermore, two Batch Three Gripens will join the program as they become available.

As previously mentioned, fundamental to Gripen operations is the Bas90 philosophy of dispersed fields. While most nations have built hundreds of hardened aircraft shelters (HAS) on their air bases to prevent destruction of their aircraft on the ground, Sweden relies on a concept of protecting its assets by dispersing them in the open. The Gulf War, in particular, reinforced the value of this strategy when that conflict saw the destruction of Iraq's aircraft by modern precision-bombing techniques while they were inside their shelters. In the event of a war, all *Flygvapnet* peacetime air bases will be abandoned completely and each *flygflottilj* will disperse its aircraft in small groups around the country, and operate them from rural highways. This has been the policy since the 1930s.

The requirement for road-based operations has strongly influenced the air force's choice of equipment and organizational methods. All aircraft types, whether fighters or transports, have the capability to take off and land on runways no more than 2,650 ft (800 m) long and 52 ft (16 m) wide. In addition, between-mission servicing requirements must be possible under relatively primitive field conditions, being quick and simple to perform. This is a tall order for a fourth-generation jet but, despite the challenge, Saab has made it a reality for the Gripen. Another Bas90 requirement is that all support functions have to be mobile so they can be dispersed along with the aircraft.

At present, *Flygvapnet* operates six primary peacetime air bases and has 16 reserve war bases available for dispersed operations. Prior to 2000 the number was 24. Each Bas90 war base covers an area measuring approximately 12 x 19 miles

(20 x 30 km) and consists of one 6,600-ft (2000-m) primary runway (usually at an airfield) and three or four satellite 2,650-ft (800-m) secondary runways, which are usually strips of hardened and widened highway, all connected by normal roads. To the sides of these roads are up to 100 small open areas, usually well-camouflaged 'pockets' in the woods — although shelters tunneled out of rock are also utilized in northern Sweden — from which aircraft turnarounds can be performed. The various war bases also include pre-positioned fuel depots and concealed bunkers for command and control purposes. In addition to the Bas90 war bases, some 50 other sites are available for dispersed operations, including civilian light aircraft runways.

An element of Bas90 is the notion that aircraft will change their ground bases frequently and, ideally, never land at the same place from which they departed. The purpose is to make target identification difficult for a potential attacker. Consequently, a highly effective logistics system is required to make the system work. Accordingly, *Flygvapnet* has organized 16 so-called Basbat85 base battalions tasked with servicing and re-arming fighters under dispersed field conditions. One Basbat85 consists of eight fully mobile groups, each crewed by

Saab JAS39 Gripen

Both photos on this page were taken during air show appearances. At left, an F7 Gripen is seen during the UK's 1998 International Air Tattoo and below, 14 aircraft are shown in formation during a display at the home of F7 in Sweden.

six technicians and equipped with three trucks carrying all the necessary tools, fuel and ammunition to handle a turnaround for one fighter. From its camouflaged hideout the group is supposed to be positioned by the runway when a fighter returns from a mission — ready to direct it to a designated parking space, make the turnaround and then move out once the fighter takes off. The unit then has to locate to another position to handle a subsequent turnaround. If necessary, a TP84 Hercules can move Basbat85 units between war bases, flying ammunition and mobile ground equipment at treetop height between the short highway strips.

Ideally, the operational turnaround time for a Gripen in fighter configuration should be less than 10 minutes and, for one armed for ground attack missions, just 20 minutes. Short turnaround times, reliability and ease of maintenance thus were among the guiding factors in Gripen development. It would have been pointless to develop a highly advanced and efficient fighter that did not fit into *Flygvapnet's* Bas90 strategy. Furthermore, to ensure they stay at the top of their game, Gripen units regularly conduct Bas90 practice exercises. Typically, these last for one or two weeks during which 24-hour 'swing-role' missions are performed in the field. Basbat85 crews might consist of just one experienced technician and five conscripts — the latter needing only a few weeks of training before being able to perform such duties.

Fault-finding on the Gripen is a relatively simple task. A safety check is automatically run on an HDD on starting up the APU. Faulty line replacement units are highlighted by the report and technicians can go straight to the source of the problem rather than have to hunt around for hours. During a sortie, the pilot is advised of any serious problems that arise while airborne but not about any minor ones. Should there be a serious fault, the pilot receives relevant information about the systems affected on his HDD and can immediately request a computerized check list that tells him the best actions to take — like 'fly smoothly,' 'leave the aircraft at flight idle,' 'avoid icy conditions,' etc. Once safely back on the ground, the pilot enters instructions for what is referred to as a Quick Report on the HDD. Later, a technician can climb into the cockpit and call up the failure report for details relating to each malfunction identified during the flight.

The air force is now in the process of replacing its 16 Basbat85 units with eight Basbat04 base battalions (one for each Gripen division). Basbat04 has been developed as part of a general *Flygvapnet* transformation aimed at taking the service from being a traditional Cold War, anti-invasion defense force to a more flexible and deployable defense organization. Basbat04 will offer greater mobility in that it will function independently of any infrastructure other than runways, and be capable of deploying anywhere in Sweden or internationally. Whereas Basbat85 spread aircraft and equipment over a huge area, Basbat04 will operate in a more concentrated manner. It will be capable of supporting operations at two locations simultaneously while being led as a single unit. Furthermore, Basbat04 is designed to be fully deployable for international operations on 30 days notice.

Superfighters

PRODUCTION ORDERS

So far *Flygvapnet* has ordered a total of 204 Gripens in three production batches. Batch One consisted of the 30 JAS39A single-seaters ordered in 1982 (serials 39101 through 39130). The first example to be handed over to the air force, during a ceremony at Linköping on 8 June 1993, was 39102 because 39101 went to Saab. The final Batch One aircraft was delivered on

offers higher power output and lower maintenance costs, and will be introduced with serial 39207. *Flygvapnet* plans to retrofit the new APU to all of its Gripens.

The air force's most recent order was signed on 26 June 1997 and covers 64 Batch Three aircraft to be built to an upgraded configuration. Comprising 50 single-seat JAS39Cs (serials 39227 through 39276) and 14 two-seat JAS39Ds (serials 39815 through 39828), deliveries are scheduled to take place between 2003 and 2007. Besides more capable avionics, these aircraft

will have an inflight refueling capability via a retractable probe on the right-side of the cockpit, and will also carry an on-board oxygen generating system to facilitate longer missions. Gripen prototype 39-4 was fitted with an aerial refueling system by Flight Refuelling Ltd. in late 1998 that was successfully tested using RAF VC10 tankers. From 2003 onwards, *Flygvapnet* will equip some of its TP84 (C-130 transports) with podded underwing refueling systems so they can serve as Gripen refuelers. On a separate front, the possibility of adding thrust-vectoring to the JAS39 was studied with the Eurojet EJ200 engine, but subsequently shelved for budgetary reasons.

At the 1995 Paris Air Show, British Aerospace (now BAE Systems) and Saab officially announced the formation of a new partnership to jointly market, adapt, manufacture and support the Gripen in the export arena. Saab felt British Aerospace would provide better access to overseas markets than it could otherwise achieve on its own because of the British company's marketing network. On the manufacturing side, Linköping still

This two-seater visited South America as part of a Saab/BAE Systems sales effort, and is seen here in Chile. While much has been done to try and interest a number of South American air forces in the new fighter, early export successes have come from elsewhere — notably South Africa and Eastern Europe.

13 December 1996, some three and one-half years later. The contract covering the first 30 aircraft was for a fixed price, which almost broke the company because of the costs associated with the aircraft's teething problems, especially the FCS. The first Gripen took 604 days to construct but, by the time Batch One deliveries ended, Saab had reduced this to 200 days per aircraft. One JAS39A within the batch was never completed as planned due to the fact the prototype two-seater (serial 39800) was inserted into the production run. As a result, no JAS39A carries the serial number 39130 because that aircraft rolled off the line as 39800.

The initial Gripen order also included an option for a further 110 aircraft, which was converted to a firm contract on 3 June 1992. Batch Two comprised 96 JAS39As (serials 39131 through 39226) and 14 two-seat JAS39Bs (serials 39801 through 39814). The two-seater is 26 inches (66 cm) longer than the JAS39A, and carries no built-in cannon because the second cockpit had to be accommodated. The internal fuel load is slightly less than the single-seater but otherwise the JAS39B has similar equipment and performance to the 'A' model, and is fully combat capable. The first Batch Two aircraft was handed over to *Flygvapnet* on 19 December 1996 and deliveries will run through 2003. For these aircraft the fixed-price concept was abandoned in favor of a 'target price' that splits any cost overruns or underruns between Saab and the FMV.

Besides the avionics differences previously described, Batch Two models feature a new US-built Hamilton Sundstrand auxiliary power unit (APU) in place of the original French-built Microturbo TGA15 APU. The original unit does not conform to the latest Swedish environmental laws in terms of noise levels, and its fatigue life is too short. The quieter Sundstrand unit

Batch Three Gripens represent the most capable version of the JAS39. Among improvements, the aircraft will be fitted with retractable inflight refueling probes.

carries out most of the export work, although BAE assembles the main landing gear units in the UK. However, there are plans to move assembly of some fuselage packages to BAE's Brough plant, as well.

The export variant of the Gripen is referred to internally as the JAS39X, and is based on *Flygvapnet's* Batch Three JAS39C/D standard. While still retaining its inherent Gripen features like fly-by-wire, low radar signature and datalink, additional capabilities incorporated into the baseline JAS39X include air-to-air refueling, an on-board oxygen generating system, a FLIR/laser designator pod, a helmet-mounted display and English-language systems. Furthermore, the cockpit will be NVG-compatible. NATO-standard weapons pylons can be fitted if required but exactly how an export Gripen will be configured is to be determined by the customer, and that is likely to vary from nation to nation. At present Saab/BAE

Systems is producing 18 aircraft per year but the current export program calls for 28 export models annually. Saab/BAE views 400 export sales as a realistic overall goal.

The first Gripen export success has come from an unexpected source. As the type has long been marketed to potential customers in Eastern Europe and South America, it was assumed it would come from one of those regions. Instead, South Africa ordered 28 examples in November 1998 as replacements for its Cheetah 'Cs' and 'Ds' operated by No. 2 Squadron. The contract calls for nine two-seat Gripens to be delivered in 2007-9, followed by 19 single-seat models during 2009-12. The Pilkington/Denel-developed Guardian HMD has been selected for those aircraft, and will be integrated with South Africa's A-Darter off-boresight air-to-air missile.

The second export customer was Hungary. In November 2001 that country signed a 10-year lease with the Swedish government for 14 fully NATO-interoperable fighters — 12 single-seat Gripens and a pair of two-seaters, and has the option of buying the aircraft thereafter. Initial deliveries will begin towards the end of 2004 and all aircraft are to be operational with a squadron at Kecskemét in 2005. These examples will comprise some of the early production Gripens now surplus to *Flygvapnet* needs, and will be modified in accordance with specifications developed by Saab/BAE at Hungary's request. The work will be carried out at *Flygvapnet* maintenance workshops. In December 2001, Hungary's northern neighbor, the Czech Republic, announced it wanted 20 single-seat and 4 two-seat Gripens to replace its MiG-21 fighters. Again, the aircraft will be fully NATO-interoperable. Subject to successful conclusion of those contract negotiations, the first of two planned Czech Air Force JAS39 squadrons should be operational by late 2005.

Potential customer interest in the Gripen remains high and Saab/BAE is actively marketing the fighter to Austria, Poland and Brazil. The type is a candidate to replace Austria's Saab 35OE Drakens — that country's requirement extending to 24 single-seaters and six two-seaters. Retirement of the old airframes is expected between 2005 and 2012. In addition, negotiations are underway with Poland, which wants to obtain 60 fighters in the near future. It has expressed interest in 16 used aircraft for the short-term plus 44 new aircraft for delivery by late 2008. Meanwhile, Brazil is looking to purchase up to 24 new fighters as replacements for its F-5s. The Saab/BAE team also anticipates a number of opportunities in the ASEAN region, where several countries will have to replace older-generation fighters in the years ahead. In many markets the Gripen faces competition from the Lockheed Martin F-16 Fighting Falcon, Boeing F/A-18 and Dassault Mirage 2000-5 and its greatest window of opportunity may be 2005-10. By then, large numbers of current-generation jets will wear out yet future rivals like the Lockheed Martin F-35 JSF will not be ready for export service.

In May 2002, as part of its bid to meet Brazil's requirement for a new fighter, Gripen International submitted a revised proposal to the Brazilian Air Force that couples the proposed sale with certain technology transfers. This would enable that nation not only to support and maintain the fighter locally, should the JAS39 be chosen, but to further develop the type during its service life. Two months before, the company announced a Memorandum of Understanding with Brazil's VEM-VARIG Engineering and Maintenance, for industrial cooperation — something required under the terms of that government's tender process.

Superfighters

SPECIFICATIONS

Wing span (incl. launchers)	27 ft 6.75 in (8.40 m)
Length – single-seat version, excl. pitot tube	46 ft 03 in (14.10 m)
– two-seat version, excl. pitot tube	48 ft 06 in (14.80 m)
Height	14 ft 09 in (4.50 m)
Wheel track	7 ft 10 in (2.40 m)
Wheel base – single-seat version	17 ft 00 in (5.20 m)
– two-seat version	19 ft 04 in (5.90 m)
Empty weight	12,560-14,599 lb. (5700-6622 kg)
Max. takeoff weight	30,850 lb (14000 kg)
Normal takeoff weight (air defense config.)	18,700 lb (8500 kg)
Maximum speed	Mach 1.15 at sea level
	almost Mach 2 at altitude
Acceleration (Mach 0.5 to Mach 1.1 at low altitude)	30 sec.
Climb rate (brake release to 33,000 ft/10,000 m)	120 sec.
Turn performance	20°/sec. sustained
	30°/sec. instantaneous
Range (with drop tanks)	1,864 miles (3000 km)
Service ceiling	65,600 ft (20000 m)
g limits	max. 9g sustained / min. 3g
Thrust-to-weight ratio in fighter role	At max. takeoff weight — 1.0
	As fuel is consumed — 1.5
Accommodation	JAS39A – Pilot, JAS39B – Second pilot or systems operator
Power plant	Single Volvo Aero RM-12 turbofan rated at 12,140 lb st (54 kN) dry and 18,100 lb st (80.51 kN) with afterburner
Armament	Single 27-mm Mauser BK27 cannon AIM-9L Sidewinder (RB 74), AIM-120 AMRAAM (RB 99) IRIS-T air-to-air missiles, AGM-65 Maverick (RB 75) air-to-surface missiles RB 15F anti-ship missiles, DWS 39 anti-armor dispenser weapon KEPD 150 Taurus SOMs

On the opposite page, the old meets the new. At the 1997 Paris Air Show, a P-51D Mustang from the Breitling Fighter Collection flew in formation with a Gripen. Stig Holmström, a former Saab test pilot and the first man ever to fly the JAS39, rode in the back seat of the old warbird during the event.

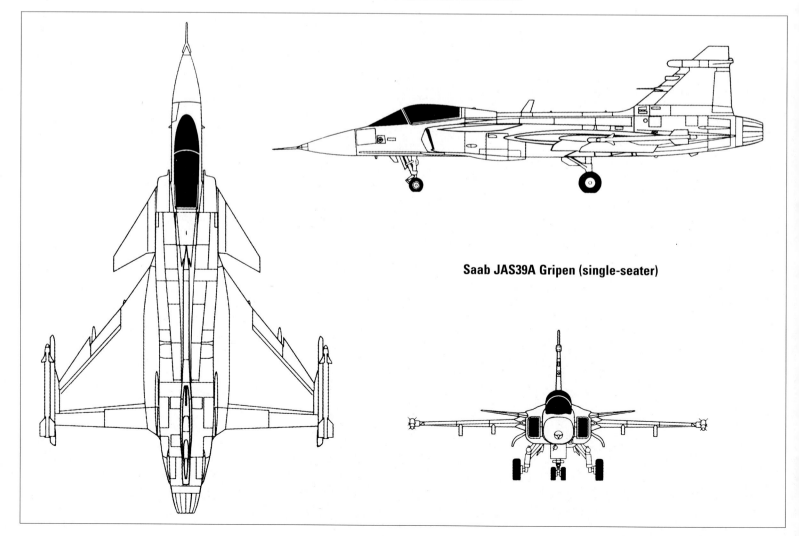

Saab JAS39A Gripen (single-seater)

CHAPTER 5

Dassault Rafale

The imposing form of a Rafale M rises above the steam from the catapult of the carrier *Charles de Gaulle*. When it came to Rafale procurement, the needs of the *Aéronavale* were considered more pressing than those of the *Armée de l'Air*, so the first operational aircraft were delivered to Landivisiau to form *Flottille* 12F. In so doing, a true air defense capability was restored to the carrier air group.

DEVELOPMENT & FLIGHT-TESTING

The origins of Rafale development date back to the mid-1970s when the French Navy (*Aéronavale*) and Air Force (*Armée de l'Air* or AdA) began looking at future replacement options for aircraft either then in service or about to enter service. In an effort to reduce costs, both services agreed on a common requirement and issued a common request for proposals.

Stringent French Ministry of Defense requirements called for a true swing-role fighter that could operate day or night, in all weather conditions and cover the spectrum of air-to-air and air-to-ground operations. Until now this has required an assortment of different types like the Jaguar, Mirage F1C/R/T, Mirage 2000/N, Super Etendard, Etendard IVPM and F-8P Crusader. Furthermore, the design had to offer affordable life-cycle costs through low fuel consumption, low maintenance, and long airframe and engine service lives.

European cooperation was a way to help reduce costs associated with new fighter development but the agreement France had entered into with Britain, Germany and Italy stalled over the issue of the proposed aircraft's weight. France's armed forces wanted a swing-role platform in the 9-tonne (19,840-lb) class for aircraft carrier compatibility, whereas the other parties were committed to a heavier air defense fighter in the 10-tonne (22,045-lb) class. The European program gave rise to the Eurofighter Typhoon.

The first Rafale — the white-painted demonstrator Rafale A

— was unveiled at Saint-Cloud near Paris in a ceremony led by the late Marcel Dassault in December 1985. From then on, initial progress was swift and the type made its first flight from the Dassault flight-test center in Istres in southeastern France, on 4 July 1986. To limit the risks traditionally associated with a first sortie, the aircraft was fitted with two proven General Electric F404-GE-400 turbofans, the same engine that powers the US F/A-18A/B Hornet. The demonstrator had all-moving canard foreplanes, an advanced fly-by-wire (FBW) flight control system (FCS) and a large delta-wing, and was first displayed outside France at Britain's Farnborough air show in September 1986. However, in May 1990, a Snecma M88 turbofan replaced the port-side F404 and 'supercruise' in dry thrust was achieved with the new power plant when the aircraft flew at Mach 1.4. Rafale A was retired in January 1994 after 865 sorties.

A severe blow to the program came with the fall of the Berlin Wall and collapse of the Soviet Union. These events led to a considerable drop in French defense spending and a drastic reorganization of the AdA, which resulted in near-immediate withdrawal of the Mirage 5F fleet and a decision to upgrade 55 Mirage F1Cs to Mirage F1CT tactical fighter configuration. Budgets that might have been used to accelerate the new fighter program thus were swallowed up, and research and development was further slowed as the AdA devoted more resources to updating some of its Mirage 2000Cs.

To meet its various mission needs (air defense, air superiority, precision attack, nuclear strike and reconnaissance), the service indicated it would require two Rafale variants — a

For some years the Rafale A technology demonstrator was on display at Istres, outside the EPNER (test pilot school) building. It was subsequently moved to a display site outside Dassault's Saint-Cloud facility, although it was later removed after local authorities complained about the sharp rise in traffic accidents on the road outside!

Rafale B301, the first production aircraft, made its maiden flight from the plant in Bordeaux with Dassault chief test pilot Yves Kerhervé at the controls and Philippe Deleume, the plant's chief test pilot, in the rear seat. In December 1998 it was delivered to the French Flight Test Centre. B301 initially flew without FSO. Magic 2s on the wingtips will become a rare sight as Standard F2 introduces the MICA IR.

On the fin of the Rafale Marine prototype displayed at Farnborough'96, was recorded the total number of flights flown to date by the new fighter. The number was updated daily throughout the period of the show.

single-seater designated the Rafale C ('C' for *chasseur*, meaning fighter) and a two-seat version designated the Rafale B ('B' for *biplace*, meaning two-seater). Painted in a black scheme, Rafale prototype C01 first took to the air over Istres in May 1991. For budgetary reasons, however, the planned second single-seat prototype was never built.

C01 differed significantly from the earlier demonstrator. While the overall configuration was retained, the 'C' prototype was fractionally smaller and lighter. Furthermore, other changes designed to reduce the fighter's radar cross-section (RCS) were apparent. These included a gold-coated canopy, a re-profiled fuselage/fin junction, the use of radar-absorbing materials (RAM) and more rounded wing-root fairings. Also, more extensive use of composite materials was made, contributing to a simultaneous reduction in weight and RCS. C01's canards were constructed using superplastic forming diffusion-bonded titanium, while carbon fiber was used for the wings.

Essentially, Dassault engineers developed a very simple fighter with fixed air intakes and no dedicated airbrake to help reduce maintenance requirements. At the same time, however, Dassault pioneered the use of such advances as a fully redundant, very high-pressure (350-bar/5,000-lb sq in) hydraulic system and variable-frequency alternators that boost reliability and safety. These particular ideas proved so successful they have been adopted by some other aircraft manufacturers — for the Airbus A380, for instance.

Like the Mirage 2000, the Rafale was conceived from the outset to meet NATO interoperability standards, and Dassault engineers strictly adhered to NATO 'Stanags' (Standard Agreements). Consequently, all of the Rafale's major systems are fully compatible with NATO's. The type's radios come with Have Quick secure capabilities and the Rafale's inflight-refueling equipment can be used with NATO probe-and-drogue systems. Furthermore, the IFF system is completely interoperable, and the Multifunction Information Distribution System – Low Volume Terminal (MIDS-LVT) has been designed in cooperation of other NATO members. Interoperability also extends to weapons. The GBU-12, one of the most widely available air-to-ground stores, has already been qualified on the Rafale and the fighter's 14 fully NATO-compatible hardpoints offer the flexibility to carry a wide variety of other ordnance. It is

assumed the Rafale will be qualified for such ordnance as Mk 82/83/84 'dumb bombs' and GBU-22/24 Paveway III LGBs in the near future.

Rafale C01 was primarily used for flight-envelope expansion and to test the M88-2 engines. Later, it was used for weapon firing/separation testing (the gun and Magic IIs) and man-machine interface validation. At one point, however, it was felt C01 was getting too old and should be retired. Instead, it will be retained for further engine testing and will participate in the M88-3 development program.

Since the introduction of the two-seat Mirage 2000N in the mid-1980s, the AdA has been keen to operate two-seat tactical fighters. Initially, it intended to procure just 25 two-seat Rafales for conversion training purposes. Studies made following the Gulf War, however, indicated two-seaters were much better adapted to complex attack missions. The workload in single-seat Jaguars and Mirage F1s was deemed too high under poor weather and demanding combat conditions. Experience gained from two-seat Mirage 2000N and 2000D operations proved that burden-sharing between the pilot and weapon system operator (WSO) was the better solution for air-to-ground missions in high-threat scenarios. Another key driver is the need for increased operator functionality.

Rafale B01, the only two-seat prototype, first flew in April 1993 and has been used for fire-control/weapon system testing, including the RBE2 radar and SPECTRA electronic warfare suite. It subsequently took part in weapon separation and heavy-load trials, and the fighter regularly flew with three 528-gal (2000-lit) drop tanks, two Apache/Scalp cruise missiles and four air-to-air missiles. It even took part in numerous flying displays in that configuration, to demonstrate the agility of the aircraft under extreme load conditions. Compared with the single-seat variant, the two-seater is 771 lb (350 kg) heavier but carries 106 gal (400 lit) less fuel. Nevertheless, it is fully combat-capable and the front and rear cockpits are similar, so either the pilot or the WSO can perform the mission tasks. However, it is generally agreed that the pilot in the front cockpit will deal with air-to-air modes while the WSO in the back seat will handle air-to-ground functions.

The *Aéronavale* has had a long-standing requirement for a new carrier-borne fighter to supplant its aging Dassault Etendard IVPMs, Vought F-8P Crusaders and, ultimately, its Dassault Super Etendard Modernisés. At one stage, the F/A-18

Hornet was seriously considered as a replacement but a naval variant of the new French fighter was deemed more appropriate. A lack of funding delayed development of a carrier version, however, and the French Navy was forced to modernize its old Crusaders in order to maintain a modicum of air defense capability.

While a number of changes had to be introduced for Rafale carrier operations, the single-seat naval variant retains a high degree of commonality with its air force counterpart. As a consequence, the multispar wing cannot be folded. This reduces complexity and weight but limits the number of aircraft that can be stored aboard ship, both on deck and in the hangar. What might otherwise have been a problem has been mitigated by the larger size of the *Charles de Gaulle* — the latest nuclear-powered carrier to enter French service — compared with the

older *Clémenceau* and *Foch*.

'Navalization' led to the Rafale M ('M' for *Marine*), which has a strengthened airframe, massive tail hook, reinforced main undercarriage to absorb higher vertical velocities, and a power-operated built-in ladder to improve cockpit accessibility and reduce the need for ground support equipment. In addition, the 'M' is equipped with a new fin-tip Telemir system that allows the aircraft's inertial navigation system to exchange data with the carrier's navigation suite. It also has a carrier-based microwave landing system. The most obvious modification is the longer nosewheel strut, which gives the aircraft its noticeable nose-up attitude and forced elimination of the front centerline weapon pylon. To increase interoperability with US aircraft carriers, the nosewheel leg also incorporates a launch-bar coupled with a 'hold-back' system that would allow

Aéronavale Rafales to operate from American 'flat-tops.' The consequence of all such modifications is a Rafale Marine heavier than its air force counterpart by about 1,100 lb (500 kg) — a figure slightly less than that anticipated when the naval variant was designed. Needless to say, the new aircraft represents a considerable improvement over the old F-8P Crusader and is designed to meet likely threats through 2030 and beyond.

After an in-depth study, the *Aéronavale* procurement plan was amended to include a two-seat variant, the Rafale N ('N' for Naval). It will have very high commonality with the single-seat Rafale M but will carry slightly less fuel: 9,888 lb (4485 kg) instead of 10,362 lb (4700 kg). Dassault engineers have begun

signaled the start of the type's full naval development.

The aircraft first underwent catapult testing in the United States at NAS Lakehurst in New Jersey, in the summer of 1992. Testing had to be conducted there because the last suitable European facility, the catapult test bench at RAE Bedford in the UK, was closed following withdrawal of HMS Ark Royal from Royal Navy service. A second round of tests involving M01 took place at Lakehurst in January-February, before the first actual landings were made aboard the *Foch* in April 1993. For these Yves Kerhervé, Dassault's chief test pilot, was at the controls. Rafale M02 first flew at Istres in November 1993 while M01 was at Lakehurst for its third series of tests during

development of the new version and it is clear some modifications will have to be introduced. Adoption of the beefed-up airframe and nosewheel has already forced elimination of the 30 M 791 cannon in order to make room for the relocated equipment. In addition, reinforced canopy hinges will be required to deal with the strong winds encountered on carrier decks.

Carrier-suitability trials were carried out quite early in the development program when the Rafale A demonstrator flew approaches to the since-retired carrier *Clémenceau*. Although not carrier-capable, the Rafale A was subjected to further testing with the *Foch* to confirm its ability to fly more slowly around the ship, despite its heavier weight compared with its predecessors. Two dedicated navy prototypes were later built, Rafales M01 and M02, and delivery of M01 in December 1991

November and December. Subsequent trials, both at Lakehurst and aboard the *Foch*, allowed the fighter to be tested under extreme conditions — including takeoffs and landings with 330-gal (1250-lit) and 528-gal (2000-lit) external fuel tanks fitted. The first 'traps' and launches aboard the *Charles de Gaulle* were performed in July 1999 by Yves Kerhervé in M02. Today, the aircraft is still used for Standard F2 development but M01 has been withdrawn from service. In June 2001, for the week of the le Bourget air show, the latter was on static display in the Place de la Concorde in central Paris.

Reports indicate the Rafale M has excellent 'bring-back' capabilities and is able to 'trap' with heavy unexpended ordnance. For the test program, all prototypes have carried a fixed refueling probe to the right of the nose, ahead of the wind-

screen, to enable inflight refueling from co-located C-135FRs during long-duration test sorties.

Developing the Snecma M88 engine for the Rafale was a daunting task but the power plant is reported to be capably meeting the needs of the new fighter. Demanding air combat and low-altitude penetration requirements made the adoption of an innovative engine essential. It had to exhibit a high thrust-to-weight ratio, low fuel consumption in all flight regimes and long engine life. Snecma responded with a state-of-the-art, twin-spool turbofan that now powers every variant — representing France's third generation of fighter engines (after the Atar family of the Mirage III/IV/V/F1 and M53 of the Mirage 2000). The program was officially launched in 1986 and the first bench trials were performed in February 1989. The power plant's initial flight (fitted to the Rafale A) was in February 1990 and qualification was obtained in early 1996, with the first production engine delivered at the end of that year. According to Snecma, development and production engines have accumulated almost 23,000 functioning hours so far, of which 8,000 have been bench-running hours. Prototype engines have logged 11,000 flying hours and close to another 4,000 hours have been flown by series M88-2s.

Having to run at much higher temperatures than previous-generation engines, the M88 incorporates innovative solutions to meet high performance and durability requirements. It utilizes advanced technologies such as integrally-bladed compressor disks ('blisks'), a low-pollution combustor, single-crystal high-pressure turbine blades, ceramic coatings, revolutionary powder metallurgy disks, and composite materials. Additionally, the M88 has been optimized to prevent it from compromising the Rafale's overall IR signature, and its smoke-free emissions make the aircraft more difficult to detect visually. Light, compact and fuel-efficient, the M88-2 is rated at 11,236 lb st (50 kN) dry and 16,854 lb st (75 kN) with afterburner. It is equipped with a fully-redundant Snecma full authority digital engine control (FADEC) that allows it to accelerate from idle to full afterburner in less than three seconds. 'Carefree' engine handling allows the throttle to be slammed from combat power to idle and back to combat power again anywhere in the flight envelope. Furthermore, it is fully capable of handling minor engine faults without the need to warn the pilot. The compressor utilizes a three-stage low-pressure fan and a six-stage high-pressure compressor. Peak engine temperature is 1850 K (1577 °C / 2,870°F) with a pressure ratio of 24.5:1. At maximum dry power, specific fuel consumption is in the order of 0.8 kg/daN.h, increasing to 1.8 kg/daN.h with afterburner.

A staged approach was adopted for development of the power plant, and the first 29 production engines were produced to M88-2 Stage 1 standard. All subsequent turbofans ordered by the French MoD will be built to the improved M88-2 Stage 4

standard, which features an extended time-between-overhauls (TBO) due to a redesigned high-pressure compressor and turbine. Tailored to simultaneously excel in low-altitude and air combat flight regimes, the M88 offers a combination of extremely high thrust and very low operating cost.

Snecma indicates it has secured orders for 160 M88s, and the French MoD will eventually acquire about 700 engines for the 294 Rafales now on order. Production at Melun-Villaroche currently runs at the rate of four per month but will increase to six per month in due course. Furthermore, the flexibility is there to increase output in the event of export orders, and the M88 is also available to power other types like the German Mako trainer.

While the M88 was designed to excel during both low- and high-level operations, and to respond instantly to pilot throttle movements, a few potential customers have expressed concerns that the engine is not really powerful enough for some roles — typically for air-defense/air superiority missions. Snecma has thus launched development of a new variant of the M88 dubbed the M88-3, which will be rated at 20,225 lb st (90 kN) with afterburner. This represents a 20 percent increase in output over the original M88-2 but improvements are not limited to thrust alone. Durability is also expected to improve and a customer can even select a 16,854-lb st (75-kN) 'peacetime' rating for the engine that will be implementable through a ground procedure that takes just a few minutes. A cockpit switch is even under consideration to allow the pilot to choose a rating during flight.

Efforts are being been made to retain a high degree of commonality between the M88-2 and the M88-3. According to Snecma, the engine components will be about 40 percent interchangeable. The M88-3 features a redesigned low-pressure compressor for a higher airflow — 159 lb (72 kg) per second instead of 143 lb (65 kg) — a new high-pressure turbine, new stator vane stage, modified afterburner and an adapted nozzle. Engine weight will increase from 2,017 lb (915 kg) for an M88-2 Stage 1 engine to 2,171 lb (985 kg) for an M88-3, and while the M88-2 and M88-3 will be interchangeable, the M88-3 will require slightly enlarged air intakes to permit higher airflow. The new fixed intakes can be retrofitted easily to existing airframes and have been shaped so as not to increase drag or the RCS.

The new engine will improve the Rafale's takeoff distance,

climb rate and sustained turn rate and, although more powerful, the M88-3 will have the same specific fuel consumption as the M88-2. Full-scale development of the M88-3 was launched in 2001 and qualification is planned for 2005. The flight-test program will comprise 200 hours using Rafale C01, and initial deliveries are anticipated in 2006.

From the start the Rafale was designed to carry a large fuel load — the internal tanks of a single-seater hold 1,519 gal (5750 lit) — and the fighter is equipped with no fewer than five wet points. Two types of external tanks are available with 330-gal (1250-lit) supersonic tanks capable of being fitted to any of the five wet pylons, while 528-gal (2000-lit) drop tanks can be mounted on the centerline and inner wing stations. As previously stated, the Rafale is also equipped with a fixed inflight refueling probe. For air forces undertaking extremely long range missions, Dassault Aviation also has conceived two 304-gal (1150-lit) detachable conformal fuel tanks (CFT) that can be mounted on the upper surface of the wing/fuselage blend. Offering less drag than traditional tanks and freeing underwing stations for armament carriage, the CFTs bring the Rafale's maximum external fuel load up to 2,853 gal (10800 lit) and can be mounted or removed in less than two hours. All Rafales have built-in CFT capability and the tanks can be adapted to any variant of the fighter, including naval and two-seat versions. Using two-seat prototype B01, with test pilot Eric Gérard at the controls, CFTs were first flown from Istres on 18 April 2001. Supersonic speeds have already been demonstrated — the CFT-equipped fighter reaching Mach 1.4 — and various configurations have been tested successfully, like air-to-air with MICA missiles; and a long-range strike with three 528-gal drop tanks, two Scalp standoff missiles and four MICAs. The CFTs are reported to have negligible impact on aircraft handling.

Now in full operational service, the Rafale is one of the most advanced fighters flying today. With future development of the RBE2 active array and M88-3 engine now strongly backed by the French MoD, the Rafale is a serious contender in the export market and several foreign countries have expressed interest. Ongoing updates will help ensure the aircraft remains at the forefront of Dassault's export effort. One upgrade under serious consideration for the future is another RCS-reduction idea. Dassault is pushing ahead with a new system to shroud external weapons. The new stealthy shapes would be ejected prior to weapon release. Alternatively, tube-launched missiles might be adopted.

Recent competitions have highlighted the issue of exportability of high-tech fighters — an area in which Dassault finds itself well placed. Whereas the USA often has been reluctant to supply, even to their closest allies, software source-code for their weapon systems, French manufacturer have no such qualms, which has certainly helped the company build strong ties with its customers.

An M88-2 is mounted in a test rig. As the engine is compact its accessories are easily accessed for maintenance.

Painted in black, Rafale C01 is seen here with two wingtip-mounted Magic II IR-guided, air-to-air missiles. This older weapon will be replaced in Rafale service by two MICA IRs.

Rafale M01 is readied for launch from the deck of the *Foch*. The aircraft is armed with two Magic II and two MICA air-to-air missiles, and is fitted with two 1250-litre drop tanks.

Dassault Rafale

1. Kevlar composite radome
2. Thales RBE2 electronically-scanned look-down/ shoot-down multimode radar scanner
3. Fixed (detachable) inflight refueling probe
4. Front sector optronics (FSO) – Infrared scanner/ tracker (IRST)
5. FSO – Passive visual sight, low-light television (LLTV)
6. Forward-looking optronic system module
7. Airflow sensors, pitch and yaw
8. Total temperature probe
9. Radar equipment module
10. Dynamic pressure probe
11. Cockpit front pressure bulkhead
12. Instrument panel shroud
13. Rudder pedals
14. Canopy emergency release
15. Electro-luminescent formation lighting strip
16. Alternative nose undercarriage assembly, Rafale M
17. Catapult strop link
18. Deck approach and identification lights
19. Drag strut
20. Hydraulic retraction jack
21. Nosewheel bay
22. Port side console panel
23. Engine throttle lever with display imaging controls, and hands-on throttle and stick (HOTAS) control system. Sidestick controller for digital fly-by-wire control system on starboard side
24. Elbow rest
25. Pilot's wide-angle holographic head-up display (HUD)
26. Frameless windscreen panel
27. Canopy, open position
28. Thomson-CSF ATLIS II laser designator pod, carried on starboard intake pylon
29. ATLIS II mounting pylon adapter
30. Rear-view mirrors (three)
31. Pilot's helmet with integrated sight display
32. Cockpit canopy, hinged to starboard
33. Pilot's SEMMB (license-built Martin-Baker) Mk 16F 'zero-zero' ejection seat
34. Forward fuselage/cockpit section all-composite carbon-fiber structure
35. Lateral equipment bays, port and starboard
36. Nose undercarriage pivot mounting
37. Nosewheel door-mounted lower UHF antenna
38. Taxiing lights
39. Hydraulic steering jacks
40. Twin nosewheels, forward-retracting
41. Hydraulic retraction and lock strut
42. Port engine air intake
43. Boundary layer splitter plate
44. Ventral intake suction relief door
45. Port forward oblique SPECTRA ECM antenna
46. SPECTRA RWR antenna
47. Onboard oxygen generation system (OBOGS)
48. Canopy center arch and support frame
49. Embedded electrically charged canopy emergency breaker
50. Circuit breaker and diagnostic panel
51. Avionics equipment bays
52. Canard foreplane hydraulic actuator
53. Foreplane hinge mounting

54. Environmental Control System (ECS) equipment bay
55. Canopy emergency release
56. Cockpit pressurization outflow valves
57. Canard foreplane hinge fitting
58. Starboard canard foreplane
59. Carbon-fiber foreplane structure with honeycomb core
60. Starboard navigation light
61. Air system heat exchanger exhaust
62. Center-fuselage aluminium-lithium primary structure
63. Intake ducting
64. Fuselage integral fuel tankage, total internal capacity 1,407 US gal (5325 liters)
65. Port main longeron
66. SATCOM antenna
67. Dorsal spine fairing housing systems ducting
68. Anti-collision beacon
69. Starboard fuselage integral fuel tank
70. Kevlar composite wing/fuselage fairing panels
71. Starboard wing integral fuel tank
72. Wing pylon hardpoints
73. Leading-edge slat hydraulic jacks and position transmitters
74. Slat guide rails
75. Starboard two-segment automatic leading-edge slats
76. Starboard external fuel tank
77. GIAT 30 M 791 30-mm cannon located beneath starboard wing root
78. Forward RWR antenna
79. Wingtip fixed missile pylon/ launch rail
80. MATRA MICA air-to-air missile (IR version)
81. Rear RWR antenna

82. Starboard outboard elevon
83. Elevon hydraulic actuator
84. Wing carbon-fiber skin paneling
85. Inboard elevon
86. Fuselage aluminium-lithium skin paneling, carbon-fiber ventral engine bay access panels
87. Auxiliary power unit (APU) intake grilles
88. Microturbo APU
89. Wing panel attachment forged and machined fuselage main frames
90. Engine compressor intake with variable guide vanes
91. Snecma M88-2 afterburning turbofan engine
92. Forward engine mounting
93. APU exhaust
94. Carbon-fiber engine bypass duct
95. Rear engine mounting
96. Fin attachment main frames
97. Fin root bolted attachment fittings
98. Rudder hydraulic actuator
99. Carbon-fiber multi-spar fin structure

© Mike Badrocke

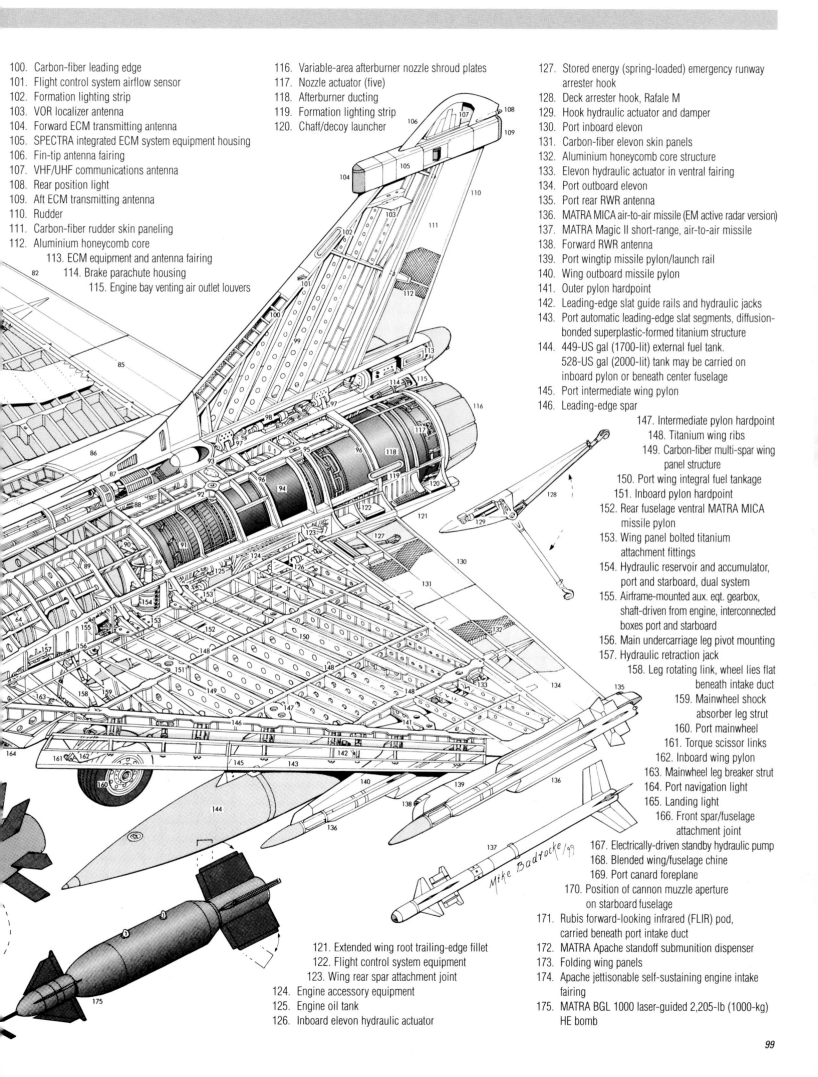

100. Carbon-fiber leading edge
101. Flight control system airflow sensor
102. Formation lighting strip
103. VOR localizer antenna
104. Forward ECM transmitting antenna
105. SPECTRA integrated ECM system equipment housing
106. Fin-tip antenna fairing
107. VHF/UHF communications antenna
108. Rear position light
109. Aft ECM transmitting antenna
110. Rudder
111. Carbon-fiber rudder skin paneling
112. Aluminium honeycomb core
113. ECM equipment and antenna fairing
114. Brake parachute housing
115. Engine bay venting air outlet louvers

116. Variable-area afterburner nozzle shroud plates
117. Nozzle actuator (five)
118. Afterburner ducting
119. Formation lighting strip
120. Chaff/decoy launcher

121. Extended wing root trailing-edge fillet
122. Flight control system equipment
123. Wing rear spar attachment joint
124. Engine accessory equipment
125. Engine oil tank
126. Inboard elevon hydraulic actuator

127. Stored energy (spring-loaded) emergency runway arrester hook
128. Deck arrester hook, Rafale M
129. Hook hydraulic actuator and damper
130. Port inboard elevon
131. Carbon-fiber elevon skin panels
132. Aluminium honeycomb core structure
133. Elevon hydraulic actuator in ventral fairing
134. Port outboard elevon
135. Port rear RWR antenna
136. MATRA MICA air-to-air missile (EM active radar version)
137. MATRA Magic II short-range, air-to-air missile
138. Forward RWR antenna
139. Port wingtip missile pylon/launch rail
140. Wing outboard missile pylon
141. Outer pylon hardpoint
142. Leading-edge slat guide rails and hydraulic jacks
143. Port automatic leading-edge slat segments, diffusion-bonded superplastic-formed titanium structure
144. 449-US gal (1700-lit) external fuel tank. 528-US gal (2000-lit) tank may be carried on inboard pylon or beneath center fuselage
145. Port intermediate wing pylon
146. Leading-edge spar
147. Intermediate pylon hardpoint
148. Titanium wing ribs
149. Carbon-fiber multi-spar wing panel structure
150. Port wing integral fuel tankage
151. Inboard pylon hardpoint
152. Rear fuselage ventral MATRA MICA missile pylon
153. Wing panel bolted titanium attachment fittings
154. Hydraulic reservoir and accumulator, port and starboard, dual system
155. Airframe-mounted aux. eqt. gearbox, shaft-driven from engine, interconnected boxes port and starboard
156. Main undercarriage leg pivot mounting
157. Hydraulic retraction jack
158. Leg rotating link, wheel lies flat beneath intake duct
159. Mainwheel shock absorber leg strut
160. Port mainwheel
161. Torque scissor links
162. Inboard wing pylon
163. Mainwheel leg breaker strut
164. Port navigation light
165. Landing light
166. Front spar/fuselage attachment joint
167. Electrically-driven standby hydraulic pump
168. Blended wing/fuselage chine
169. Port canard foreplane
170. Position of cannon muzzle aperture on starboard fuselage
171. Rubis forward-looking infrared (FLIR) pod, carried beneath port intake duct
172. MATRA Apache standoff submunition dispenser
173. Folding wing panels
174. Apache jettisonable self-sustaining engine intake fairing
175. MATRA BGL 1000 laser-guided 2,205-lb (1000-kg) HE bomb

Superfighters

AVIONICS

Like every modern combat aircraft, the Rafale is dependent on technology for air dominance and its advanced avionics suite comprises several different systems, all closely integrated to maximize pilot situational awareness. Among them are sensors, the electronic warfare suite, and navigation and identifi-

time to tactics management. The pilot can now concentrate on fight rather than flight. Additionally, the Rafale's multi-channel weapon system can simultaneously deal with airborne and ground threats. Pilots will be able to attack targets on the ground while engaging the enemy fighters presenting the greatest threat. For example, even with the radar in air-to-surface mode, the FSO will be fully capable of detecting and tracking hostile interceptors.

At the core of the Rafale's capabilities is the Modular Data Processing Unit (MDPU) composed of line-replaceable modules. Built from commercially available off-the-shelf elements, the MDPU enhances avionics and armament integration. Thanks to its redundant, open and modular architecture, the system is highly adaptable and new avionics and new ordnance now under

Both the pilot and WSO have access to the same information from the aircraft's system, allowing them to tailor workshare to particular requirements. In general, the pilot would concentrate on the air threat while the WSO works against surface targets. By mid-2002 all 13 Standard F1 Rafales will be flying. This includes 10 for the French Navy, plus two Bs and one C that will be used as trials machines for the follow-on Standard F2 batch.

cation equipment and displays. In essence, there is no primary sensor because the Rafale's radar, Front sector optronics (FSO) and SPECTRA electronic warfare suite all contribute to situational awareness, and the data obtained from the various sources is fuzed into a single tactical picture displayed on a central eye-level screen collimated to infinity. All of the sensors have inherent advantages and drawbacks. The passive FSO has excellent countermeasures resistance, and its angular resolution is better than that of the radar. On the other hand, the radar is very accurate in range at long distances, and can track more targets than the FSO, while the SPECTRA suite can analyze enemy radar emissions to precisely identify an emitter. The data fusion system combines and compares the data gathered by those sensors to accurately position and positively identify targets.

Going beyond a simple correlation, the combined systems allow a pilot to gather an accurate and unambiguous tactical picture. Previously, pilots were forced to rely on their brains to process the information obtained by their radars and eyes, and build a mental image of the evolving situation. The Rafale's avionics suite has taken over the processing role to considerably reduce pilot workload, allowing aircrews to devote more

development will be capable of easy adoption. Furthermore, the system has been conceived with growth in mind, so that modifying the aircraft from one standard to another will not be a problem. Noteworthy is the fact that the MDPU is not fitted to Standard F1 Rafale Ms, which are equipped with older technology systems. However, the MDPU will be fitted to the first production Air Force Standard F1 Rafales — B301, B302 and C101.

The adoption of specialized phased-array radars in the B-1B Lancer and MiG-31 'Foxhound' did not go unnoticed by French planners who quickly recognized this revolutionary technology represented the way forward. The trend was confirmed when the USA made it clear the F-22 Raptor and future fighters are to be equipped with phased-array radars, as well. Accordingly, French radar specialists embarked on an ambitious research and development program to develop indigenous, electronically scanned (e-scan) radars to equip a wide variety of warfighting systems, including warships and new combat aircraft. The Rafale was the first aircraft to benefit from this massive research effort.

E-scan radars offer a quantum leap in efficiency over mechanical planar antenna radars. As they do not need complex actuators to point the antenna, they are inherently more reliable and more stealthy. Beam-shifting is extremely precise and nearly instantaneous in both vertical and horizontal planes, ensuring a very high 'revisiting rate' on detected targets in search-while-track mode. Modern air combat tactics have been devised to counter mechanical scanning radars operating in track-while-scan mode, with a pair of fighters usually splitting to confuse the interceptor. In such a scenario, some of the dispersed enemy aircraft inevitably will fall off the screen. However, against a fighter equipped with an e-scan radar operating in search-while-track, the tactic would be totally ineffective. Even more important is the capability of being able to share time between modes, so that different tasks can be conducted simultaneously. Powerful data processors and unmatched beam agility enable the Rafale to fully interleave functions within a given mode. The radar combines search, track and missile-guidance functions, processing them simultaneously, while the superior fighter/missile datalink gives better fire-control capabilities in adverse environments — thus increasing the overall lethality of the Rafale's weapon system. In addition, fixed-array radars considerably reduce signature returns to enemy aircraft. Together, these factors contribute to the enhancement of combat efficiency and stealthiness.

Developed by what is now Thales Airborne Systems, the *Radar à Balayage Electronique 2 plans* or RBE2 (two-axis) electronic scanning radar is the first airborne look-down/shoot-down multimode e-scan radar designed and produced in Europe. Developing such a compact and high-performance radar was challenging because the RBE2 had to offer long range detection yet fit into the relatively small nose of the Rafale. Furthermore, the radar and related electronics had to be capable of withstanding the shock of carrier landings. Flight-testing began using a Mystère 20 (serial 104) in July 1992 and, at one point, no fewer than five *Centre d'Essais en Vol* aircraft — three Mystère 20s and two Mirage 2000s (serials 501 and 504) — were involved in RBE2 development, before testing aboard Rafales B01 and M02 began. Today, Rafales M1, B301 and B302 also participate in radar development and the first production RBE2 was delivered in October 1997. The radar is already in operational service with French naval aviation although the systems on Standard F1 Rafales are only capable of air-to-air modes. Subsequent radar sets will have improved capabilities and culminate with Standard F3, which will introduce comprehensive air-to-surface modes including automatic

A cockpit test rig at Istres (top) allows test pilots and engineers to simulate highly complex mission profiles and scenarios. Taxiing his Rafale, a *Flottille* 12F pilot models the new lightweight CGF-Gallet helmet developed for France's air arms. This headgear is fully compatible with the two helmet-mounted display (HMD) systems currently competing for the Rafale contract (JHMCS and Topsight E). Also evident is the Mk 16F ejection seat, which is reclined at 29° to improve high-*g* tolerance.

terrain-following. The RBE2 is now totally qualified for air-to-air combat, and air-to-ground functions actively are being developed in preparation of the Standard F2.

Due to its unique waveform design and electronic scanning management, the RBE2 can perform long-range detection and tracking of up to 40 air targets in look-down or look-up aspects, in all weathers and in severe jamming environments. Interception and firing data are calculated for eight priority targets, which can be engaged with MICA BVR/air combat active radar seeker missiles fired at the rate of one every two seconds. Using its electronic scanning antenna, the radar is fully capable of tracking the other 32 targets while updating the MICAs with mid-course corrections via the secure radar-to-missile link. Thus, very long-range multiple firings are possible, offering an exceptionally high 'kill' probability rate, even against maneuvering enemy fighters. For air-to-ground strikes, the radar has dedicated functions for low- and high-level navigation, target-aiming, searching and tracking of moving and fixed targets, as well as ranging and terrain-avoidance/following. In the latter mode the RBE2 looks ahead to build a constantly changing, wide-angle, three-dimensional profile of the area to be overflown. Using electronic scanning technology, terrain-avoidance is optimized to improve survivability while flying at extremely low altitude and high speed.

Through the use of open architecture, the RBE2 offers significant growth potential. For instance, a synthetic aperture radar (SAR) mapping mode is actively being developed for Standard F3 Rafales. It will allow crews to 'paint' from stand-off distances, and thereby obtain high-resolution maps of surface targets in any weather, day or night, and to designate a precise aiming point to the fighter's weapon system. Airborne trials

Superfighters

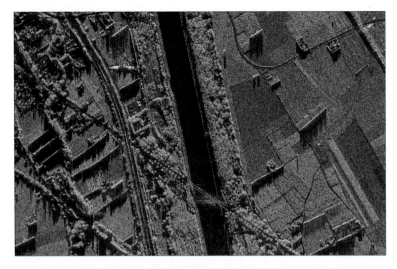

An impressive SAR capability is being developed for the RBE2, as demonstrated by this 'patch map' obtained by a development radar. Using such images, the WSO can designate targets for the system, which slews other sensors to peer at the designated location.

have already started using a flying test bed, and the SAR mode is expected to be fully qualified on the Rafale in 2006. Anti-ship attacks require specific modes, and the RBE2 will be able to detect, track and engage ships, even in high sea states. An air-to-sea radar surveillance mode will be introduced on Standard F2 Rafales, and the fighter's weapon system will be capable of firing anti-ship missiles with the advent of Standard F3.

To complement the radar, the Rafale is fitted with a comprehensive optronics suite composed of three systems: the aforementioned FSO (OSF in France), the Damoclès laser designation pod, and the *Pod de Reconnaissance Nouvelle Génération* (Pod Reco NG/New Generation Reconnaissance Pod). Mounted on top of the nose, ahead of the windshield, the FSO allows an uninterrupted view of the forward sector. Operating in different IR wavelengths, it provides discreet long-range detection, multi-target angular tracking and range-finding for air and surface targets — considerably enhancing the Rafale's stealthiness as the fighter is thus able to covertly detect and identify enemy aircraft without using its own radar and betraying its own presence. The FSO is made up of two modules — the IR sensor (an IRST) and the TV system — coupled with an eye-safe laser rangefinder, and their functions are clearly complementary. Surveillance and multi-target tracking is the job of the starboard IR surveillance module, while target tracking, identification and ranging is handled by the port TV/laser module. Whatever rules of engagement restrictions might apply, the FSO minimizes the risk of fratricides ('blue' on 'blue') and allows instantaneous battle damage assessment. Although this unique surveillance and identification system has been

A Rafale and Mirage 2000 at extreme range, captured by the FSO. The suite is fully integrated with the radar and other systems, allowing it to be cued by the radar at long range for identification or raid assessment, and for continued passive tracking of targets. It also incorporates a laser rangefinder — allowing slant range and offset point data to be fed to the computer for bomb release.

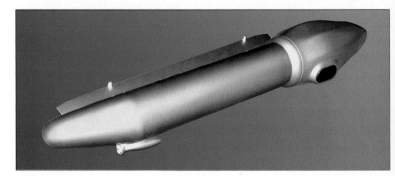

A model of the Pod Reco NG which will provide the Rafale with state-of-the-art digital reconnaissance capabilities. The nose section rotates to allow horizon-to-horizon operation, and the pod also has a function that allows it to automatically track linear features like roads.

thoroughly tested on a Dassault Falcon 20, plus Rafale prototypes M02 and B01 and series aircraft B301 and B302, it will not be incorporated into production aircraft until the first Standard F2 Rafale is delivered.

Produced by Thales, the new-generation Damoclès laser designation/targeting pod has been designed for use in conjunction with existing and future laser-guided ordnance like Paveway LGBs and AASM precision weapons. The 550-lb (250-kg) Damoclès represents the next generation of pod following the ATLIS that equips *Armée de l'Air* Jaguars and *Aéronavale* Super Etendards, and the PDL-CT/PDL-CTS fitted to the Mirage 2000D. The new staring array detector and laser technologies chosen for the Damoclès offer extended detection and recognition ranges, permitting laser-guided weapons to be delivered at substantially greater ranges and from higher altitudes. This considerably reduces the aircraft's vulnerability to short- and medium-range air defense systems. Two fields of view are available to aircrew: wide (4° x 3°) and narrow (1° x 0.5°), and the pod is fitted with an eye-safe (wavelength 1.5 μm) laser rangefinder, a laser designator fully compatible with NATO's Stanag 3733 (wavelength 1.06 μm), and a laser spot tracker (wavelength 1.06 μm). Additionally, its greatly improved resolution means the system can be used for standoff reconnaissance and battle damage assessment.

The Damoclès has been conceived for considerably lower maintenance requirements and costs than earlier designs, and can withstand the shocks associated with carrier landings. It is currently being qualified on Mirage 2000-9 and Super Etendards, and should be qualified on the Rafale in 2003. Already, it has been ordered by the *Aéronavale* for its Standard 5 Super Etendard Modernisés, and is likely to be adopted by both services for their Rafales. Additionally, it has been selected by the United Arab Emirates for recently ordered Dassault Mirage 2000-9s (30 of which have been purchased, along with 33 earlier Mirage 2000s brought up to dash 9 standard). From 2010, a joint British-French electro-optic targeting pod called JOANNA (for Joint Airborne Navigation and Attack), will be introduced on Rafales to supplant the Damoclès. Flight-testing of JOANNA is due to start in 2005.

For reconnaissance missions, electro-optics represent the wave of the future and the Pod Reco NG will make good use of this technology. Also designed and produced by Thales, this system will be fielded by suitably modified Mirage 2000Ns and Rafale tactical fighters. The system's performance is still classified but it is understood it will allow exceptionally good high-resolution images to be acquired from standoff distances. For maximum efficiency, the sensors use different wavelengths, and the pod features state-of-the-art digital recorders. Additionally, it will be equipped with a datalink to relay data in a timely and accessible way for real-time interpretation. For targets of opportunity, it is envisaged the pilot will be able to slew the pod's sensors using his helmet-mounted display (HMD). A total of 23 Pod Reco NGs are to be acquired, including eight for the *Aéronavale*.

In terms of 'man-machine' interface, Rafale systems have been tuned to reduce aircrew workload and the aforementioned sensor fusion system is not the only novelty to be introduced. The Rafale's HMD and voice control system will

considerably enhance aircrew situational awareness and is to be adopted on Standard F3 aircraft, while implementation of the Voice, Throttle And Stick (VTAS) concept will revolutionize air combat. Development of the voice control system began in the early 1990s. Extensive testing was conducted initially using Alpha Jets and Mirage IIIs before full-scale trials were undertaken on the Rafale. Word recognition represented a major hurdle at first, as cockpit noise changes with aircraft speed, altitude and *g*-loading. A pilot's voice is also affected by stress and extreme *g* forces, and Thales and Dassault engineers progressively had to solve the problems encountered. Now, however, a customer can choose between vocabulary options offering recognition of between 90 and 300 words. Recognition rates are claimed to be better than 95 percent and response time is under 200 milliseconds. As an added bonus, the system adds to flight safety by helping reduce pilot workload in emergency situations.

Initially, the Sextant Topsight full-face HMD with an integrated oxygen mask was designed for the Rafale. The program

unprecedented capabilities to French fighter pilots with shots 'over the shoulder' becoming a reality, greatly increasing combat efficiency. The Topsight E system appears to be the front-runner, and could first enter service on Mirage 2000-5Fs before being implemented on Standard F3 Rafales in 2008. The system can be fitted to a wide variety of helmet designs, including the lightweight CGF-Gallet type that was recently ordered by the AdA and is used now by Dassault aircrew and *Flottille* 12F Rafale pilots.

While some detractors have questioned the purchase of so many two-seat Rafales by France's armed services, and criticized the 'man-machine' interface, proponents argue that with its wide-angle HUD, touch screens and innovative central display collimated to infinity, the Rafale possesses one of the most modern cockpits in service or under development anywhere in the world. The two-seat configuration will allow new missions to be undertaken and, as has been announced already, Rafale B/Ns will be utilized as high-speed command aircraft during complex attack sorties, and as control posts for unmanned combat aerial vehicles (UCAV). The back-seater will be able to assess time-critical data and intelligence obtained via the datalink and make key decisions while the pilot handles the aircraft. Indeed, the mixed-fleet concept of fighters and UCAVs undoubtedly will be a requirement in dense electromagnetic environments, when modern air defense systems have to be destroyed to achieve air dominance without exposing pilots.

The Rafale is also equipped with two Sagem Spark ring laser-gyro inertial navigation systems with a 'hybridized' GPS, to ensure highly accurate autonomous navigation without reliance on external and vulnerable navigation aids. Their powerful and open architecture is fully capable of blending all data from various sensors (GPS, air data system and radar altimeter for terrain-matching) while performing integrity monitoring.

has been plagued with development problems and funding shortages, however, and France's armed forces are seriously considering alternatives. Two competitors are thought to be in the running: Elbit, with a variant of the Joint Helmet-Mounted Cueing System (JHMCS), and Thales Avionics (formerly Sextant) with its Topsight E. The winning HMD is required to display flight reference data and to permit weapon-aiming and engagement at large off-boresight angles. This will bring

For self-protection the Rafale is equipped with highly automated and capable defensive systems — an essential requirement given the proliferation of air defense systems over the past decade and the considerable pressure this has put on airborne electronic warfare specialists. Moreover, potentially hostile fighters are being equipped with ever more efficient fire-control systems. Designed and produced by Thales Airborne Systems in co-operation with MBDA, the Self-Protection Equipment Countering Threats of Rafale Aircraft (SPECTRA) is a state-of-the-art self-defense system fitted as a complete and totally integrated electronic warfare suite, and is mounted

B01 is seen during hardened aircraft shelter compatibility trials. The AdA is budgeting to operate a squadron of Rafales with 20 percent fewer personnel than is the case with Mirage 2000 units.

internally to keep all weapon stations free. It provides effective electromagnetic detection, laser warning and missile approach warning using passive IR detection technology; and jamming and chaff/flare dispensing in demanding multi-threat environments. The system comprises four different modules and sensors strategically positioned throughout the airframe for all-round coverage.

The latest advances in micro-electronic technology have led to a system that is much lighter, more compact and less demanding than its ancestors in terms of electrical and cooling power. Thanks to its advanced digital technology, SPECTRA offers passive long-range detection, identification and localization of threats, and allows the pilot or system to react immediately with defensive measures: jamming, decoy-dispensing, evasive maneuvers or any combination thereof. Even in a very dense signal environment, direction-finding accuracy is reported to be excellent and the time taken for signal identification extremely short, although all details remain classified.

Additionally, very high processing power ensure excellent detection and jamming performance, optimizing the response to match the threat. Incoming electromagnetic s'gnals can be analyzed, and the bearing and location of emitters determined with great precision. The exact location and types of systems detected by SPECTRA can be recorded for later analysis, giving Rafale operators a substantial built-in SIGINT/ELINT capability while minimizing the need for specialized and costly dedicated intelligence platforms. Further development will bring adoption of high-debit datalinks that will allow two Rafales to carry out instantaneous triangulations of threats, giving positional accuracy to within a few meters. SPECTRA is also fully flightline re-programmable.

As portable surface-to-air missiles have become so serious a threat in recent years, a laser warning system has been mounted either side of the nose and on the tail of the Rafale to provide 360° coverage. Essential for the detection and warning of incoming shoulder-launched, laser beam-riding missiles, the discreet IR missile-approach warner ensures a high probability of detection and low false alarm rates, even against totally passive IR-guided weapons. The exhaust plume of an incoming missile can be detected at very long-range without any emission that would betray the presence of the Rafale. Four

upward-firing launcher modules that utilize various types of cartridges — flares or electro-optic decoys — are built into the airframe, and the Rafale also has internal chaff dispensers.

SPECTRA is much more than a traditional self-defense system as it is closely integrated with the primary sensors also supplied by Thales (RBE2 multimode electronic scanning radar and FSO passive front sector optronics system). As such, it considerably improves situational awareness as all data obtained by the various means is fuzed into a single picture to provide the pilot with a clear image of the evolving tactical situation. Lethality zones, determined by SPECTRA according to the air defense weapon types detected and the local terrain, can be displayed on the color tactical screen, enabling the crew to avoid dangerous areas. Such smart data fuzion significantly increases mission success rates because aircraft survivability is improved.

SPECTRA's first flight aboard a Rafale took place in September 1996 after M02 prototype had been retrofitted. Since then the system has been thoroughly tested in very complex electronic warfare scenarios. For instance, Rafale M02 was pitted against a wide variety of the latest air defense systems during the comprehensive NATO Mace X trial conducted in August 2000, in southwest France. It is reported to have worked flawlessly against Crotale NGs, Aspics, Danish Enhanced-Hawks (DE-Hawks), Danish Army Low-Level Air-Defense Systems (DALLADS), Norwegian Advanced Surface-to-Air Missile Systems (NASAMS) — even an American SA-15 simulator and a German SA-8. The system is now in full production and already operational on *Aéronavale* Rafales. Furthermore, the suite has been designed with growth in mind and further development is envisaged, including a towed radar

Rafale C01 has been used for Magic 2 separation/firing trials, and usually carries dummy Magic 2s on the wingtips. Another common wingtip store is the 'Smoke-Magic', used to enhance the visual effect during airshow performances.

decoy and laser-based IR countermeasure directional turrets to defeat incoming IR-guided missiles. However, Dassault and Thales engineers are pretty confident that SPECTRA is already fully capable of dealing with current and anticipated future threats. Thus, such new systems are likely to be needed only in the long-term, if ever.

To rise above the fog of war, the Rafale is fitted with an extensive communications suite which comprises four radio sets. One is a V/UHF, another is an encrypted UHF and the other two are MIDS-LVTs. In modern combat, information and situational awareness are essential for success, and the futuristic network-centric warfare concept is a key enabler. One of the

most significant advances in technology, the advent of this global military 'infosphere,' will shape the future of combat operations and allow assets to exchange and share tactical data at very high rates. The impact will be to bring together in an efficient manner all of the forces in a particular 'battlespace.'

The Rafale was designed from the outset with datalink capability and, for the French services and other potential NATO-approved customers, will be equipped with the secure and interoperable MIDS-LVT Link 16 system. Jointly developed by France, Germany, Italy, Spain and the USA, the lightweight (64 lb / 29-kg) LVT can transmit and receive data at a rate of 200 Kb/s. With MIDS-LVT, each Rafale in a formation will have access to the sensor data of other aircraft, ground stations and AWACSs. Recognized as a fundamental change in air warfare tactics, datalinks offer the capability to receive targeting information for a silent interception/attack.

Mastering digital technologies has proved essential in designing the MIDS, and EuroMIDS and its American partners have developed the very light LVT, which also includes a TACAN. With its two associated antennas, the LVT offers 360° coverage. Again, the Falcon 20 and Mirage 2000 have been used as test beds and an airborne Rafale successfully exchanged data with a C3 simulator and an integration rig. In the summer 2001, two MIDS-LVT-equipped Rafales cooperated with an E-2C Hawkeye fitted with the Joint Tactical Information Distribution System (JTIDS). The first production MIDS-LVT for the Rafale will be delivered in 2003, and the system will be fully operational on Standard F2 aircraft, and future improvements are likely to see the Rafale's information-sharing capabilities developed further through the adoption of an advanced satellite communication system. For non-NATO-approved countries, Thales and Dassault have designed the LX-UHF tactical datalink, which has been selected by two customers for incorporation into their Mirage 2000s. This high-tech, jam-resistant, line-of-sight system is comparable to the Link 16.

In 1999, Thales announced that an active array for the RBE2 radar would be offered to boost export prospects. Although the innovative RBE2 already represents a giant leap forward compared with older mechanical scanning radars, the adoption of an active array will ensure the design remains fully effective in the long term. Thales began studies on active array technology in 1990, and has made much progress in the field. It has several ongoing operational programs for ground/naval and airborne applications and the development effort is being conducted in parallel with the European collaborative Airborne Multi-mode Solid-state Active-array Radar (AMSAR) program, which eventually will lead to a production radar that should

be incorporated during Rafale and Typhoon mid-life updates.

The new active array to be integrated into the RBE2 is composed of about 1,000 GaAs (gallium arsenide) solid-state transmit/receive modules, which are embedded in the antenna assembly and offer considerably better power and detection range. Better reliability will also be a benefit as the new antenna has inherent redundancy. Whereas a failure of the receiver or of the transceiver makes most radars useless, a percentage of an active array radar's transmit/receive modules can fail with minimal impact on radar performance. Moreover, the direction of the radiation beam from each module is accurately controlled, making it possible to scan an extremely wide area at very high speed. The new antenna will increase the azimuth coverage of the RBE2 from +/- 60° with the passive array to +/- 70°. This will bring it on a par with mechanical scanning radars. Additionally, the detection range will be at least 50 percent better than that offered by the passive array.

Again, the RBE2's open architecture will facilitate upgrading and the new array is totally 'plug and play.' It can be readily adapted to standard RBE2 radar sets without any changes to the processing equipment. Only a patch for the new computer program and slight modification to the wiring are required, representing a real advantage for customers needing urgent radar updates. The active array will be available in 2006 and, although no decision has been announced yet, it is widely anticipated that France's armed forces will switch to active radar technology thereafter.

The *Aéronavale* received its first four Rafale Ms (M2 to M5) in Standard LF1 (without guns and only able to fire Magic 2 missiles, and with limited RBE2 and SPECTRA modes). From M6 onwards, deliveries have been made in full Standard F1. Initial examples were subsequently raised to this standard, and *Flottille* 12F should have all 10 of its allocated F1s by mid-2002. Subsequent deliveries will be in Standard F2 configuration and those aircraft will begin replacing the Super Etendard.

WEAPON SYSTEMS

In order to take full advantage of the Rafale's load-carrying capabilities, French Air Force examples are being equipped with 14 hard points and naval versions with 13. Dassault has specified the maximum external load as 20,925 lb (9500 kg). The

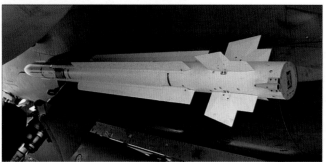

Although closely matched in overall capabilities, Eurofighter's Typhoon and the Rafale offer individual advantages in certain areas. The Rafale is deemed to offer more air-to-surface options than its rival. Both the *Aéronavale* and *Armée de l'Air* have opted for more two-seat versions than single-seaters, a weapons system officer being seen as vital for complex attack and reconnaissance missions.

external stations include five 'wet' pylons for drop tanks.

The Matra/BAe Dynamics *Missile d'Interception, de Combat et d'Autodéfense* (Interception, combat and self-defense missile or MICA) is the primary air-to-air weapon fielded by the Rafale. The lightweight (246-lb/112-kg) missile can be deployed in both beyond-visual-range and short-range situations. A jet deviation system, long fin and aerodynamic control surfaces endow the multimission MICA with exceptional agility and allow operation at load factors as high as 50*g*. Two variants will be carried by air force and navy Rafales — the radar-guided MICA EM (*Electromagnétique*) and the infrared-guided MICA IR. The airframes, warheads and motors of both missile versions are the same, ensuring substantial cost savings. The only difference is the seeker head.

The active-radar seeker in the MICA EM means the weapon is fully autonomous after launch, enabling the pilot to engage several targets simultaneously or simply turn away immediately after release to reduce the time spent in a high-threat environment and deny the enemy an opportunity to fire. Extensive testing has culminated in 'attacks' by one fighter on two widely separated targets, using two missiles. The MICA EM is currently in service on Dassault Mirage 2000-5s with the *Armée de l'Air*, Republic of China Air Force (Taiwan) and Qatar Emiri Air Force, and has been ordered by the United Arab Emirates Air Force for its Mirage 2000-9s.

The MICA IR is replacing the long-serving, Matra/BAe Dynamics Magic II short-range, IR-guided air-to-air missile and is supposed to enter service on Standard F2 Rafales. The IR seeker has many advantages and, thanks to dual-band imagery, has excellent angular resolution. It is also stealthy. The passive homing head will enable 'silent' interceptions when used in conjunction with the FSO and, when employed with the Topsight system, can be fired for an off-axis shot.

However, deployment of both weapon systems on the Rafale is not necessarily a foregone conclusion. Development of long-range missiles like the American Raytheon AIM-120 AMRAAM and Russian Vympel R-77 (AA-12 'Adder') has caused the French MoD to rethink its strategy and a longer-range missile

might be required, instead. At the Paris Air Show in June 1999, an announcement indicated the Ministry might want to join the European Meteor program — the weapon currently being developed for the EF2000 Eurofighter Typhoon. The missile is due to serve with Britain's Royal Air Force and is part of a program dubbed the Beyond Visual-range Air-to-Air Missile (BVRAAM). Another contender, already eliminated, was Raytheon's Future Medium-Range Air-to-Air Missile (FMRAAM), a derivative of the AIM-120 AMRAAM. It is to be fitted with a new guidance section and rocket/ramjet.

Participation of French forces in operations over Kosovo served to demonstrate how 'dumb' bombs will have less application in future conflicts. Increasingly, smart weapons will be needed to neutralize high-value targets while minimizing collateral damage. For this reason, Rafales primarily will be armed with guided munitions. The main air-to-ground weapons chosen for the Rafale belong to the Matra/BAe Dynamics Apache and Scalp EG stealth cruise missile family. An acronym for *Arme Propulsée Antipiste à Charges Ejectables* (meaning propelled anti-runway weapon with ejectable charges), the Apache has been designed for attacks on enemy air bases and to allow air superiority to be gained quickly. The weapon has very low IR and radar signatures that help it disappear into background clutter, and carries 10 Kriss anti-runway submunitions that are released laterally and vertically.

The Scalp EG (*Emploi Général*, meaning general purpose) is a long-range, stealthy cruise missile with one conventional but powerful penetration warhead. It is intended for use in pre-planned attacks against high-value and well-defended hardened targets. Once launched, the Scalp is fully autonomous thanks to its GPS/terrain-referencing navigation system, and the passive IR-imagery homing head is activated during final target approach. Automatic target recognition algorithms compare the actual landscape with preloaded imagery, allowing identification of the target and selection of the impact point to be made with high precision. France may purchase as many as 500 of these weapons, including 50 for the *Aéronavale*, although a serious drawback is the system's

The wingtip launch rails and rear fuselage pylons give the MICA missiles a 'free' ride in any configuration. The fuselage stations are limited to a 4*g* launch envelope, so they would normally be used to mount the active radar EM version, which is less likely to be used in hard-maneuvering combat.

A MICA air-to-air missile is tested near Cazaux, France. Infrared- and radar-guided versions will be fielded.

expense. As a consequence, it might have to be acquired in relatively small numbers.

Specialists with the French MoD have already decided that a cheaper weapon must be designed and this has led to the *Armement Air-Sol Modulaire* or AASM (meaning modular air-to-ground armament). The concept is for a family of modular, all-weather attack weapons with GPS/INS-navigation guidance, with some variants featuring a terminal-phase seeker to enhance precision qualities. The AASM kit is to be adapted for 550-lb (250-kg) bombs (or American Mk 82s) first but versions with different weights and power will also join the French inventory, including rocket-powered examples. The boosted variant of the AASM will need to have a range of up to 32 nm (60 km) when launched from 45,000 feet (13700 m), and an accuracy within three feet (one meter). Of 31 contenders for the contract, the three shortlisted candidates were Aérospatiale/ Matra Missiles, Matra/BAe Dynamics and Sagem. The latter was declared the winner in September 2000 and the first of 3,000 such weapons are due to enter *Armée de l'Air* and *Aéronavale* service in 2005.

At a later stage, a full range of air-to-surface ordnance will become available for Standard F3 aircraft. The ANF missile designed to replace the sea-skimming AM-39 Exocet is likely to

reduce technological risks associated with the ANF and help develop solutions to limit installation and ownership costs. The first air-launched variant is scheduled to enter service between 2008 and 2010 and it is widely believed the missile eventually will equip the Rafale.

The future *Air-Sol Moyenne Portée* or ASMP-A (meaning medium-range air-to-ground) standoff nuclear weapon is also likely to benefit from Vesta program technology. The new pre-strategic nuclear missile will supercede the current ASMP, which serves on air force Mirage 2000Ns and navy Super Etendards. The ASMP-A is based on the existing weapon's general architecture but will be powered by a new-generation, liquid-propellant ramjet. Featuring a long burn time, it has been designed to provide considerable range extension and allow more aggressive trajectories to be followed. The pre-feasibility phase was completed in 1996 and the feasibility/definition phase ended in 1999. Full-scale development began in 2000 and initial operational capability (IOC) on the Mirage 2000N and Rafale is expected in 2008.

GIAT Industries of France has developed the new 30 M 791 cannon for the Rafale. It is the world's only single-barrel 30-mm weapon capable of firing at a rate of 2,500 rounds per minute. This technically advanced gun fires the 30 x 150 range of ammunition designed specifically for this aircraft, possessing high penetration and incendiary qualities that combine good splinter and detonation effects. The 30 M 791 possesses a high fire-rate as well as high initial velocity (3,362 ft/1025 m per sec) to optimize hit probabilities. Mounted to the starboard engine duct, the 264-lb (120-kg) gas-powered gun is autonomous, offers instantaneous firing and also features an electrical ammunition ignition. On all Rafale variants 125 rounds will be carried, which means 21 rounds will be released during a normal one-half second burst. The gun's effective air-to-air range is 4,900 ft (1500 m), and a pyrotechnical rearming device

In 2001, B01 flight-tested the CFTs developed for export Rafales. On the intake side the aircraft carries an impressive tally of Scalp, MICA and GBU-12 launches.

be adopted although the program is currently on hold. This long-range, supersonic (Mach 2.5) fire-and-forget weapon will be propelled by a ramjet and should offer high operational efficiency in terms of range and penetration, in all weathers. High terminal agility coupled with very high speed will endow it with good defenses against antimissile weapons. The ANF project is the first member of a new family of multi-mission supersonic missiles derived from the *Vecteur à Statoréacteur* (Vesta) aerodynamics and propulsion program. It has been under development since 1996 and three test flights were scheduled for 2002. The goals of the Vesta program are to help

ejects faulty rounds after a safety time period.

However, the gun might be deleted from the new two-seat naval version to make room for avionics equipment. In the air force version, such avionics are accommodated in the area of the wheel well but the larger nose gear fitted to the naval variant precludes them from being housed in a similar fashion.

Superfighters

PRODUCTION ORDERS

In a ceremony held at Bordeaux-Mérignac, in the south-west of France, the first production Rafale was delivered to the French MoD in December 1998. That two-seater (B301) was followed by the first production Rafale M in July 1999. However, production rates remain low. Only six aircraft were delivered in 2001 and only the first 13 Standard F1 Rafales (two Rafale Bs and one Rafale C for the AdA, plus 10 Rafale Ms for the navy will have been delivered by October 2002. Assembly is taking place at four Dassault factories: Argenteuil where the fuselage is built, Martignas where the wings are constructed and Biarritz which is responsible for the fin — with final assembly at Bordeaux-Mérignac.

The original plan called for 250 Rafales for the AdA but this was reduced by 16 aircraft subsequently, and the service has also amended its procurement plan. It now wants 95 single-seat and 139 two-seat models — for a total of 234 examples. The revised split between single- and two-seaters is based on operational experience gained with the service's two-seat Mirage 2000N/Ds. [It is worth noting that the US Navy likewise has increased the percentage of Super Hornet two-seaters within its order] While plans initially called for the *Aéronavale* to receive 86 single-seat Rafale Ms, budget cuts reduced the overall number to the aforementioned 60, and the service also decided it needed 'N' models to be included within its order. While the final split between naval single-seat and two-seat aircraft is still to be announced, the breakdown is likely to be 25 M single-seaters and 35 N two-seaters.

It was assumed the first Rafale N would take to the air in 2005, and that initial delivery to an operational unit would be made in 2007. However, the recently announced budget cuts could have an impact on these timings. Overall, the most likely outcome is that deliveries of all 294 F1, F2 and F3 Standard aircraft will be completed by about 2020.

To reduce research and procurement costs and limit risks, a stepped development and delivery approach has been adopted by Dassault and the French MoD. The first three air force aircraft (two-seaters B301 and B302, and single-seater C101) and the first 10 naval fighters (M1 through M10) were delivered as Standard F1 aircraft. This configuration is one dedicated to

air-to-air combat and air defense missions, with MICA EM radar-guided missiles and Magic II short-range air-to-air missiles operational. However, the RBE2 electronically-scanned radar is not fitted with air-to-ground modes. Standard F1 Rafale Ms entered service in 2000, and the first unit to be equipped was *Flottille* 12F at Landivisiau, in Brittany, which was created in May 2001.

Rafales B301, B302 and M1 are being used for Standard F2 development and mainly operate from Istres. However, from 2002, it was anticipated that M1 will spend about half its time at Landivisiau with *Flottille* 12F. The improved Standard F2 will allow air-to-ground attacks using advanced weapons like the Scalp cruise missile and the low-cost AASM. The FSO, Link 16 MIDS-LVT and air-to-ground modes for the RBE2 radar also will be introduced with Standard F2 Rafales. Moreover, a high-resolution three-dimensional digital database will permit automatic terrain-following at low level, and the MICA IR will replace the Magic II with these aircraft. Furthermore, an in-flight refueling pod will be adopted for naval aircraft, making 'buddy' tanker missions possible. At this time, 48 Standard F2s also are on order and full authorization for such development was signed on 26 January 2001. Of the total, 33 will be Rafale 'Air' models (for the *Armée de l'Air*) and 15 will comprise 'Ms' and 'Ns.' The first Standard F2 aircraft is due to enter service in 2004 and the first squadron is supposed to be fully operational in 2005. However, this could slip by a year.

Delivered from 2008 onwards, the final 198 Rafale B/Cs and 35 Rafale M/Ns will be swing-role Standard F3 aircraft. These will be capable of carrying out other specialized tasks like nuclear strikes using ASMP-A missiles, anti-ship attacks with Exocets or ANFs, reconnaissance missions with the Pod Reco NG, and inflight-refueling sorties with a 'buddy' tanking pod more advanced than that planned for use on Standard F2 Rafales. French Navy Rafale F3s will replace the Super Etendard and although those aircraft can fire Exocets, and some Standard 4 Super Etendard Modernisés are fitted with a belly-mounted reconnaissance system, Standard F3 Rafales will be more capable. Progress in the field of reconnaissance has been rapid in recent years, and the Pod Reco NG will significantly boost air force reconnaissance capabilities too. The pod will be fielded on the Rafale starting in 2008 and

Mirage F1CRs will be retired beginning in 2005.

In an effort to standardize the fighter fleet, all Standard F1 and F2 aircraft will be updated to Standard F3 configuration while undergoing inspection maintenance. A subsequent Standard F4 is already envisaged, and could feature yet to be announced improvements. Apart from the already budgeted MBDA Meteor long-range air-to-air missile, it is highly likely that conformal fuel tanks, the active-array electronic scanning RBE2 radar and uprated M88-3 engine being developed for the export market will be Standard 4 adoptions.

It is worth noting that while Rafale prototypes and series aircraft are quite similar there are some important differences. For instance, production Rafales have a beefed-up undercarriage for operations at higher maximum weights, and benefit from a more powerful air conditioning unit. They also have improved IR signature reduction. Prototypes were restricted to a maximum takeoff weight of almost 43,000 lb (19500 kg), while production aircraft are already cleared to an MTO of over 54,012 lb (24500 kg), and eventually will be capable of operating at 57,300 lb (26000 kg) — quite an achievement for such a small fighter.

Although the Rafales built for the *Armée de l'Air* and *Aéronavale* are meeting French requirements, it was felt the design could be improved to strengthen the Rafale's appeal in the export arena. Accordingly, Dassault, Thales and Snecma have launched the curiously dubbed 'Operation Mk 2' — a phased improvement program for the Rafale incorporating systems tailored to meet the requirements of potential foreign operators. The development of new versions has been fully funded through an agreement between the contractors and French government, and full-scale work was officially launched in 2001. As is the case for Rafales entering French service, a stepped approach has been adopted for export Rafales as well. Variants with differing equipment levels will be available as follows:

Block 05:	FSO
	Conformal fuel tanks (optional)
	Voice command
	3D digital database terrain-following system
	GBU-12 laser-guided bomb
	Mk 82 general-purpose bomb
	Scalp standoff cruise missile
	MICA IR missile with combat modes only
	Datalink
Block 10:	M88-3 engines
	Active array for RBE2
	Radar terrain-following capability
	Synthetic aperture radar (SAR) mode
	Helmet-mounted display
	MICA IR with BVR interception modes
	AASM precision weapon
	Exocet anti-ship missile
	Pod Reco NG reconnaissance pod
	Inflight-refuelling pod
Block 15:	Meteor air-to-air missile
	Follow-on avionics improvements

In contrast to the rival Eurofighter, Rafale prototypes have travelled far and wide in the hunt for export sales. Most sales jaunts have involved B01, as it can be used to give demonstration rides to interested and influential air force commanders. Here the aircraft is seen in 1998 at the Seoul International Air Show. South Korea proved to be a bright prospect for Dassault as that nation searched for a heavy fighter to fulfill its F-X requirement. the Rafale was reported to be the favored option from a technical standpoint but political considerations placed the Boeing F-15K as front-runner. The decision ultimately was delayed because of budgetary considerations.

Integration of some of these items is already going ahead, and a series of flight-tests was conducted by Dassault in 2000 to validate GBU-12 laser-guided bomb deliveries from the Rafale. Separation tests were carried out at Cazaux using the two-seat prototype B01. The GBU-12 is widely used by air forces around the world and is already in service in France on Mirage F1CTs, Jaguars, Mirage 2000Ds and Super Etendard Modernisés.

A typical configuration cleared during the trial program featured four wing-mounted GBU-12s along with four MICA and two Magic 2 air-to-air missiles, plus three 528-gal drop tanks. This combination gives the Rafale enormous fire power and very long range. In this configuration, the combat radius is said to be 800 nm (1480 km) and the Rafale can boast significant self-escort capability. Other laser-guided weapons like the 500-lb (227-kg) GBU-22 and 2,000-lb (907-kg) GBU-24 Paveway III bombs are likely to be adopted in due course. Unsubstantiated rumors also suggest Raytheon is pushing Dassault to consider clearance of the new-generation AIM-9X Sidewinder air-to-air missile on the type, which would serve to increase the missile's export prospects.

The Rafale excels at low-level flight with heavy loads. Automatic terrain-following is possible thanks to a digital terrain database, obviating the need for an emitting TF radar that could give away the aircraft's position.

On their fins *Flottille* 12F Rafale Ms wear a toned-down representation of the unit's well-known badge, which depicts Donald Duck carrying a blunderbuss.

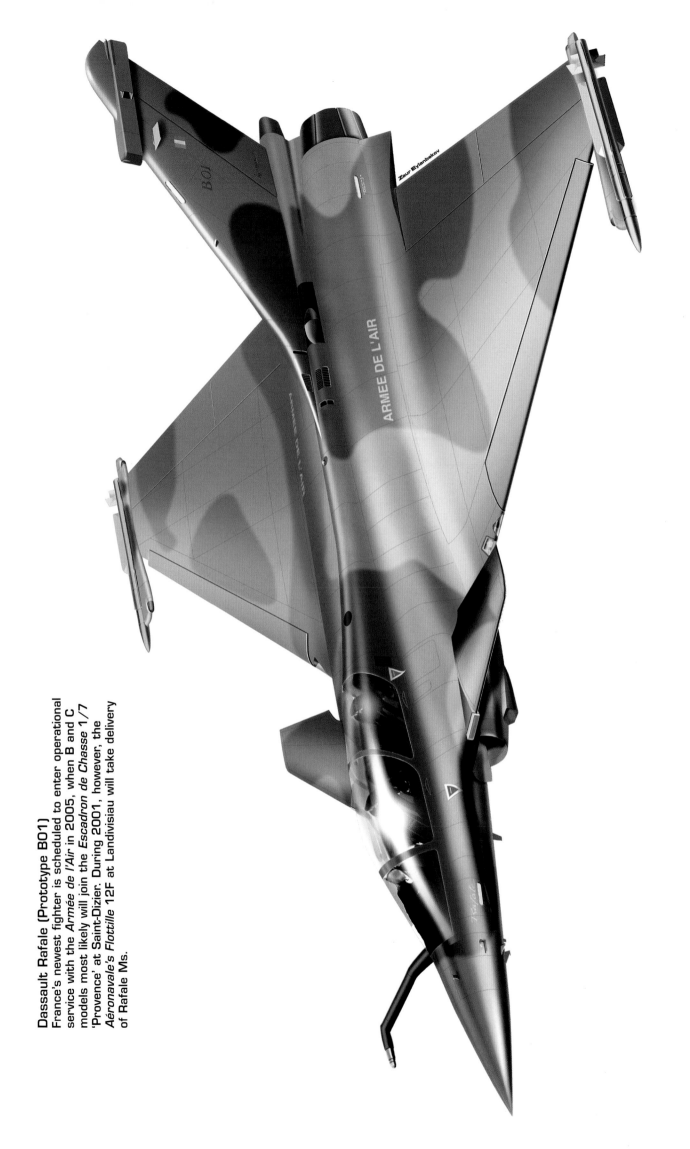

Dassault Rafale (Prototype B01)

France's newest fighter is scheduled to enter operational service with the *Armée de l'Air* in 2005, when B and C models most likely will join the *Escadron de Chasse 1/7* 'Provence' at Saint-Dizier. During 2001, however, the *Aéronavale's Flottille 12F* at Landivisiau will take delivery of Rafale Ms.

Superfighters

SPECIFICATIONS

Wing span (incl. missiles)	35 ft 9.125 in (10.90 m)
Length	50 ft 2.375 in (15.30 m)
Height	17 ft 6.25 in (5.34 m)
Empty weight	approx. 20,925 lb. (9500 kg)
Max. takeoff weight (initial version)	42,951 lb (19500 kg)
Max. takeoff weight (developed version)	49,559 lb (22500 kg)
Fuel	internal 9,911 lb (4500 kg)
Fuel	max. external 16,519 lb (7500 kg)
Max. level speed at altitude	Mach 2
Max. low-level speed	750 kts (1390 km/h)
Approach speed	115 kts (213 km/h at typical weight)
Takeoff distance	for an air defense mission 1,312 ft (400 m)
	for an attack mission 1,968 ft (600 m)
Operating range	CLASSIFIED
Service ceiling	59,055 ft (18000 m)
g limits	+9 / -3.6
Combat radius	591 nm (1093 km) for a strike mission with 12 500-lb bombs, four MICAs, one 2000-litre and two 1250-litre drop tanks. 1000 nm (1853 km) for an air defense mission with eight MICAs, two 2,000-lit and two 1,250-lit drop tanks
Accommodation	One or one pilot and one WSO, depending on variant, on Martin-Baker Mk16F ejection seats
Power plant	Two SNECMA M88-2 turbofans rated at 10,960 lb st (48.75 kN) thrust dry and 16,413 lb st (73.01 kN) with afterburner

The Thales/MBDA team is justifiably proud of SPECTRA, particularly its directional ECM capabilities. The above marking appeared on Rafale M02 during the NATO MACE X exercise in August 2000, in which SPECTRA proved itself. Below is the fin tip, location for several SPECTRA elements, including rear-facing interferometer and laser-warner on the side.

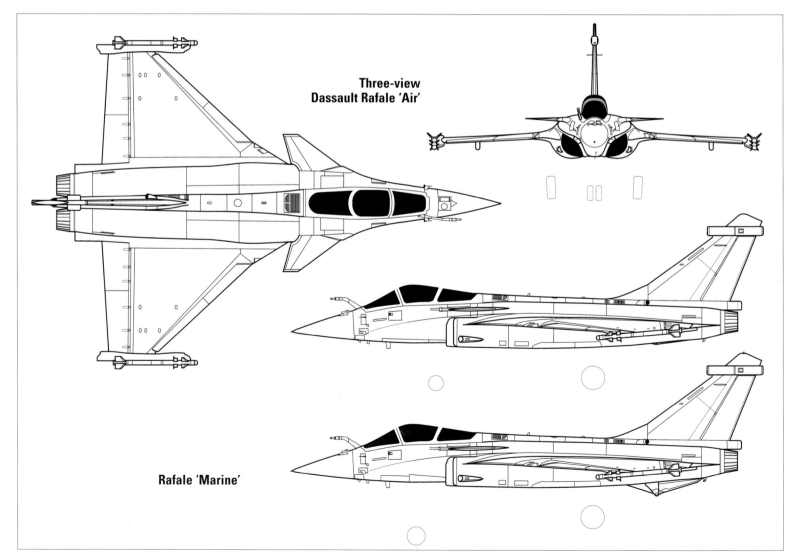

Three-view
Dassault Rafale 'Air'

Rafale 'Marine'

In the 1980s, when the Rafale was under development, it was considered current and projected avionics capabilities would alleviate much of the pilot's traditional workload, allowing him/her to concentrate on the important aspects of conducting the mission at hand. In the light of Gulf War experience, France was one of the first to admit that the workload on a single pilot would be too much in a sophisticated strike mission scenario, in a heavily-defended environment. As a result the Rafale order was revised to include a majority of two-seaters. This decision was derided by many but other programs have since arrived at a similar conclusion: Saab (Gripen), Boeing (Super Hornet), Mikoyan (MiG-29M2), Sukhoi (Su-30) and even the Eurofighter are either pursuing or studying fully 'missionized' two-seaters, capable of handling the most complex of mission taskings. These are expected to include command and control of other combat aircraft and of UCAVs.

CHAPTER 6

Sukhoi 'Super Flankers'

DEVELOPMENT OBJECTIVES

The Su-27 'Flanker' is viewed by many as the best fighter ever produced by the Soviet aircraft industry, with unmatched aerodynamic performance and superb handling characteristics, especially at high angles of attack (AoA) and in the post-stall area of the envelope. Unlike the contemporary MiG-29, the Su-27 had more than adequate range, and carried sufficient weapons to give it remarkable 'combat persistence.' However, most analysts would acknowledge that the original aircraft had major flaws — a primitive radar, old-fashioned avionics and a poor man-machine interface that severely limited the pilot's ability to utilize the aircraft without the aid of GCI controllers. It also lacked real multirole capabilities. Development of advanced Su-27 variants was well under way when the Cold War ended, with various prototypes of newer derivatives already flying. While the subsequent breakup and economic collapse of the Soviet Union did not kill these programs outright, starved of funding they progressed only at a snail's pace. Production of the Su-27 slowed to a trickle in 1991 and ceased altogether except for export, in 1993.

The basic Su-27 was developed to meet a requirement for a long-range heavy interceptor for the IA-PVO (air defense forces), to replace aircraft like the Su-15, Tu-128 and MiG-25, and augment the very fast, long-range MiG-31 'Foxhound'. A

related requirement for a similarly configured but shorter-range and lighter-weight tactical fighter resulted in the MiG-29. The basic Su-27 is broadly comparable with the MiG, both types possessing very similar aerodynamic performance and limits. The MiG-29 has been extensively evaluated, and has emerged from engagements against the best western fighter types with a formidable reputation as a close-in 'dogfighter.' Most qualified weapons instructors caution their students against trying to fight on the MiG-29's or Su-27's terms. 'Never wrestle with a pig. You both get dirty but the pig enjoys it!' runs the advice.

The two aircraft can also be compared quite closely in the beyond-visual-range (BVR) arena, since both have similar and, in some respects, common avionics. The Su-27's version of what NATO calls the 'Slot Back' radar is more powerful, and has a larger antenna, giving longer detection ranges but a similar lack of onboard processing power tends to tie the Su-27 pilot to GCI control. The two aircraft also rely on the same R27 (NATO AA-10 'Alamo') missiles, although the Su-27 can carry six or eight compared to the MiG-29's two, and can field the larger, longer-range 'ET' versions of the weapon.

For all of the aircraft's inadequacies in the BVR role, the big Sukhoi is extremely agile at low weights and especially in the low-speed/high-Alpha (high angle of attack) element of the envelope. With full internal fuel, the aircraft has significantly lower *g* limits and is much less agile, and supersonic agility also

Despite advances to the Su-27's airframe developed over the past decade, it is still the baseline Su-27 that provides the backbone of Russian air defenses. Of the many variants that have appeared, the Su-35 (below and on the opposite page) exhibits extraordinary agility, having been fitted with canard foreplanes. The Su-30KN at the bottom of the page is carrying Kh-31 (AS-17 'Krypton') anti-ship missiles along with air defense R-77 (AA-12 'Adder') and R-73 (AA-11 'Archer') missiles.

may be less impressive. Nevertheless, at low weights, and especially at low speed, the aircraft is exceptionally maneuverable and its post-stall capabilities give the Su-27 pilot an unmatched ability to point the nose of his aircraft (and thus his weapons and sensors) far away from the axis of flight, and tackle off-boresight targets. The significance of low-speed 'dogfighting' is sometimes overstated since it is notoriously unpredictable and dangerous. The wise fighter pilot will exit the area and reload with BVR missiles rather than enter a close-in fight, and if an encounter becomes a turning engagement it is usually best to maintain airspeed and energy.

Sukhoi and Russia's air forces realized the limitations of the original Su-27 and plans were put in place for a second-generation version — a multirole aircraft with a greatly

expanded air-to-ground capability, including real potential in the all-weather precision-attack role that would not prejudice its air-to-air capabilities. The new variant was intended to replace a range of Frontal Aviation types, including the MiG-23ML, MIG-27 and Su-17, as well as the original MiG-29 and Su-27. It was also intended for the same aircraft to replace the Su-27 with the IA-PVO (fighter air defense forces).

Just as the original requirement that resulted in the basic Su-27 had been divided to produce heavy and light fighters in a high/low mix, it soon became apparent that cost considerations and an unwillingness by the customer to put all of its eggs into one basket would probably require a similar lighter weight, lower-cost aircraft to augment the new Su-27 derivative. Mikoyan thus launched the MiG-29M. The new Sukhoi (Su-27M) and the MiG-29M were not strictly competitors, since it was always thought a mix of types would be procured but, as each company wanted its aircraft to gain the lion's share of the work, competition intensified as spending declined. Still, since first appearing, the Su-27 has spawned many variants besides the Su-27M air superiority fighter — the Su-30 interceptor, Su-33 shipborne fighter and Su-27IB tactical fighter bomber to mention some.

By the mid-1990s, it was increasingly clear that even for export the baseline Su-27 was no longer attractive enough to win commercial orders. Serious proposals to upgrade the Su-27 first emerged around that time and a single aircraft was painted up as a demonstrator, with the designation Su-27SMK painted on the forward fuselage. Initially, the intention was for the new version to borrow components and systems from the MiG-29SMT upgrade. Thus, it would be fitted with a Zhuk-based Fazatron-NIIR Zhemchug or NIIP N011M radar. However,

Superfighters

Two 'Flankers' refuel from an Il-78M 'Midas,' which can mount up to three UPAZ pods (two beneath the wings and one on the port rear fuselage) for tanking operations. With relatively few in service, demand for the refuelers is high and their use is often restricted to supporting the bomber fleet. Control of refueling cycles is overseen from the rear turret station (which has its guns removed), beneath which is fitted a traffic light system to direct the receiving aircraft.

Below, a pair of Su-27s are readied for a training sortie from Lipetsk Air Base, located 235 miles (380 km) south of Moscow, the center for the Russian Air Forces' (VVS) tactical know-how. Interestingly, the VVS Medical Service is currently using one of the base's Su-27UBs to study the effects of high *g*-loads on pilots during combat maneuvers. Other fast-jet tactical types operating at Lipetsk include the MiG-29 'Fulcrum' and Su-24 'Fencer.' Just visible is some of the tri-color scheme applied to a number of the aircraft as part of the 50th-year commemorative celebrations that marked victory over Nazi Germany.

these plans were abandoned, along with the idea of the Su-27SM upgrade configuration for Russia's air forces. The Su-27SMK was proposed as a more austere aircraft. For the first phase of the planned upgrade (an export model designated the Su-27SMK-I) the plan was to take the basic Su-27 fighter and integrate a retractable inflight refueling probe, GPS, improved navigation suite, radios and extra hardpoints (per the Su-30), as well as bigger integral wing tanks and provision for two external 528-gal (2,000-lit) underwing tanks. A planned second phase (dubbed the Su-27SMK-II) would have added compatibility with various precision-guided, air-to-ground weapons and up to eight R-77 air-to-air missiles. However, neither SMK version attracted orders.

Despite the early setbacks, perhaps the most astonishing development in the Su-27's story has been the way in which a dedicated long-range PVO heavy interceptor was developed to

This Su-30, factory no. 96310104007, was completed on 24 July 1996 and is operated by the air defense troops of the PVO, an organization recently amalgamated with the VVS.

Vasiliy Zolotov

As military funding dwindled, Sukhoi projects prospered while the competing products of other bureaus were cut back or canceled, even on the rare occasions when a competitor's aircraft might have been more suitable for a particular role. Sukhoi also played the political game with great expertise and enthusiasm. When it became clear new-sounding projects were more likely to obtain funding than warmed-over derivatives of existing aircraft, Sukhoi assiduously assigned new designations to what hitherto had merely been Su-27 subtypes. Thus, the Su-27IB became the Su-34 and Su-32, while the Su-27K became the Su-33. Similarly, the Su-27PU became the Su-30, and the Su-27M became the Su-35 and Su-37. An analyst once complained in 1995 that Sukhoi had produced more new designations than they had airframes. To confuse matters further, Russia's air forces obstinately refused to recognize the new designations at first and continued to use the old ones. The AV-MF (*aviatsiya voyenno-morskogo flota*/naval aviation) eventually bowed to pressure and re-designated its Su-27Ks as Su-33s.

P-42 (above, center) is a series Su-27 that laid claim to many world records during the period 1986-88, including absolute altitude and rate of climb. For its record-breaking flights the aircraft was made as light as possible — even the paint was stripped off.

fill so many different roles, and as the basis of so many variants and derivatives. The aircraft's formidable internal fuel capacity and load-carrying capabilities made it a natural choice to be the basis of even longer-range and longer-endurance fighter variants like the Su-30, and long-range strike-attack aircraft like the Su-30M and Su-27IB. However, it needs to be remembered that the Su-27 also enjoyed the advantage of being the product of the Sukhoi Design Bureau (OKB). Its liberal-leaning management gained a great deal of influence as Russia liberalized, while the company was very fortunate that its designer general, the charismatic Mikhail Simonov, sat on the Committee of the Supreme Soviet that oversaw the running of the aircraft industry. Simonov thus was able to fight for and safeguard the position of his OKB and its associated plants, and was able to ensure they became the first experimental grouping of OKB and factories together, in Russia. Under Presidents Gorbachev and Yeltsin the OKB reached a position of ascendancy over other concerns.

China's Su-30MKK, above, is a multirole aircraft with the accent on attack. It lacks the canards and thrust-vectoring of India's Su-30MKI but does have a 'missionized' rear cockpit with a multifunction display. The aircraft sold to Vietnam, to complement that country's standard Su-27K/UBKs, are also thought to lack canards.

Prior to its only operational deployment to date, the *Kuznetsov* air wing left its Severomorsk base in 1995 for a work-up at Kubinka Air Base, near Moscow. The Su-33s wear the markings of the 1st *eskadrilya* (squadron) of the 279th *korabel'nyi istrebitel'nyi aviatsionnyi polk* or KIAP, meaning shipborne fighter air regiment.

Superfighters

Su-27M / Su-35 / Su-37

Although improved multirole and air-to-ground capability was the *raison d'être* of the Su-27M (known as the T-10M within the design bureau), Sukhoi claimed the primary aim had been to improve 'dogfighting' characteristics through higher-Alpha

Despite bureau enthusiasm for the aircraft's enhanced air combat capabilities, it was always been driven by an improved air-to-ground proficiency and the core of the variant was a new N-011 multimode radar, an advanced new infrared scanner/tracker (IRST) with collimated laser and TV channels for advanced precision-guided missile delivery, and a new offensive electronic warfare (EW) suite. The aircraft also had a new

In the 1990s, the Su-35 (Su-27M) was put forward in a number of international fighter competitions, offering the benefits of exceptional range and performance. However, its relatively low acquisition cost was offset by high 'through-life' costs. Furthermore, questions remain as to the true capabilities of Russian systems. The Su-35 prototype is shown at right and depicted below.

Mark Styling

limits (up to 30 units), improve high-Alpha handling, achieve 3.5 times greater instability and achieve a lower weight. The OKB also associated the aircraft with new and ultra-long-range air-to-air missiles — and emphasized the variant's ability to operate independently of GCI control as well as integrate with airborne warning and control system (AWACS) aircraft and other fighters using datalinks for automatic target allocation.

'glass' cockpit and, to fully exploit its new canard foreplanes, was intended to have a new quadruplex digital fly-by-wire (FBW) system, although it also retained its analog equipment.

As the Su-27M was planned as a new-build aircraft, with existing Su-27s due to be 'cascaded' to the second-line and to export customers, the opportunity was taken to significantly redesign the airframe. Although external differences between

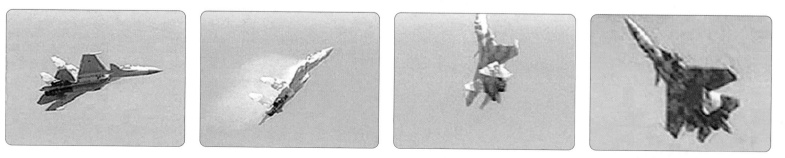

'Bort 710' is a production Su-35.

The enormous thrust-vectoring nozzles fitted to the AL-37FU engines of Su-37 'Bort 711,' an Su-35 airframe, are clearly evident in this view. In the capable hands of test pilot Yevgeniy Frolov, it has demonstrated outstanding post-stall maneuvers and enabled the design bureau to gather a wealth of performance data. The sequence below shows a maneuver performed for a show crowd. The aircraft made its first appearance outside Russia in 1996 at Farnborough, and also took part in the Paris Air Show at France's Le Bourget field, the following year.

the Su-27 and Su-27M are relatively minor, like the contemporary MiG-29M the Su-27M made extensive use of composites and welded aluminum lithium to reduce weight and increase internal volume. As an air-to-ground aircraft, however, it was expected to operate at higher loads and the undercarriage was strengthened to allow a higher maximum takeoff weight. The nose gear was entirely redesigned with twin nosewheels. The new radar allowed the use of a longer, more graceful radome, while the rear-facing radar necessitated a thicker, raised tail 'sting.' Most prototypes also gained taller tailfins, like those for the Su-27UB, but with the rudder extending down to the root and with a new flat-topped fin-cap profile.

The first Su-27M prototype flew on 28 June 1988, preceded by a number of test and trials aircraft used to verify the revised flight control system (FCS) software and the new canard foreplanes. Sukhoi optimistically boasted that the new type would enter service in 1995 and very early on began referring to it as the Su-35. The type was officially re-designated in 1993. Development continued at a slow pace even after the rival MiG-29M program was terminated but it became increasingly clear that the Su-27M would never enter full-scale service. Many were astonished by the continuation of the aircraft and the cancelation of the smaller, cheaper MiG-29K, which was widely viewed as being more flexible, better 'sorted' in the air-to-ground role, and better suited to the post-Cold War world. Three aircraft (Blue 86, 87 and

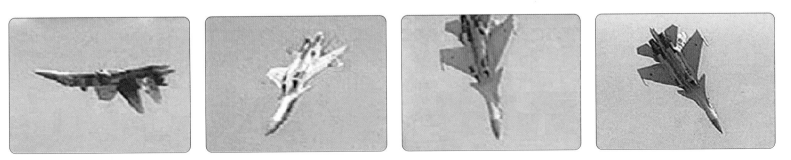

Superfighters

88), described by sources at the KnAAPO or Komsomolsk-na-Amure aviatsionno-proizvodstvennoye ob'edineniye (meaning Komsomolsk aviation enterprise) as production Su-35s, were delivered to Akhtubinsk from Komsomolsk in 1996 or 1997, although they may have been rebuilt or refurbished Su-27M prototypes. Ignoring the manufacturer, the VVS continued to refer to the aircraft as Su-27Ms.

Sukhoi claimed definitive production Su-27Ms would feature thrust-vectoring engines, and that a thrust-vectoring example would appear at Farnborough in 1994. Despite dramatic funding cutbacks, the OKB did re-engine the eleventh and final Su-27M development airframe with thrust-vectoring power plants. That aircraft undertook its maiden flight on 2 April 1996 with the nozzles locked full aft. The aircraft was funded by the OKB, with no formal requirement for vectoring nozzles from the air forces, and became a trials aircraft for proposed thrust-vectoring export versions of the 'Flanker.' The aircraft, re-designated the Su-37 by the bureau, demonstrated impressive levels of agility and was able to match maneuvers performed by the X-31, doing so reliably and predictably at air show heights. While development continues, it is uncertain if the Su-35/-37 has a future. Russia's Air Forces have not expressed much interest and its fate may be determined by the strength of export orders. Alternatively, it might simply become a technology demonstrator for such programs as the Su-30MK.

The Su-37 is the first Russian fighter to incorporate vectored thrust and is powered two Lyulka-Saturn/Moscow engines, each rated at 28,219 lb st (125.5 kN). With no formal requirement from Russia's air forces for a thrust-vectored variant, Sukhoi pursued the concept at its own expense, re-engining the eleventh and final Su-27M development aircraft with a view to using it as a demonstrator and, hopefully, to generate export interest. '711' undertook its maiden flight on 2 April 1996.

Su-27PU / Su-30

The Su-30KI designation emerged in 1998, applied to a single-seat aircraft that appeared to be painted in the basic Chinese camouflage scheme, with a disruptive pattern applied over the

proposal to upgrade Russia's in-service Su-27s — replacing the Su-27SM. This program is confusingly referred to by Sukhoi as the Su-30KI, although the air forces doubtless use neither the Su-30 designation nor the 'KI' suffix. Whatever its designation, the upgraded Su-27 may gain a day/night precision-attack capability by using the new UOMP Sapsan optronic targeting

While Sukhoi has developed many potential variants of the Su-27, there has been scant interest from both domestic and foreign customers. In an effort to attract export sales, the bureau developed the multirole Su-30MK — promising enhanced performance and better weapons options. Below is the demonstrator seen at Zhukovskiy.

pod, which contains a laser designator and collimated thermal imager. The upgrade managers are also thought to be hoping to incorporate the N-011VE radar, a new mission computer, expanded ECM/EW capabilities and an Su-30MKK 'glass' cockpit.

The Su-27PU was developed to meet a long-standing requirement to replace the Tu-128 used to defend Russia's most isolated frontiers in the frozen north. This required an aircraft with considerable range and endurance, yet one that would still be able to deal with modern threats, including low-level bombers and even cruise missiles. The Su-27 already had considerable range but, with inflight refueling, would be capable of flying even longer missions — but thereby stretch the capacity of a single pilot to the limit. Therefore a decision was taken to produce a dedicated long-endurance fighter based on the airframe of the Su-27UB but with full operational equipment and a

top of the wings and fuselage, and the outer faces of the tailfins. The aircraft was based on the standard single-seat Su-27 but was fitted with the retractable inflight refueling probe associated with the Su-30, Su-32, Su-33, Su-34 and Su-35/37. Informed sources suggested it was once the prototype or demonstrator for the Indonesian single-seat Su-30 before Asia's economic crisis halted that program.

The extent to which the aircraft incorporated the Su-30's extended-endurance features, apart from its refueling probe, GPS and Western VOR/DME navigation equipment, remains uncertain. Retaining its *Kommercial Indonesian* KI designation suffix, the Su-30KI made its maiden flight on 28 June 1998, and was then sent to the Chkalov Flight Test Center at Akhtubinsk for evaluation. It was also used for launch trials of the RVV-AE (AA-12 'Adder') air-to-air missile, and as the basis for Sukhoi's latest

Canards and 15°+- thrust-vectoring nozzles equipped the first Su-30MKI prototype. On this variant, the nozzles were outward-canted by 32° to improve low-altitude maneuverability.

constraints brought the program to a halt. However, Sukhoi continued to develop the aircraft, adding limited air-to-ground capabilities to arrive at the Su-30M, known to export customers as the Su-30MK. The first foreign customer was India, which ordered 40 examples for delivery in batches with progressively improved capabilities. As deliveries progressed, the plan called for early aircraft to be shipped back to the factory for conversion to the highest standard. The first eight were to be delivered in Su-30K configuration, while follow-on batches were to introduce planned improved multirole avionics, canard foreplanes and thrust-vectoring engines.

Unfortunately, deliveries did not keep pace with the agreed schedule, and the aircraft actually delivered turned out to be basic Su-27UB trainer-standard aircraft, albeit with inflight refueling probes. Some reports suggest the first eight aircraft, delivered in March 1997, were not even new but hastily reconditioned secondhand trainers. By the end of 2000, India was still waiting for its multirole extended endurance models, let alone aircraft with canard foreplanes and thrust vectoring engines.

The moment of impact when the Su-30MKI's tail section hit the ground during a demonstration the day before the 1999 Paris Air Show. Despite a burning engine, the pilot applied full power and used thrust-vectoring to bring the striken jet to a near vertical position — and gain sufficient height for him and his navigator to make a successful ejection at an altitude of well under 300 ft (100 m). Below is the second Su-30MKK prototype (Bort 502), which underwent trials with Bort 501 at the Gromov LII Flight Research Institute.

The Su-30MKK variant ordered by another customer, China, lacks thrust vectoring and canards but does incorporate an advanced 'glass' cockpit and expanded air-to-ground capability. Sixty are on order and deliveries have already begun. Local production of the standard Su-27 (as the J-11) is expected to end after the 80th aircraft, when Shenyang will switch to production of the Su-30MKK. Meanwhile, a similar aircraft with the simple Su-30K designation has been ordered by Vietnam.

Enjoying pre-eminence in production of two-seat trainers, the Irkutsk plant took the lead with the Indian Su-30 program, while Komsomolsk seized control of the Su-30MKK project for China. As a consequence, Novosibirsk has been left with an extremely thin order book, finding work only on the Su-27IB program and its derivatives, for which production orders are still awaited.

retractable inflight refueling probe. In addition, a backseater would assist the handling pilot during transit or combat air patrols (CAP), providing an extra pair of eyes and by managing the weapons system while the frontseater concentrated on maneuvering the aircraft. The new version also gained new navigation equipment and avionics.

The first Su-27PU prototype made its maiden flight in the fall of 1988 and although the variant (referred to by Sukhoi simply as the Su-30, or Su-30K for export) was ordered into production at Irkutsk, only a handful were delivered before funding

The size and positioning of the hydraulic airbrake employed by the 'Flanker' is similar to that of the F-15 Eagle. Depending on the variant, the Sukhoi's approach speed is between 143 and 149 mph (230-240 km/h) and the landing roll is in the 2,000 – 3,000-ft (600 – 900-m) range.

In Russian service the Su-30 is essentially a missionized Su-27B with additional communications links for use in the interceptor leader role. However, the designation also covers a number of export variants. Depicted is the Su-30KI, a single-seat improved Su-27 originally intended for sale to Indonesia.

Andrey Zhirnov

1. Pitot static tube
2. Pitot static tube wiring
3. Radar dielectric nose cone
4. N001VE radar antenna
5. Nose equipment compartment
6. Antenna
7. Angle-of-attack vane
8. Inflight refueling probe
9. Inflight refueling probe extension system
10. Light for illuminating refueling drogue
11. Infrared search and track sensor
12. Cockpit windscreen
13. ILS-31 head-up display
14. Forward cockpit instrument panel
15. K-36DM ejection seat
16. Head-up display repeater
17. Rear cockpit instrument panel
18. Upward-hinging canopy structure
19. Rear view mirrors
20. Back-up pitot static tube
21. Equipment compartment
22. Radio compass non-directional antenna
23. GSh-301 30-mm cannon
24. Cannon ammunition belt
25. Shell extractor
26. Nosewheel strut
27. Twin nosewheels
28. Nosewheel mudguard
29. Strut-mounted landing lights
30. Nose gear door
31. Engine air intake
32. Intake spill doors

33. Boundary layer bleed-off slots
34. Auxiliary intake slots
35. Anti-FOD intake screen
36. Air intake screen actuator and damper
37. Air intake moveable ramp
38. Intake ramp actuator
39. No. 1 fuel cell
40. Fuel tank filler cap
41. Radio antenna
42. Airbrake
43. Hydraulic airbrake actuator
44. Electric wiring runs
45. Control linkages
46. Radio compass
47. No. 2 fuel cell
48. Fuel system units

49. Engine air duct
50. Main landing gear
51. KT-156D mainwheel
52. Undercarriage bay door
53. Undercarriage bay door actuator
54. Main undercarriage wheel well
55. Wing/center section joint
56. Wing panel structure
57. Two-section leading-edge slat
58. Leading-edge slat control hydraulic device
59. Leading-edge slat hydraulic actuator
60. Wing fuel cell

© Aleksey Mikheyev

61. Flaperon hydraulic actuator
62. Flaperon
63. Static wicks
64. Wingtip missile launch rail
65. Navigation light (green, starboard)
66. Ventral fin
67. Horizontal stabilizer
68. Horizontal stabilizer pivot

69. Horizontal stabilizer hydraulic actuator
70. Vertical fin
71. Air intake for heat exchanger
72. Rudder
73. Rudder hydraulic actuators
74. Rudder hydraulic control box

75. Fin torsion box structure
76. UHF/VHF radio antenna
77. Electronic equipment antennas
78. Rear navigation light (white)
79. Lyul'ka-Saturn AL-31F engine
80. Aircraft accessory gearbox
81. Oil tank
82. Variable engine exhaust nozzle
83. Tailboom
84. Hinged cover for brake chute container
85. Brake chute container
86. Chaff/flare dispensers
87. No. 4 fuel cell
88. Fuel system units

89. Radar warning receiver antenna
90. R-73 short-range air-to-air missile
91. Wing-mounted Sorbtsiya active ECM pod
92. R-77 medium-range air-to-air missile
93. AKU-170 launch pylon

94. R-27ET medium-range air-to-air missile
95. R-27ER medium-range air-to-air missile
96. KAB-500Kr precision-guided bomb
97. Kh-31P anti-radiation missile
98. AKU-58 launch pylon
99. Kh-31A anti-ship missile
100. Kh-29T air-to-surface missile
101. BetAB-500 bomb

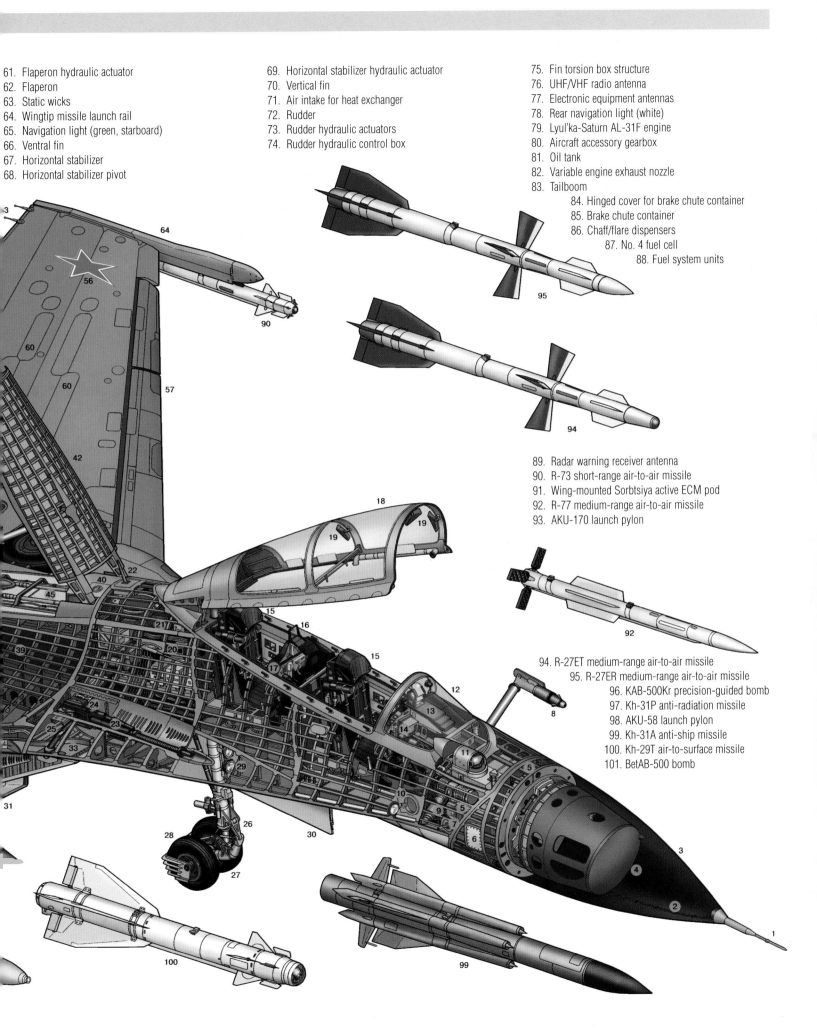

Superfighters

Su-27K / Su-33

The inability of the Yak-38 'Forger' to undertake realistic air superiority missions severely limited the usefulness of the Soviet Navy's Project 1143 ASW cruisers (*Kiev*, *Minsk*, *Novorossiysk* and *Baku*), and a decision was taken to develop a larger, more powerful carrier capable of accommodating STOL aircraft rather than just STOVL aircraft and helicopters. The outcome was the Project 1160 carrier, developed to embark an air wing of MiG-23s for air superiority, plus a strike component

allow operation of the new Yak-141 and MiG-29K, as well as the Su-27K according to Sukhoi — despite the aircraft's size.

A dominant feature of Russian fighter development over many decades has been the fierce competition between the two great design bureaus: Sukhoi and MiG. This was no less so when Russia's navy sought a new carrierborne fighter. Thus, it is useful to chart the progress of the navalized 'Flanker' in this light and to note the comparatives with its rival platform. The process began with conceptual designs for the Su-27K and MiG-29K shipborne projects in 1978, and both featured a high level of commonality with their land-based counterparts in

A service Su-33 (foreground) alongside the Su-27KUB, the prototype for the twin-seat naval 'Flanker' (Su-33UB). With this variant, Sukhoi aims to greatly expand the family's capabilities — envisaging roles like AEW for the type.

After building two Su-27K prototypes, Sukhoi began series production of seven Su-27K/ Su-33s, the first of which (T10K-3) is seen taxiing on the deck of the carrier, which was renamed *Admiral of the Fleet of the Soviet Union Kuznetsov* in October 1990. This batch of aircraft was used for both factory and service tests, and was followed by 24 full-production aircraft. As well as trials at Saki, the Su-27K/33 test fleet has undertaken occasional trials aboard the carrier itself.

of Su-24s. However, Sukhoi was concerned that the Su-24 would be too heavy for carrier operations and, in 1973, succeeded in persuading the Navy that a maritime version of the projected T10 should be used instead. Carrier Project 1153, which followed, was intended to embark a similar air wing with MiG-23Ks and Su-25s and, perhaps, some of the larger Su-27Ks. However, this failed to gain funding. Instead, the Navy examined the possibility of building a fifth Project 1143 ship with an increased displacement and modifications to

general layout, power plant, avionics and armament. There were, however, a number of important differences. The seagoing versions were to be given folding wings, reinforced landing gear, an arrester hook and a modified navigation suite, as well as additional anti-corrosion protection for their airframes, power plants and equipment.

As far as the normal and maximum takeoff weights were concerned, the Su-27K would be 1.5 times heavier than the MiG-29K and its internal fuel capacity roughly twice as large, resulting in a combat radius 1.5 times greater. The MiG-29K could boast the same combat radius and time on station only when fitted with external fuel tanks (one belly-mounted and two under the wings), which considerably reduced its capability to carry missiles. In terms of fire power, the Su-27K was far ahead of the MiG-29K as well. Along with the same 30-mm, 150-round cannon and two K-73 'dogfight' air-to-air missiles, the Su-27K mounted six K-27 medium-range air-to-air weapons, while the MiG-29K hauled just four — two of which had to be sacrificed whenever drop tanks were mounted. Unlike the MiG, the Sukhoi could fire the so-called 'swept-up' version of the medium-range missile — the extended-range K-27E , as well. However, the Su-27K's strengths were paid for in its larger dimensions and higher cost, which limited the number of such fighters that could be assigned to an air wing.

To develop support systems for the launch and recovery of carrierborne aircraft (catapult, arresting gear, optical and radio landing systems) and to train future naval pilots, it decided to establish a research and training center in the Crimea, not far from the town of Saki. The center was dubbed Nitka (meaning 'thread') since the center's abbreviated designation was NITKA (for Aviation Research and Training Complex).

Development of a carrierborne 'Flanker' was begun at an early stage of the program, and the third prototype, T10-3, was involved in the first ski-ramp trials at Saki. It made its first ramp takeoff on 28 August 1982, a week after a test MiG-29 had done the same. The T10-3 introduced outward-canted fins.

1984, the new T-2 ramp was ready and the first takeoff, utilizing that aircraft, was undertaken by Nikolai Sadovnikov on 25 September. On 1 October 1984, Valeriy Menitskiy flew MiG-29 No. 918 from T-2.

The Nitka complex was used not only for ramp-takeoff and arrested-landing trials but also for testing the equipment to be mounted on the ship. This included the Luna-3 optical landing system, which used lights of various colors to alert the pilot to glide-path deviations, a homing radar beacon system, and a short-range navigation and landing radar system. During the summer of 1986 another Su-27, the experimental T10-24 — by this time fitted with canards, was used for trials at Nitka and, a year later, it was succeeded by another prototype, the T10U-2. This was one of the first series-produced Su-27UB two-seaters, fitted with an inflight refueling probe and arrester hook. In addition to pilots from the Sukhoi, MiG and LII, Air Force pilots like Col. Yuriy Syomkin and Col. Vladimir Kondaurov from the Akhtubinsk-based Air Force Research Institute were involved in the program and expected to carry out state trials of the shipborne aircraft. Some time later, Col. Timur Apakidze and Col. Nikolai Yakovlev, followed by other Northern Fleet pilots, were officially allowed to accomplish deck landings on their own after practice at the Nitka facility.

Right after the 1984 governmental resolution was issued, both design bureaus launched initial and then detailed designs of their navalized variants. The Su-27K (T-10K) was to be derived from the production Su-27 fighter (T-10S), with the

In 1981, the Soviet General Staff ordered a reduction in the displacement of the Project 1143.5 aircraft carrier which was then under development, as well as the abandonment of work on a catapult-assisted launch system. The developers were told to look for some other means of launching their aircraft from a carrier. Sukhoi and Mikoyan design bureau leaders, supported by specialists from the LII Flight Research Institute and Central Aero- and Hydrodynamics Institute (TsAGI) proposed a ramp-assisted takeoff method for the high thrust-to-weight ratio fighters. For takeoff, the fighters were to use the 'springboard' ramp in the carrier's bow, developed earlier to assist Yak-41 VTOL/STOL fighters fitted with a full combat load.

In the summer of that same year, the proposal for Su-27 and MiG-29 tests at the Nitka facility was authorized. For this purpose, it was necessary to equip the center with a representative takeoff ramp in order to ascertain if fourth-generation fighters could make unassisted carrier takeoffs. Ramp trials began at Saki in the summer of 1982, involving upgraded prototypes that included the third Su-27 initial configuration prototype (T10-3) and the seventh MiG-29 flying prototype (No. 918). The first takeoff from the T-1 ramp was undertaken by a MiG-29 on 21 August, with design bureau test pilot Aviard Fastovets at the controls. A week later, Nikolai Sadovnikov flew the T10-3 off the ramp. The initial trials pointed up the need for a substantial change in the ramp's profile, however, with the cylinder-type surface giving way to a cubic curve. While the upgraded ramp, designated the T-2, was under construction arresting gear-assisted landings were tested during the 'down time.'

Despite the unsuitability of the T-1 ramp's shape, the Nitka trials in 1982-83 confirmed the soundness of the 'non-assisted' principle. On 18 April 1984, the Central Committee of the Communist Party of the Soviet Union (CPSU) and the USSR Council of Ministers decreed that Sukhoi should develop a carrierborne air defense (AD) derivative of its Su-27, designated the Su-27K. MiG was instructed to develop a lighter multirole shipborne fighter (the MiG-29K) capable of attack duties against naval and shore-based targets. In line with developing the ship-based Su-27K, Sukhoi launched a follow-up Nitka-trials phase for which the bureau had prepared an experimental prototype designated the T10-25 — using one of the first production Su-27s. By the summer of

Where the MiG-29K really scored over the Su-33 was in its systems. The cockpit was based on that of the MiG-29M (9-15), with two large monochrome CRT displays controlled by HOTAS (hands on throttle and stick) rather than by buttons around it. If either the MiG-29M or MiG-29K had gone ahead, they would have been the first Russian combat aircraft to have featured a Western-style 'glass' cockpit, although the technology is dated by today's standards. Another key element of the MiG-29K was the RVV-AE/R-77 missile, a Russian equivalent of the AIM-120. Like the AMRAAM, the R-77 is an active-radar weapon that can be used in fire-and-forget mode in short-range engagements. The weapon also forms an important part of Sukhoi's Su-33M upgrade proposal. Shown below is 'Bort 312,' the second MiG-29K (9-31) prototype, which was used primarily for avionics and systems testing.

Superfighters

A development Su-27K (T10K-7) displays the folding wings and tailplanes of the design, and also the heavy air-to-air missile load consisting of various R-27 variants and R-73s.

avionics and weapons suites remaining virtually the same, and with double-slotted flaps, outboard drooping ailerons and a primitive but effective carrier landing system incorporated. The aircraft's primary tasks were to provide air defense for the carrier battle group in all weathers, from sea-level up to around 88,000 ft (approx. 27000 m), and deal with hostile ASW rotary-wing and fixed-wing aircraft, troop-carrying helicopters and AEW planes — using K-27E air-to-air missiles in BVR situations and K-73s and the 30-mm cannon when close in. A multi-role Su-27K variant was expected to be developed during Phase 2, utilizing the avionics and weapons suites of the Su-27M multirole tactical fighter then under development.

To facilitate carrier deployment, a number of steps were taken to navalize the land-based aircraft. A stronger landing gear was incorporated and the whole airframe was reinforced to enable non-flare touchdowns to be made at high sink rates and g-loadings. An arrester hook was added and, to enhance lift characteristics and control during takeoffs and landings, the efficiency of its high-lift devices was improved. The wing area of both the Sukhoi and MiG was increased by roughly 10 percent and the Su-27K gained all-moving canard foreplanes, while both aircraft featured an all-axes FBW control system. As the Sukhoi would not be able to take off from the ramp at its normal MTOW, however, it was also provided with a neat retractable inflight refueling probe. The radar was improved to provide increased capability in the 'look-down' mode against sea clutter, and datalinks were provided to allow the aircraft carrier to take over the role of a GCI station. However, the variant was viewed primarily as an air superiority fighter and the MiG-29K as the carrierborne attacker.

To increase the takeoff thrust-to-weight ratio, both types were outfitted with engines featuring an 'emergency thrust mode' that ensured a brief increase in afterburning thrust. They were also fitted with refueling probes to extend their combat radius and time-on-station. Furthermore, the requirement to be

stowed above and below deck in large numbers necessitated both aircraft having folding wings, which roughly halved the Su-27K's width and reduced the MiG-29K's by 35 percent. To allow the Su-27K to use the deck edge lift, with its 26-ft (8-m) limit, the Sukhoi's stabilizer had to fold as well. In addition, both type's flight and navigation systems were complemented with special short-range radio navigation aids, and special attention was paid to protecting the fighters from saltwater corrosion by sealing individual components. Overall, these measures led to a 10-12 percent increase in weight over their land-based equivalents and flight performance was impacted accordingly. However, since the Su-27K's fuel capacity was 2.1 times that of the MiG-29K, its range exceeded that of its rival's by over 80 percent at high altitude and by 33 percent at sea level.

The difference between the fighters' normal takeoff weight was around 40 percent, but the Su-27K's maximum weight exceeded that of the MiG-29K by a factor of 1.5. At normal takeoff weight, the Su-27K's specific wing loading remained 10-15 percent lower, which led to lower approach and lift-off speeds, according to pilots who flew both aircraft. The Su-27K was responsive enough at an approach speed of 149 mph (240 km/h), whereas the MiG-29K's controllability tended to degrade at 155 mph (250 km/h) — a substantial difference as far as carrier landings are concerned.

Outfitted with the same 150-round GSh-301 cannon and an equal number of R-73 missiles (four per type in the standard configuration), the Su-27K can carry as many as eight R-27E medium-range weapons (six R-27ER semi-active radar homing and two R-27ET heat-seeking air-to-air missiles) with a range of 40 to 50 miles (65-80 km). The MiG-29K's inventory includes only two R-27ER/ET air-to-air missiles and two basic R-27R/T weapons with a range of 31 miles (50 km). By contrast, instead of R-27s, the MiG-29K can carry advanced RVV-AE active radar homing missiles with a range of 37 miles (60 km). The standard RVV-AE count is four but they can also be mounted on the R-73 hardpoints. Such a loadout means the MiG-29K's chances of surviving an engagement are better than those for the Su-27K with its eight R-27Es. In terms of air-to-surface capabilities, the Su-27K — with its 1,102-lb (500-kg) and 551-lb (250-kg) gravity bombs and 'dumb' rockets — was no match for the MiG-29K. The latter would be armed, in addition to its unguided ordnance, with air-to-surface precision-guided munitions like the Kh-31A antiship missile, Kh-29T TV-homing AGM, Kh-31P and Kh-25MP anti-radiation missiles, as well as KAB-500Kr smart bombs.

While the Su-27K was a clear winner in terms of absolute air performance, the MiG-29K introduced many advanced features and promised to be the better aircraft from a systems point of view. However, the innovations of the MiG were in an early stage of development, and would take some time and a lot of money to bring to service fruition. With the Soviet Union's collapse imminent, time was fast running out for the MiG team. By early 1986, the Project 1143.5 heavy aircraft-carrying cruiser was nearing completion at the Nikolayev-based shipyard. Both aircraft design bureaus were busy as construction of the first Su-27Ks and MiG-29Ks approached the final stage.

Sukhoi was the first to show off its aircraft. The initial Su-27K prototype (T10K-1) took the air under the control of test pilot

Depicted as seen during a visit to the Pushkin overhaul plant in the summer of 1999, this Sukhoi Su-33 is from the 2nd Squadron of the 279th *korabel'nyi istrebitel'nyi polk* (shipborne fighter regiment). Home base for the 279th KIAP is Malyavr (Severomorsk-3), near Murmansk, although training is performed on the dummy deck at Saki, Crimea, and the work-up for the Mediterranean cruise was undertaken at Kubinka, near Moscow.

Vasiliy Zolotov

Viktor Pugachov on 17 August 1987. The second prototype (T10K-2) followed in December. After factory testing, the airframes were re-deployed to the Crimea for tests at the Nitka complex. On 23 June 1988, test pilot Toktar Aubakirov undertook the maiden flight of the first MiG-29K prototype (No. 311) and the next year it was ferried to the Crimea too. Pilots from both bureaus flew numerous ramp takeoffs and arrested landings there before the *Tbilisi* left the shipyard's outfitting quay on 21 October 1989, and headed to the naval testing area near Sevastopol.

Preparations and familiarization flights over the *Tbilisi* lasted just over a week and the long-awaited day for the first real deck landing was set for 1 November 1989. Viktor Pugachov in the second Su-27K prototype (the first having crashed), and then Toktar Aubakirov in MiG-29K (No. 311), became the first Russians to conventionally land jet fighters on the deck of a ship. That same day, Aubakirov made the first takeoff from the carrier. Development trials ended on 22 November when the carrier returned to base for final outfitting and equipment installation. During the three-week test period a total of 227 sorties and 35 deck landings were recorded, of which 20 were made by Pugachov, Yuriy Syomkin and Yevgeniy Frolov in the Su-27K, and 13 by Aubakirov, Vladimir Kondaurov and Anatoliy Kvochur in the MiG-29K.

The carrier — which had its keel laid as the *Riga* but was launched in December 1985 as the *Leonid Brezhnev* and completed as the *Tbilisi* — was renamed the *Admiral Kuznetsov* before commissioning on 25 December 1990. A year later it cruised to Severomorsk. By then, KnAAPO had rolled out the first production Su-27K fighters (redesignated the Su-33 some time after the historic deck landing of 1 November). Through-

out 1990-1991, seven production Su-33s (factory designations ranging from T10K-3 to T10K-9) were constructed for factory and service testing purposes. September 1990 saw the second MiG-29K prototype (No. 312) join the trials, while the Moscow Aircraft Production Association (MAPO) — nowadays the MiG Russian Aircraft Corporation's Voronin Production Center — laid down the first production MiG-29K.

The Su-33 (Su-27K) commenced its official trials in March 1991, with the MiG-29K following in August at the Air Force Research Institute's Crimean affiliate airfields, before heading to the *Admiral Kuznetsov*. Having seven flying aircraft available (both T10K-1 and T10K-8 had crashed by then), Sukhoi's program went with a swing whereas Mikoyan's lagged behind, hampered by the availability of only two MiG-29K flying prototypes and a number of problems with the advanced avionics, new power plant and other technical novelties.

Experiencing enormous political upheaval, the Soviet Union broke apart and the subsequent military budget deficit led to suspension of aircraft carrier construction. In early 1992, at the Nikolayev-based shipyard (now owned by independent Ukraine) assembly of the *Varyag* carrier was terminated even though the ship was already 70 percent completed. In February of the same year, the nuclear-powered *Ulyanovsk* — construction for which had started in November 1988 and which was assessed at 20 percent complete — was cut up for scrap metal. Given the poor prospects for construction of any new aircraft carrier, further development of a second naval fighter was deemed unaffordable. Production Su-33s built to that point — a total of 24 examples — were considered sufficient for the *Kuznetsov*'s air group and, consequently, official tests for the MiG-29K were terminated in August. Both prototypes were

The Su-33 'Flanker-D' takes a lot of stopping, requiring a strong arresting system. Proponents of the MiG-29 point to its much lighter weight, necessitating a lighter and less beefy arresting system, although the 'Fulcrum's' approach speed is a few knots higher. Furthermore, the Su-27 takes up a lot more deck space. Aboard the post-refit *Gorshkov*, for example, 24 MiG-29Ks can be accommodated as opposed to just 12 Su-33s.

mothballed — No. 311 having flown 320 sorties and No. 312 having taken to the air 106 times.

As with the Su-27M's continuation at the expense of the MiG-29M, many felt the wrong aircraft had been canceled. The MiG-29K was more versatile than the Su-27K, and its small size meant that more could have been embarked within a carrier's limited deck and hangar deck space.

Official testing of the Su-33 continued for another three years, ending in December 1994 with the recommendation to field the aircraft. It joined the inventory of the 279th Naval Fighter Regiment and officially entered service three and one-half years later, on 31 August 1998. Almost three years before, however, in December 1995, the *Kuznetsov* had left for the Mediterranean and its first long ocean cruise. During the three-month voyage the vessel covered more than 10,000 miles (16000 km), traversing two oceans plus the Barents, Norwegian, Mediterranean, Ionian and Adriatic seas. Embarked aboard were 13 Su-33 fighters, along with two Su-25UTG trainers and 9 Ka-27 helicopters. All in all, more than 400 fixed-wing sorties were conducted during the voyage.

In time, cessation of Yak-38 operations made useless the *Kiev*, *Minsk* and *Novorossiysk* — and they were duly decommissioned in 1993. Like the Project 1123 helicopter carriers, *Moskva* and *Leningrad*, they were sold in the late 1990s at scrap rates. Some went to India, some to China and some to South Korea. Only the *Minsk* survived, converted by the enterprising Chinese into a floating museum near the city of Shenzhen. A similar fate is in store for the unfinished *Varyag*, which is supposed to become an entertainment center off the coast of Macao.

By the mid-1990s, Russia's naval forces had just two carriers at their disposal, of which only the *Kuznetsov* was a potential combatant — with an Su-33 fighter and Ka-27 helicopter carrier air group embarked. The other vessel, the Project 1143.4 *Admiral Gorshkov*, was idle at a Northern Fleet naval base until it drew the attention of India, which was interested in supplying its own navy with up-to-date carriers. Negotiations began in 1996 with a view to converting the vessel to a medium, multipurpose carrier with ramp-assisted takeoff and arrested landing capabilities. The Nevskoye Design Bureau (NPKB), which had developed the *Gorshkov* and the rest of the Project 1123 and 1143 carriers, devised a suitable conversion. To turn the *Gorshkov* into a multipurpose carrier, the NPKB determined it would be necessary to strip the vessel of its attack missile and artillery features — particularly the Bazalt anti-ship missile system — and extend the flight deck. In addition, the ship would be fitted with a takeoff ramp like that of the *Kuznetsov* as well as three arresting gear units.

The new design called for a flight deck length of 919 ft (280 m), with a 656-ft (200-m) takeoff runway and a 649-ft (198-m) landing runway. The upper deck fighter/helicopter parking area was increased to 25,834 sq ft (2400 m^2), and two elevators with lifting capacities of 30 and 20 tonnes (66,139 and 44,092 lb / 30000 and 20000 kg), respectively, would lower the aircraft into the 426 x 75 x 18.7-ft (130 x 23 x 5.7-m) internal hangar. So configured, the ship can house 34 aircraft including up to 24 MiG-29K-class fighters or 12 Su-33-class fighters, along with several Ka-27 helicopters. The vessel's electronic equipment is to be upgraded with an optical landing system and a TV aircraft landing control system. Not only will the modernized electronics provide target acquisition, close navigation, final approach, radio beaconing, control and communications, but also combat command and control of the aircraft.

It is not surprising that the possibility of fulfilling the Indian contract galvanized old rivalries between the Sukhoi and Mikoyan teams. The latter proposed its updated MiG-29K carrierborne multirole fighter, derived from the production MiG-29 and utilizing a wealth of expertise gained from building the MiG-29K (9-31) prototype and advanced avionics and weapons for the future MiG-29SMT (9-17) tactical fighter derivative. Sukhoi, meanwhile, offered its Su-33MK, an export multirole variant of the production Su-33, upgraded with features developed for the Su-30MK multirole fighter family.

The Su-33 upgrade program will fit the aircraft with an improved fire control system designed to launch the new RVV-AE air-to-air missile and air-to-surface guided munitions. The upgraded Su-33 weapon systems will include the Kh-31A active radar-homing, anti-ship missile; Kh-31P anti-radiation missile; Kh-29T(L) TV-homing (laser beam-riding), multipurpose missile; Kh-59M TV-command missile; KAB-1500Kr or six KAB-500Kr guided bombs. Furthermore, the possibility of fitting the fighter with a Moskit (Mosquito) or Yakhont (Ruby) heavy anti-ship missile is also under consideration. The upgraded Su-33 is also expected to be outfitted with new navigation and communications suites, more efficient ECM systems and an up-to-date cockpit data presentation system that features two large, color liquid-crystal displays (LCD) and a more sophisticated head-up display (HUD).

Even more impressive capabilities might be embodied into the Su-33 two-seat derivative. Sukhoi and KnAAPO built the first Su-27KUB twin-seat, side-by-side combat trainer prototype in 1999. In addition to a new forward fuselage, the aircraft has a larger wing area with the so-called adaptive deflecting leading-edge slat, plus canards, a larger stabilizer, larger ventral fins and rudders, as well as a number of other performance-enhancing improvements. It made its maiden flight was on 29 April of that year, kicking off the factory testing phase for which production is being arranged by KnAAPO. That year saw the type's first tests at the Nitka complex and on the *Kuznetsov*.

While Sukhoi continues to market the Su-33, its large size, primitive avionics and lack of multirole capabilities make it a poor choice for the operators of small carriers. India, which ultimately bought the refurbished *Admiral Gorshkov*, preferred to go with MiG-29Ks. According to experts, Su-33-class aircraft are too big to be deployed on small and medium-size carriers like the post-refit *Gorshkov*, and the future Indian carrier ADS. The reality is that MiG-29K fighters are simply better suited.

This Su-33 is from the 1st Squadron of the 279th *korabel'nyi istrebitel'nyi aviatsion'nyi polk* and is depicted launching a Yakhont fourth-generation anti-ship missile.

Su-27IB / Su-32 / Su-34

Known internally by the Sukhoi OKB as the T-10V, the Su-27IB tactical fighter-bomber's most visible difference from the standard Su-27 is the widened forward fuselage to accommodate side-by-side crew placement. It features a high 'glass' cockpit encased in 0.7-in (17mm-) thick titanium alloy, to afford crew protection from anti-aircraft fire. Another luxury is the depth of the cockpit, which allows the aircrew to stand fully upright and stretch their legs during long missions — as well as a toilet and an area between the seats to stretch out and sleep. The aircraft is even equipped with K-36DM ejection seats that have a back massage feature.

With its long range and prodigious load-carrying capabilities, the Su-27 was a natural basis for a tactical strike/attack aircraft to

replace the Su-24 'Fencer.' However, the development of the Su-27IB has been extraordinarily protracted and has followed a tortuous path.

Displayed with some of its weapon options, the Su-27IB can carry (from left to right) the TV-guided Kh-59M (AS-18 'Kazoo' ASM), with a range of 71 miles (115 km); and the Mach-3 Kh-31 (AS-17 'Krypton') antiradar-antiship missile. Also shown is the APK-9 datalink pod for the Kh-59M and, beneath the fuselage is a mockup of the proposed Alfa ASM.

Design of what became the Su-27IB began when Sukhoi first started work on the navalized Su-27K, initially under the designation Su-27KM-2, and later as the Su-27KU. The program was shelved in the late 1980s, as the carrier program drew down. However, in August 1990, a TASS photographer aboard the *Kuznetsov* captured a new type flying a dummy approach. It was described at the time as the Su-27KU — a new shipborne trainer. The aircraft, designated T-10V-1 by the OKB, made its maiden flight on 13 April 1990 with Anatoliy Ivanov at the controls, although not under the Su-27KU designation. It was converted from a standard Su-27UB and fitted with a new nose built by the Novosibirsk factory. When construction began, the new aircraft may have been intended as a prototype for the Su-27KU but by the time it was rolled out it had gained a new purpose, that of a trials and proof-of-concept platform for the Su-27IB bomber. When the aircraft was photographed again, at a static display for CIS leaders at Minsk-Machulische, in February 1992, the truth came out. The aircraft bristled with a variety of air-to-ground weapons and although the sign in front of the air-

craft was covered while TASS photographers were admitted, it slipped to reveal the true Su-27IB designation.

Production of subsequent aircraft was moved to the former 'Fencer' line at Novosibirsk and the first example built there, T-10V-2, made its maiden flight on 18 December 1993, with Igor Votintsev and Yevgeniy Revunov at the controls. The flight took

52 minutes. Novosibirsk-built aircraft differ from the initial prototype in several respects. Each is equipped with a reinforced landing gear and twin, tandem main wheels. Each has a fuller 'hump' behind the cockpit, a longer 'sting' protruding from between the engines that houses a warning radar, and modified vertical fins. The Su-27UB's oversized fins were retained for T-10V-1 but proved too large during flight-tests. As a consequence, standard Su-27 fins have been retained on later examples. Another noticeable difference is the sharp edge of the wing-root extensions.

Production aircraft are expected to incorporate fully automatic terrain-following and hostile fire-avoidance, while the canards will alleviate gust response in low-level flight. However, only four examples have been built to the planned production standard — the first making its maiden flight on 28 December 1994.

When T-10V-2 was shown early that same year, the aircraft was referred to for the first time as the Su-34 and it is possible this will become its official designation when it enters service. When displayed at the Paris Air Show in 1995, however, it was designated as the Su-32FN — the letters suggesting a proposed export maritime-strike version. In fact, Sukhoi has since promoted the basic aircraft to export customers as the maritime strike-configured Su-32FN and multirole Su-32MF. The original 'IB' designation stands for *istrebitel-bombardirovshchik*, meaning tactical fighter-bomber. Flying at high speed and low altitude, an operational radius of 375 miles (600 km) is claimed for the variant — extending to 700 miles (1130 km) at high altitude, and by a further 40 percent if additional fuel tanks are carried. Being air refuelable, however, the Su-27IB's effective range is ultimately limited by the endurance of its crew and the availability of tankers.

T-10V-5 was the first example to be fitted with a fire-control system and was flight-tested on 28 December 1994. Central to the system is the B004 radar built by the Leninets Design Bureau in St. Petersburg. This multifunction radar incorporates electrical scanning and is capable of detecting and engaging targets in the air, on the ground and on water. Offering better combat capabilities, it can track and engage multiple targets simultaneously, and has a much higher-resolution display and better jamming resistance. Reports also suggest the Su-27IB can carry any of Russia's tactical air-to-surface missiles, and the Su-32FN variant has been depicted carrying two Moskit heavy antiship missiles and three (planned) multipurpose Alfa ASMs. It is also claimed the aircraft can carry Kh-65S subsonic cruise

of the aircraft and its armament systems have been conducted at the flight-test center in Akhtubinsk. At 45 tonnes (99,208 lb / 45000 kg), with a full load of fuel and ordnance, the Su-27IB is 50 percent heavier than the original Su-27. This has required extensive testing to be conducted on the platform itself and the question of more powerful engines has had to be addressed. Unlike the seven prototypes built within the research and development program, production aircraft will be powered by new-generation Lyulka-Saturn AL-41F turbofans each rated at 39,342 lb st (175 kN) with afterburning. The new engine provides almost 40 percent more thrust than the AL-31F and is more fuel efficient. It is expected to enhance performance significantly by providing much better acceleration, a higher cruise speed and improved range.

Building tactical reconnaissance and electronic warfare aircraft is now an urgent issue for Russia and such variants are being developed from the Su-27IB. The prototype Su-27R reconnaissance platform was flight-tested by Oleg Tsoy in the spring of 1997, at the Leninets facility. Now undergoing further testing, the aircraft is expected to enter service at some point in the future. Just how many Su-27IBs might be built will depend on a number of factors including export interest. By 2015-2020, however, it is likely Russia's air forces will need at least 550 aircraft (including a reconnaissance platform) to replace a similar

missiles, which have a range of 155-175 miles (250-280 km), as well as the Mach 5 Kh-15S aeroballistic missile serving with strategic air forces. Like the rest of the 'Flanker' family, the Su-27IB is fitted with a GSh-301 cannon in its starboard wing root, capable of firing 180 rounds.

Although optimized for strike missions, the aircraft is well equipped for air-to-air combat. It may not prove equal to an opponent during close-in fighting because of its high weight and limited g-loads but, for BVR encounters, it is well served by its advanced radars and weapons. Capable of firing air-to-air missiles having ranges of 125-185 miles (200-300 km), the Su-27IB can usefully adopt the role of long-range interceptor.

Despite insufficient funding, development of the Su-27IB has continued over the years and, since 1997, state acceptance tests

number of Su-24s now with the fleet. In the meantime, the Novosibirsk factory has been struggling with the cost of the few examples it has built because of late payments from the state. Clearly, foreign sales will be important to the project and the aircraft has been widely advertised to potential buyers. In 1998, a Chinese military delegation visited Novosibirsk, and India has expressed interest. This is not surprising since both countries fly jets from the same family and soon will begin licensed production of the Su-27 and Su-30. However, the

Perhaps the most important new aircraft program for Russia's air forces is the Su-34, a 'Flanker' derivative designed to replace the Su-24 and other types in the strike/attack/anti-ship roles. Eight pre-production aircraft (including two static test examples) have been built, to be followed by a production batch of 10. Construction is taking place at the Novosibirsk plant. Shown below is the one production aircraft built in 1996 and used for show appearances at Paris and Zhukovskiy the following year.

Russian government has not yet issued an export license for the variant, and no production models have rolled off any line. That said, of Russia's current fighter-bomber projects, there is no doubt the Su-27IB is at the top of the list.

It should be noted that a single example was deployed to Mozdok in late 1999 and flew combat sorties over Chechnya alongside Su-24s and Su-25s, in the hands of air force test and evaluation crews.

Sukhoi Su-27IB/Su-32FN 'Bort 45'

'Bort 45' was the third Su-27IB to fly, going aloft on 28 December 1994. Six months later it was displayed at the June 1995 Paris Air Show, the first appearance of a side-by-side 'Flanker' in the West. Painted in this garish color scheme, the aircraft was described as an 'Su-32FN', a supposed anti-ship attack version. It is likely that it did not differ in any significant detail from the standard Su-27IB/34, although Sukhoi was extolling the virtues of the Sea Dragon avionics system (with Sea Snake radar), which included ASW sonobuoys (dropped from a centerline pod) and associated processing equipment. In recent years, Sukhoi has described the Su-32 designation as applying to export versions of the Su-27IB/34. As well as its overseas demonstrations, 'Bort 45' is heavily involved with tests and clearance trials for the Russian Air Forces' Su-27IB/34, and may have been involved in a reported combat evaluation over Chechnya in 1999. The test fleet is now believed to number six, the latest of which ('Bort 47') flew in August 2000.

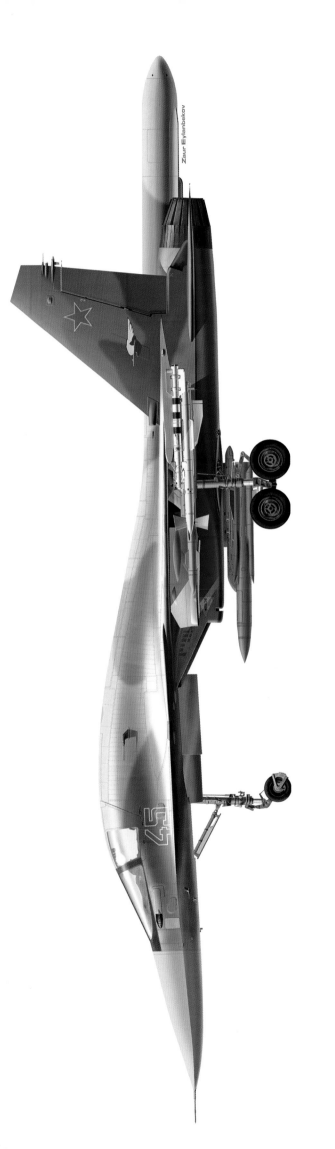

Zaur Eylanbekov

Superfighters

PRODUCTION ORDERS

After a false start and a complete redesign because the original aircraft suffered excessive drag, handling problems and inadequate performance, the production (original) Su-27 entered service with the IA-PVO in late 1986, reaching a peak of about 500 aircraft prior to the breakup of the USSR. By early 1996, the VVS had about 130 Su-27s in service, with 300 more operated by PVO regiments and about 30 more were in service with the AV-MF. Apart from some 20 or so Su-33s (Su-27Ks), three Su-27Ms (Su-35s) and five Su-30s (Su-27PUs), all were baseline Su-27s or Su-27UB trainers.

An estimated 380 'Flankers' are in service with Russia's air forces today within a tactical fleet numbering 1,800 aircraft, excluding trainers and stored airframes. Worldwide, the total number of 'Flankers' in service is probably less than 500. Since production ended, the relatively small number of export aircraft for China, India and Vietnam were probably produced from airframes already under construction (or even completed) for canceled Russian orders. Some Russian sources suggest that five Su-30s and three Su-35s were commissioned after 1994, but even these aircraft are likely to have used Su-27 airframes already taking shape on the Komsomolsk and Irkutsk production lines.

The prospects of Russia's military ordering large numbers of Su-27PU long-range interceptors, Su-27IB tactical bombers and Su-27M advanced tactical fighters has evaporated, and even continuing the development programs has proved difficult. Attention has had to turn from domestic to export customer potential but even here, Sukhoi has been unable to make much impact. Baseline first-generation 'Flankers' have been sold in small numbers to traditional Soviet export customers but have failed to break into new markets.

Despite allocating a variety of new designations to a number of Su-27 versions, no genuine new-generation 'Flankers' have yet to be delivered to a customer. Yet the impression sometimes given is quite the opposite. During 2000, Sukhoi indicated it expected orders in the following four-year period to total $7 billion, and listed Indonesia and the Royal Malaysian Air Force as likely customers for the Su-30. As if the lack of orders was not bad enough, 'Flanker' work has had to be divided between the three competing production plants at Komsomolsk, Irkutsk and Novosibirsk. Irkutsk seized the lead on the Indian Su-30 program while Komsomolsk monopolized the Chinese 'Flanker' program, including two-seaters. That left the Novosibirsk facility limited to work on the Su-27IB and its derivatives. All three plants have been operating as part of the Sukhoi Aviation Military-Industrial Complex (AMIC), alongside the OKB, since August 1996.

The first head of that new holding organization was Aleksey Fedorov, the director of IAPO and his appointment confirmed the increasing muscle of the production plants over the hitherto dominant design bureaus, which believed that plant directors would inevitably place industrial considerations over scientific and engineering interests. The OKB was able to re-assert its primacy with the appointment on 29 May 1999 of Mikhail Pogosyan as Fedorov's replacement. Behind the

scenes, meanwhile, Inkombank and ONEXIMbank have struggled for control of the OKB although probably for short-term, speculative reasons. A transition to full privatization, however, has become less likely and most expect a partially privatized Sukhoi to remain under central control. At the same time, the complex attempted to reduce its dependence on foreign sources, replacing components previously supplied by organizations located in non-Russian former Soviet republics. This will simplify matters in the long term but has led to short-term dislocation and many difficulties.

During President Yeltsin's last period in office, First Deputy Prime Minister Yuriy Maslyukov, overseeing the aircraft industry, proposed merging the Sukhoi and Mikoyan OKBs, an idea greeted with hostility by both organizations. Before Maslyukov was removed from office, however, he appointed a senior Sukhoi executive (Nikolai Nikitin) to lead the Mikoyan OKB. Under the current president, Vladimir Putin, moves towards major mergers have recommenced.

While the small, cheap and relatively lightweight MiG-29 was widely exported, the Su-27 was not offered to Russia's Warsaw Pact allies during the Cold War, nor to non-aligned but traditional customers for Russian combat aircraft like India. Only after the end of the Cold War, and a collapse in Soviet/Russian orders, did the OKB seriously start marketing the aircraft to export customers. The Sukhoi OKB and Russian defense ministry have taken the lead with respect to secondhand Su-27 sales, though these have been patchy at best.

The Su-27's major export success came in 1991, when China ordered 24 Su-27SKs and two Su-27UBKs (or 20 Su-27SKs and four UBKs according to some sources). These have equipped the 9th Fighter Regiment of the 3rd Air Division at Wuhan and were augmented by a further batch of 22 Su-27SKs and two UBKs (16 Su-27SKs and six UBKs according to some sources). Some of these aircraft were then deployed to Liancheng where 17 were damaged in a hurricane during April 1997 — three reportedly beyond repair. The Chinese order represents the type's biggest export project to date. Officially designated Su-27SKs, they are believed to be identical to those serving with the Russian Air Forces, although some sources have suggested they have Zhuk-27 radars.

China signed a license with Russia in February 1996 under

The breakup of the Soviet Union left Ukraine with a formidable number of combat aircraft on its soil that included Su-27s. The newly independent nation substantially reorganized its air forces in the years that followed and brought them under a single unified command. Today, Ukraine has operational 'Flankers' stationed at its air bases at Mirgorod and Belbek.

which it would manufacture up to 200 Su-27s to supplement the original 48 Russian-built aircraft. Sukhoi supplied US $150 million worth of production tooling in 1997 for what was expected to total six or seven aircraft per year initially, rising to 15 after 2002. In fact, the first two Su-27s assembled at Shenyang had to be grounded and rebuilt by Russian technicians following their maiden flights and, by early 2000, only five locally-manufactured aircraft had been built. Delays to Chinese-built Su-27s then led to delivery of a further batch of 20 or more Russian-supplied Su-27UBs, to be included in the 'umbrella' figure agreed for Chinese license production. Some sources suggest these latest aircraft are (or will eventually become) multirole Su-30MKK two-seat strike fighters. In fact, that nation has ordered 60 Su-30MKKs and the first 10 were delivered during late 2000.

It seems unlikely Sukhoi will score much success with new 'Flanker' variants unless they are fitted with more modern systems and updated cockpits. Given that new Western fighters entering or soon to enter service represent 'new thinking' in terms of design, technologies and capabilities, the old Su-27 airframe will be hard pressed to match such qualities.

Meanwhile, the Russians have tried hard to ensure the Chinese will not be able to produce further unlicensed aircraft for re-export, and has not granted any license for engine or avionics manufacture, which represents at least 30 percent of the aircraft's value.

Another customer emerged in 1995, when Vietnam received the first of seven Su-27SKs and five Su-27UBKs for a squadron that has operated from Phan Rang and Cam Ranh Bay. In addition, Kazakhstan received an initial six Su-27s in part payment for debts, including rent owed by the Russian government for use of the Baikonur Cosmodrome, and four more were delivered in 1997. Russia has promised to deliver a total of 32 aircraft. Syria has also received about eight second-hand Su-27s, these being delivered to a frontline regiment with detachments based at Minakh (home of the Air Force Academy) and Damascus, during mid 2000.

In areas of conflict where many other nations would be cautious about selling advanced combat aircraft, the Su-27 did win some small-scale sales successes. Ethiopia, for example, took delivery of eight secondhand Su-27s in 1998 and used them to great effect against neighboring Eritrea's equally new MiG-29s, shooting down at least two of them. Angola received another eight — probably from Belarus, where Angolan pilots underwent conversion training on the aircraft, with technical support from the Ukraine. More recently (and arguably showing even greater desperation) Sukhoi has attempted to promote various Su-27s to Australia (Su-30MK, Su-32FN and Su-35/37), New Zealand (Su-27 or Su-30), Chile, Greece, Indonesia, Malaysia, Singapore and South Africa, but without success.

At one time, it seemed likely the Su-27 might win orders as an adversary aircraft, although the US company Greystone Technologies' ambitious plans were defeated by the regulatory problems inherent in operating civil-registered Su-27s in the USA. It has been reported that at least one was shipped to America in an An-124 on 26 November 1995. Japan was reported to be interested in acquiring two aircraft as 'aggressors' but apparently was unable to do so because Sukhoi was unwilling to sell fewer than six. However, two JASDF pilots did undergo a $300,000 training, familiarization and evaluation program in 1988.

For all the hype surrounding the various 'Super Flankers,' only a modest handful of minimum-change Su-33s have been delivered to the Russian Navy, while the small number of Su-30s delivered to the PVO and Indian Air Force are little more than probe-equipped Su-27UB trainers. Bickering between the Sukhoi OKB and its main production plants at Irkutsk, Komsomolsk-na-Amur and Novosibirsk has not helped the Su-27's sales prospects but the fundamental problem remains the same. The basic 'Flanker' was a great vintage in its day but changing the label is no longer enough. The Su-30, Su-32, Su-34, Su-35 and Su-37 now being marketed by Sukhoi lack real credibility and have been unable to win open-market competitions.

The Su-27's superb airframe/engine combination remains extremely impressive and while there is every indication the OKB has successfully integrated canard foreplanes and thrust-vectoring with a new FBW FCS, the basic Su-27's avionics are no longer viewed as adequate. Furthermore, new-generation Russian avionics remain untried and unproven. The market now demands a more sophisticated and advanced product. Unfortunately, there are still some who are reluctant to recognize the fundamental weaknesses of the Su-27 and, sometimes, there has been an unwillingness to provide potential customers with sufficient information to stimulate interest.

Furthermore, while senior players in the Soviet aerospace industry may sometimes express their willingness to integrate foreign weapons and, to a lesser extent, avionics into their aircraft to meet the needs of export customers, this rarely happens. Not one Western missile has been integrated with any frontline Su-27 or MiG-29, for example. Even the integration of new Russian weapons and avionics with existing types can be painfully slow. Under the original 1996 contract, for example, India expected to receive its 40 Su-30MKIs in four batches — each batch progressively closer to the definitive, fully-equipped version. All were to have been delivered by 1999-2000 — the last batch featuring advanced ground attack avionics, canard foreplanes and thrust vectoring. In reality, India had received only 18 aircraft by the end of 2000 — apparently to basic Su-27UB trainer standard only.

Computer simulations used in development of the Eurofighter and other advanced western fighters used a thrust-vectoring, canard-equipped Su-27 as a baseline threat, assuming parity in radar and weapons. No such 'Flanker' exists and none is even planned. Nothing short of such an aircraft is likely to be enough to restore the 'Flanker's' once fearsome reputation.

Superfighters

SPECIFICATIONS

SU-27

Wing span	48 ft 3 in (14.71 m)
Length, without probe	72 ft (21.95 m)
Height	19 ft 6 in (5.93 m)
Empty, operating weight	36,112 lb (16380 kg)
Fuel, maximum weight	20,723 lb (9400 kg) internal
Normal takeoff weight	51,015 lb (23140 kg)
Maximum takeoff weight	62,391 lb (28300 kg)
Maximum speed	1,429 mph (2300 km/h)
Maximum speed at sea level	870 mph (1400 km/h)
g limit	+9
Ceiling	60,700 ft (18500 m)
Approach speed	140 mph (225 km/h)
Takeoff distance	2,133-2,297 ft (650-700 m)
Landing distance	2,034-2,297 ft (620-700 m)
Ferry range	2,312 miles (3720 km)
Maximum range with 10 AAMs	1,740 miles (2800 km)
Operational radius at high altitude	677 miles (1090 km)
Operational radius at low altitude	261 miles (420 km)
Accommodation	Pilot
Power plant	Two Lyulka-Saturn/Moscow AL-31F turbofans, each rated at 27,558 lb (122.6 kN) with afterburner
Mission Sensors	S-27 (N001) radar with a search range of 62 miles (100 km) for a fighter-type target head-on, OEPS-27 infrared search/track device coupled with a laser rangefinder (tracking range 31 miles/50 km) and Shchel-3U helmet-mounted target designator
Armament	6 medium-/extended-range R-27/R-27E (AA-10 'Alamo') AAMs plus 4 R-73 (AA-11 'Archer') short-range AAMs Or 8,818 lb (4000 kg) of bombs and unguided rockets GSh-30-1 single-barrel 30-mm cannon with 150 rounds in starboard wing LERX
Self-protection System	32 x APP-50 chaff/flare dispensers in tailboom. Provision for 2 Sorbtsiya-S jamming pods suspended on wingtips

SU-30

Per Su-27, except:

Height	20 ft 10 in (6.36 m)
Maximum internal fuel	20,723 lb (9400 kg)
Normal takeoff weight	54,520 lb (24730 kg)
Maximum takeoff weight	67, 131 lb (30450 kg)
Maximum speed	1,336 mph (2150 km/h)
Maximum speed at sea level	839 mph (1350 km/h)
g limit	+8.5
Ceiling	57,415 ft (17500 m)
Maximum range	1,864 miles (3000 km)
Maximum range at sea level	789 miles (1270 km)
Accommodation	2 in tandem
Power plant	Per Su-27
Mission Sensors	As for Su-27 plus tactical datalink enabling a group commander flying an Su-30 to assign targets to other fighters
Armament	Per Su-27
Self-protection System	Per Su-27

SU-33

Wing span	48 ft 3 in (14.71 m)
Length, without probe	69 ft 6 in (21.19 m)
Height	18 ft 9 in (5.72 m)
Maximum takeoff weight	72,752 lb (33000 kg)
Maximum speed	1,429 mph (2300 km/h)
Maximum speed at sea level	808 mph (1300 km/h)
g limit	+8, -2
Ceiling	55,775 ft (17000 m)
Approach speed	149 mph (240 km/h)
Maximum range	1,864 miles (3000 km)
Maximum range at low altitude	621 miles (1000 km)
Accommodation	Pilot
Power plant	Two modified Lyulka-Saturn/Moscow AL-31F3 turbofans, each rated at 28,214 lb (125.5 kN), with emergency afterburning added plus anti-corrosion protection
Mission Sensors/Self-protection	Per Su-27
Armament	Standard Su-27 weapons plus R-27EM AAMs specialized for use over sea against low-altitude air targets

SU-34

Wing span	48 ft 3 in (14.71 m)
Length	81 ft 4 in (24.81 m)
Height	19 ft 11.5 in (6.08 m)
Maximum fuel	26,676 lb (12100 kg) internally, plus 15,873 lb (7200 kg) in drop tanks.
Maximum takeoff weight	97,797 lb (44360 kg)
Maximum speed	1,181 mph (1900 km/h)
Maximum speed at sea level	808 mph (1300 km/h)
g limit	+7
Ceiling	45,930 ft (14000 m)
Takeoff distance	4,134 ft (1260 m)
Landing distance	2,953 ft (900 m)
Ferry range	2,796 miles (4500 km)
Operational radius (low alt., max fuel)	702 miles (1130 km)
Operational radius (low alt., internal fuel)	373 miles (600 km)
Accommodation	2 – side by side
Power Plant	Currently two Lyulka-Saturn/Moscow AL-31F turbofans, each 27,558 lb (122.6 kN) Future production version to be powered by two Lyulka-Saturn AL-41Fs each rated at 39,342 lb (175.0 kN).
Mission Sensors	Leninets/St Petersburg B004 phased-array radar in nose, with terrain-following and terrain-avoidance capabilities, offering search ranges of 56 miles (90 km) for a 3 m² target or 19 miles (30 km) for a surface vehicle or 84 miles (135 km) for a warship Rear-facing air-to-air radar in tailboom tip
Armament	Up to 17,637 lb (8000 kg) on 12 pylons, including all current and future Russian tactical air-to-surface weapons plus short- and medium-range AAMs, plus GSh-301 cannon in starboard wing root firing 180 rounds
Self-protection	Khibiny system coupling warning receivers, active electronic jammer and chaff/flare dispensers Rear-facing air-to-air radar in tail

Su-35

Wing span	48 ft 3 in (14.71 m)
Length	72 ft 9 in (22.18 m)
Height	21 ft 1 in (6.43 m)
Weights	
Empty, operating	40,565 lb (18400 kg)
Maximum fuel	22,928 lb (10400 kg) internally plus
	2 drop tanks each holding 529 gal (2000 lit)
Normal takeoff weight	56,593 lb (25670 kg)
Maximum takeoff weight	74,936 lb (34000 kg)
Maximum speed	1,553 mph (2500 km/h)
Maximum speed at sea level	870 mph (1400 km/h)
g limit	+9
Ceiling	58,402 ft (17800 m)
Climb rate	45,275 ft per minute (230 m/s)
Required runway length	3,937 ft (1200 m)
Maximum range	1,988 miles (3200 km)
Max. range at low altitude	864 miles (1390 km)

Su-35 (CONTINUED)

Mission Sensors	N011 with flat slotted antenna or N011M phased-array antenna offering maximum maximum search range for a fighter-type target of 50-62 miles (80-100 km) Rear-looking N012 radar in thicker tailboom OLS-27K electro-optical search/track device and Shchel-3UM helmet-mounted sight
Armament	Up to 17,634 lb (8000 kg) of weaponry on 14 pylons, including all modern Russian AAMs and tactical ASMs GSh-30-1 single-barrel 30-mm cannon
Self-protection	System coupling warning receivers, active electronic jammers and chaff/flare dispensers
Accommodation	Pilot
Power plant	Two Lyulka-Saturn/Moscow AL-31FM turbofans, each rated at 28,219 lb (125.5 kN) Optional vectored-thrust AL-31FP engines

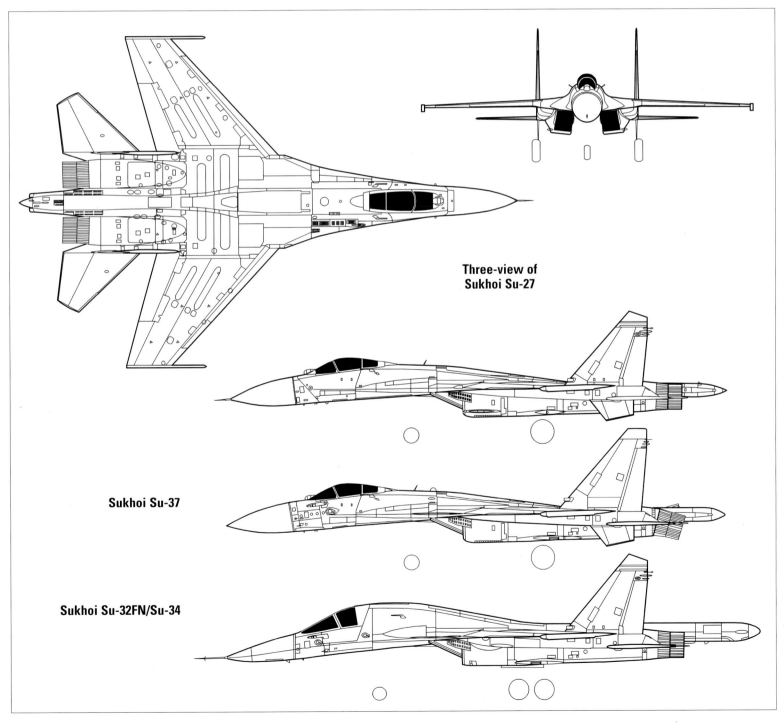

Three-view of Sukhoi Su-27

Sukhoi Su-37

Sukhoi Su-32FN/Su-34

Appendix 1   'Superfighter' Comparative Sizes

F-22A Raptor   **F-35 JSF**   **Eurofighter Typhoon**

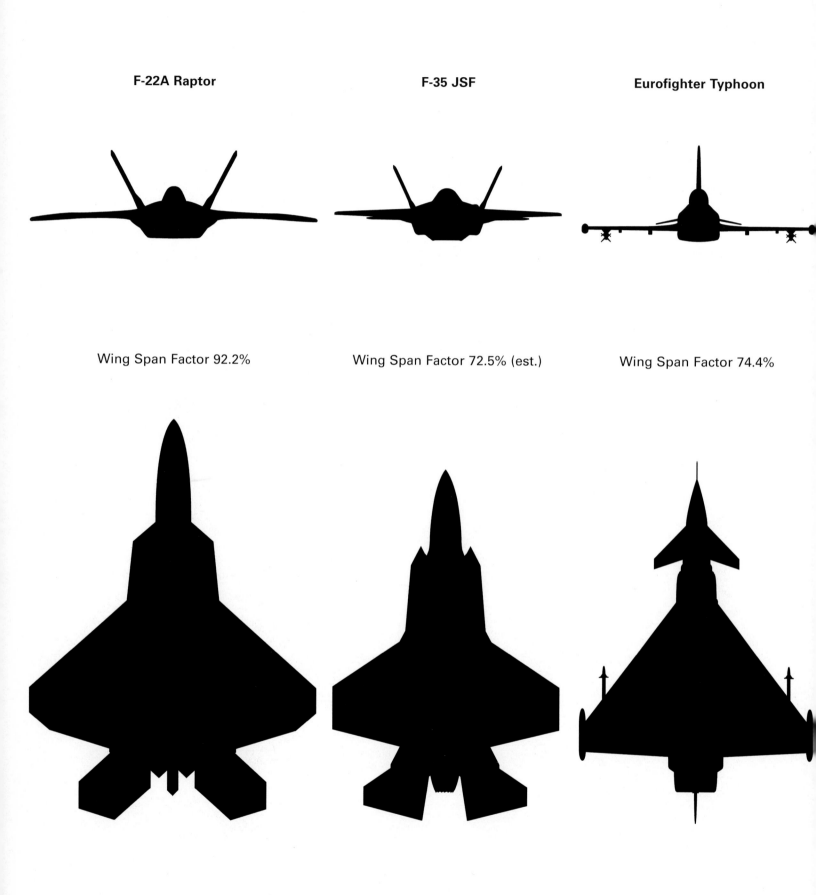

Wing Span Factor 92.2%   Wing Span Factor 72.5% (est.)   Wing Span Factor 74.4%

Overall Length Factor 86.2%   Overall Length Factor 74.7% (est.)   Overall Length Factor 72.7%

Saab Gripen

Dassault Rafale

Sukhoi Su-27 'Flanker'

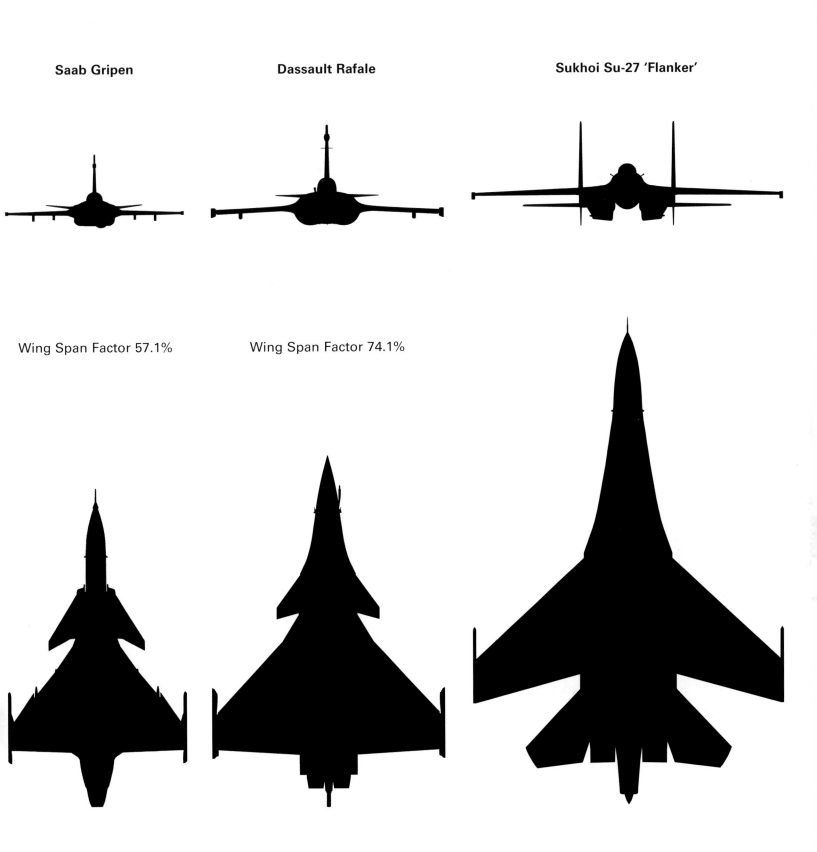

Wing Span Factor 57.1%

Wing Span Factor 74.1%

Overall Length Factor 64.2%

Overall Length Factor 69.7%

Wing Span and Overall Length Factors reflect comparisons with the Su-27 'Flanker' ('Flanker' = 100%)

Appendix 2   Key Program Dates

Lockheed Martin F-22A Raptor

1971	Birth of the ATF concept
1981	Serious studies for ATF commence
1986	US Navy expresses interest in joining ATF program
31 October 1986	Lockheed and Northrop awarded contract to build two prototypes each
27 August 1990	Northrop/McDonnell Douglas YF-23 makes first flight
29 September 1990	Initial Lockheed YF-22 (PAV1) makes first flight
30 October 1990	Second Lockheed YF-22 makes first flight
20 December 1990	First firing of an AIM-120 AAM conducted from internal weapons bay
28 December 1990	YF-22 completes flight-test program after 74 flights, having flown above Mach 2 and sustained Mach 1.58 without afterburner
23 April 1991	Lockheed declared winner of ATF program
25 April 1992	Second YF-22 suffers landing accident (due to PIO) and never flies again
April 1994	Lockheed Martin directed to develop nominal air-to-surface capability for F-22
9 April 1997	First EMD F-22A (4001) rolled out at Marietta, Georgia
May 1997	Total production number for F-22s reduced to 339 aircraft under Quadrennial Defense Review
10 July 1997	Plans for two-seat version officially shelved
7 September 1997	4001 makes maiden flight
21 November 1997	AN/APG-77 AESA radar flown for first time
5 February 1998	4001 flown to Edwards AFB aboard C-5B
17 May 1998	4001 enters test program at Edwards
29 June 1998	4002 (PAV2) makes maiden flight
26 August 1998	4002 flies to Edwards under its own power
July 1999	US Congress votes to eliminate F-22 production funds for FY2000
6 March 2000	Third F-22A (4003, with the first fully representative internal structure) makes its maiden flight
15 March 2000	4003 delivered to Edwards
25 July 2000	First AIM-9 launched by 4002
24 October 2000	First AIM-120C launched
2 November 2000	4001's flight duties ended when aircraft delivered to Wright-Patterson AFB in Ohio for static tests
15 November 2000	4004 undertakes maiden flight
5 January 2001	Block 3 avionics software flown aboard 4005
5 February 2001	4006 makes maiden flight
March 2001	Assembly of first production aircraft (01-4018) begun
15 August 2001	Low-rate initial production (LRIP) authorized
September 2001	First two guided AIM-120 launches undertaken
5 January 2002	4007 (first with integrated weapon/sensor suite) delivered to Edwards
25 April 2002	Block 3.1 software (DIOT&E standard) makes first flight aboard 4006
April 2003	Dedicated Operational test and Evaluation (DIOT&E) set to begin
2004	Full-rate production authorization expected
Late 2004	First operational F-22A fighters due to arrive at Tyndall AFB, Florida (AETC) and Langley AFB, Virginia (for 1st FW)
December 2005	1st FW expected to achieve IOC
2006	Earliest time Block 5 software delivery is expected
2009	Three squadrons (24 aircraft each) expected to be operational at Langley

Lockheed Martin F-35 JSF

January 1986	Agreement covering Harrier replacement signed by NASA and the UK's Royal Aeronautical Establishment (later DERA)
1987	US Marine Corps decides an advanced STOVL will replace its Harriers and F/A-18s
1989-90	DARPA funds STOVL design studies
1991	DARPA convinces US Navy to to issue draft requirement, impressed by Lockheed-GE proposal
March 1993	Contracts issued to Lockheed and McDonnell Douglas for ASTOVL/CALF project. More companies subsequently join
1993	Individual service fighter programs canceled (JAST is born)
Summer 1994	Northrop bids on CALF
Late 1994	Northrop agrees to collaborate with McDonnell Douglas and British Aerospace on JAST
1996	JAST Office issues Request for Proposals for prototypes
November 1996	LM and Boeing selected for next JSF phase
Early 1997	Formal contracts issued

Early 2000	JORD issued requesting EMD proposals
August 2000	GE tests core of proposed JSF120-FX engine for future-lot deliveries (2010)
24 August 2000	P&W F119-614 turbofan is run in full afterburner for first time
7 September 2000	Development and integration of X-35A's avionics completed
18 September 2000	X-32A (Boeing) makes first flight
13 October 2000	X-35A taxi trials commence
24 October 2000	X-35A undertakes maiden flight
7 November 2000	X-35A undertakes first aerial refueling
21 November 2000	X-35A flies at Mach 1.05
22 November 2000	X-35A CTOL trials end
16 December 2000	X-35C undertakes maiden flight
28-29 December 2000	Lift-fan assembly and vectoring nozzle fitted to X-35A (Aircraft then redesignated the X-35B)
3 January 2001	FCLPs commence with X-35C
February 2001	Lockheed Martin and Boeing submit proposals
22 February 2001	X-35B begins hover pit testing at Palmdale
10 March 2001	F119-611S power plant run up to full dry power in hover configuration
11 March 2001	X-35C ends test schedule at NAS Patuxent River, Maryland
22/23 May 2001	JSF Program Office complete first flight-readiness review prior to STOVL trials
23 June 2001	X-35B makes first vertical takeoff and landing
9 July 2001	X-35B makes first transition from STOVL to CTOL mode
16 July 2001	X-35B makes first transition from wingborne flight to vertical landing
20 July 2001	'Mission X' achieved (STOVL-mode short running takeoff, followed by supersonic dash, followed by vertical landing)
30 July 2001	X-35B completes flight-test program
Mid-August 2001	Lockheed Martin and Boeing submit final bids
26 October 2001	Lockheed Martin declared JSF winner
May 2002	Canada, Turkey and Denmark become JSF program partners (joining USA and UK)
2006	First F-35 fighter expected to fly
2008	Initial deliveries to the USAF and USMC expected
2012	Initial UK deliveries anticipated

Eurofighter Typhoon

1977	Trinational (British, French, German) discussions begin concerning new combat aircraft
26 May 1983	EAP technology demonstrator construction authorized
16 December 1983	Outline European Staff Target issued by France, West Germany, Italy, Spain and UK
11 October 1984	Full European Staff Target issued
1 August 1985	Italy, West Germany and UK agree to proceed with ACA design, similar to EAP
2 August 1985	France leaves discussions to develop its ACX design (Rafale)
2 September 1985	Spain agrees to stay with ACA design consortium
8 August 1986	EAP flies for first time
23 November 1988	Full-scale development contract placed, for intended in-service date of 1995
11 May 1992	First prototype (DA1) transferred to Manching airfield
6 June 1992	DA1 begins engine runs of interim RB.199s
January 1994	Four nations agree on revised European Common Staff Requirement
27 March 1994	DA1 undertakes Eurofighter's first flight
6 April 1994	DA2 makes first flight with RB.199 power
4 June 1995	DA3 undertakes maiden flight. First aircraft with EJ200 engines
January 1996	Revised workshare agreed
Mid-1996	ECR.90 (Captor) radar begins flight trials in BAC One-Eleven
31 August 1996	First flight made by two-seater DA6
27 January 1997	DA7 makes first flight
24 February 1997	DA5 joins test fleet, fitted with ECR.90 radar
14 March 1997	Two-seater DA4 flies for first time
15 December 1997	First Sidewinder launch undertaken by DA7
17 December 1997	DA7 jettisons AIM-120 for first time
January 1998	Inflight refueling trials begin, using RAF VC10
17 June 1998	Drop tank jettison trials begin
September 1998	Batch 1 production order finalized
October 1998	EF.2000 named Typhoon for export purposes
December 1998	Construction of major subassemblies begins
June 1999	Pit-drop tests begin of air-to-surface weaponry

October 1999	Flight trials with production-standard EJ.200-03Z engines begin in DA3
December 1999	First flight to Mach 1.6 with three external tanks
8 September 2000	Final assembly of production aircraft begins
March 2001	DA5 undertakes Captor radar trials in 20-target tests
June 2001	DA7 launches ASRAAM for first time
November 2001	First firing of an infrared flare
5 April 2002	First production aircraft (IPA2) flies at Caselle
8 April 2002	IPA3 flies from Manching for first time
15 April 2002	IPA1 joins test fleet
April 2002	DA4 undertakes first guided AMRAAM launch
2002	First deliveries to operational evaluation/conversion units
2004/5	First operational squadrons to be formed
2010	Advanced Tranche (Batch) 3 aircraft due to enter service

Saab Gripen

1976	B3LA future fighter studies begin
30 June 1982	First contract signed covering five prototypes and 30 Batch 1 aircraft
9 December 1988	First flight of Gripen prototype (39-1) undertaken
2 February 1989	39-1 is lost in landing accident
4 May 1990	First flight of second prototype (39-2) is made
20 December 1990	First flight of two-seater prototype (39-4) is made
25 March 1991	39-3 flies for first time. First Gripen to have full avionics suite, except radar
23 October 1991	39-5 flies. First aircraft with radar
1991	Weapons trials begin with Rb 74 Sidewinder launch
3 June 1992	Batch 2 production authorized, covering 96 JAS 39As and 14 JAS 39Bs
10 September 1992	First production aircraft (39101) flies
8 June 1993	First production aircraft (39102) delivered to F7 at Såtenäs
18 August 1993	39102 lost during air show over central Stockholm
29 April 1996	Two-seat JAS 39B prototype (39800) flies
20 August 1996	First flight of a Batch 2 aircraft (39131)
22 November 1996	First production JAS 39B two-seater (39801) flies
13 December 1996	Batch 3 production authorized for 50 JAS 39Cs and 14 JAS 39Ds
19 December 1996	First Batch 2 aircraft delivered
1 November 1997	First squadron (1./F7) declared operational
27 August 1998	First captive flight of KEPD-150 weapon
18 November 1998	South Africa selects Gripen
30 September 1999	First Gripens arrive to begin equipping F10 at Ängelholm
October 1999	Testing of KEPD-350 weapon begins
10 December 2001	Czech Republic selects Gripen
20 December 2001	Hungary selects Gripen
late 2004	First Gripens due for delivery to Hungary
2007	South African deliveries due to begin

Dassault Rafale

June 1982	First public revelation of ACX studies
13 April 1983	Formal approval to build two (later one) ACX technology demonstrators
2 August 1985	France leaves Eurofighter discussions to develop Rafale independently
14 December 1985	Rafale A technology demonstrator unveiled at St Cloud
4 July 1986	Rafale A technology demonstrator makes first flight, from Istres (F404 engines) and achieves Mach 1
31 August 1986	Public debut of Rafale A at Farnborough air show
14 February 1987	French government decides to proceed with Rafale combat aircraft
4 March 1987	Rafale A achieves Mach 2
30 April 1987	First dummy approaches made to a carrier deck
21 April 1988	Full-scale development authorized
27 February 1990	First flight of Rafale A with one M88 engine in the port bay
29 October 1990	Rafale C unveiled at St Cloud
19 May 1991	Rafale C01 makes first flight from Istres (Mach 1.2)
13 June 1991	Rafale C01 makes public debut at Paris air show
12 December 1991	Rafale M01 makes first flight
13 June 1992	Rafale M01 begins dummy-deck trials in USA (at NAS Lakehurst, New Jersey)
10 July 1992	RBE2 radar begins flight trials in Falcon 20
23 December 1992	Dassault receives production authorization
26 March 1993	First production order for two aircraft (one B/ one M)
19 April 1993	Rafale M01 undertakes first carrier landing on *Foch*

20 April 1993	First carrier launch accomplished
30 April 1993	First flight of Rafale B01
8 November 1993	First flight of Rafale M02
24 January 1994	Last (865th) flight of Rafale A
September 1996	First flight with SPECTRA EW suite aboard (M02)
October 1997	First production RBE2 radar delivered
June 1998	First flight of a production aircraft (B301)
December 1998	First production aircraft (B301) handed over to French armed forces at Mérignac
July 1999	First carrier operations by M01/M02 on carrier *Charles de Gaulle*
July 1999	First production Rafale M delivered to *Aéronavale*
July 2000	MICA EM qualified on Standard F1 Rafale
4 December 2000	First two Standard LF1 Rafales (M2 and M3) delivered to Landivisiau
26 January 2001	Authorization given for Standard F2 development
18 April 2001	First flight of B01 equipped with conformal fuel tanks
May 2001	*Flottille* 12F reformed at Landivisiau
May 2001	First major deployment by Rafale Ms to *Charles de Gaulle* in Exercise Trident d'Or
2004	First Standard F2 aircraft due to enter service
2005	First Standard F2 squadrons due to become operational (*Flottille* 11F, EC 7)
2008	Scheduled delivery of first Standard F3 Rafales

Sukhoi 'Super Flankers'

1969	Work begins on new PFI interceptor to replace Su-15, Tu-128 and Yak-28P
1971	Sukhoi project becomes TPFI (heavy interceptor)
20 May 1977	T10-1 first prototype flies at Zhukovskiy
20 April 1981	Redesigned T10S makes first flight
3 September 1981	T10S-1 crashes
November 1982	First production Su-27 rolled out
1 September 1984	First arrested landing (by T10-25) on Nitka dummy deck at Saki, Crimea
7 March 1985	Su-27UB two-seater flies for first time
May 1985	T10-24 flies with canard foreplanes fitted
27 October 1986	P-42 (T10S-3) sets first of many time-to-height records
October 1986	Su-27 enters service
17 August 1987	First flight of Su-27K
28 June 1988	First flight of Su-27M (Su-35)
31 March 1989	First inflight vectoring of thrust, using Su-27LL-PS test bed
June 1989	Su-27 debuts in the West at the Paris air show
1 November 1989	First deck landing by Su-27K
31 December 1989	Maiden flight of Su-27PU (Su-30) prototype
13 April 1990	Maiden flight of Su-27IB (Su-34) prototype
June 1992	Initial deliveries of Su-27SK to China
March 1993	First production Su-33s delivered to Russian Navy
18 December 1993	First production-standard Su-34 flies
24 December 1995	*Kuznetsov* carrier leaves port with Su-33s aboard for the type's only full-scale deployment
2 April 1996	Su-27M 'Bort 711' (Su-37) flies with thrust-vectoring nozzles
9 March 1999	Maiden flight of Su-30MKK thrust-vectoring aircraft for China
29 April 1999	Su-27KUB (Su-33UB) flies for the first time
6 October 1999	Su-33UB lands on *Kuznetsov* for the first time
26 November 2000	First pre-production standard Su-30MKI makes first flight
2001	Avionics upgrades made to Russian air force single- and twin-seat Su-27/Su-30s
6 March 2001	Su-27UBM (s/n 20) and Su-30KN (s/n 302) delivered by IAPO

Appendix 3   Glossary of Acronyms

AAM — Air-to-Air Missile
AASM — Modular Air-to-Ground Armament (France)
ACC — Air Combat Command
ACFC — Air-Cooled Flight-Critical
ACP — Audio Control Panel
ACT — Active Control Technology
AD — Air Defense
AdA — *Armée de l'Air* (French Air Force)
ADF — Air Dominance Fighter
AESA — Active Electronically Scanned Array
AEW — Airborne Early Warning
AEW&C — Airborne Early Warning and Control
AFFTC — Air Force Flight Test Center
AFOTEC — Air Force Operational Test & Eval. Center
AFTI — Adv. Fighter Technology Integration
AGM — Air-to-Ground Missile
AIL — Avionics Integration Laboratory
AMI — *Aeronautica Militare Italiana* (Italian AF)
AMIC — Aviation Military-Industrial Complex
AMRAAM — Advanced Medium-Range AAM
AMSAR — Airborne Multi-Mode Solid-State Active-Array Radar
AMU — Audio Management Unit
ANF — *Anti-Navir Futur* (Future Anti-ship)
AoA — Angle of Attack or High-Alpha
APU — Auxiliary Power Unit
ARB — Auxilliary Reserve Base
ASEAN — Assoc. of South East Asian Nations
ASM — Air-to-Surface Missile
ASMP-A — Medium-Range Air-to-Ground
ASRAAM — Advance Short-Range AAM
ASTA — Aircrew Synthetic Training Aid
ASTOVL — Advanced STOVL
ASW — Anti-submarine Warfare
ATF — Advanced Tactical Fighter
ATFLIR — Adv. Targeting Forward-Looking Infrared
AV-MF — Russian Naval Aviation
AWACS — Airborne Warning and Control System
Bort — Aircraft No. (Russian)
BVR — Beyond Visual Range
BVRAAM — Beyond Visual-Range AAM
CAD — Computer-Aided Design
CALF — Common Affordable Lightweight Fighter
CAP — Combat Air Patrol
CAS — Close Air Support
CATB — Cooperative Avionics Test Bed
CCDU — Communication Control Display Unit
CDA — Concept Demonstration Aircraft
CDL39 — Communication and Datalink 39
CFC — Carbon-Fiber Composite
CFT — Conformal Fuel Tank
CINC — Commander(s) in Chief
CIP — Common Integrated Processors
CIS — Commonwealth of Independent States
CNI — Communications, Navigation & Identification
COTS — Commercial-Off-The-Shelf
CRT — Cathode Ray Tube
CT/IPS-E — Cockpit Trainer/Interact. Pilot Stns. - Enhcd.
CTF — Combined Test Force
CTIP — Continuous Technol. Insertion Program
CTOL — Conventional Takeoff and Landing
CV — Carrier Capable Variant
DAB — Defense Acquisition Board
DALLADS — Danish Army Low-Level Air-Def. System
DARPA — Defense Adv. Research Projects Agency
DASS — Defensive Aids Subsystem
DE-Hawks — Danish Enhanced-Hawks
DemVal — Demonstration Validation
DERA — Defence Evaluation and Research Agency
DIOT&E — Dedicated Operational Test and Evaluation
DIRS — Distributed Infrared System
DVI — Direct Voice Input
DVI/O — Direct Voice Input/Output
ECM — Electronic Countermeasures
ECS — Environmental-Control System
EdA — *Ejército del Aire* (Spanish Air Force)
EFI — Eurofighter International
EM — *Electomagnétique* (Radar-guided)
EMD — Engineer. and Manufact. Development
EMP — Electromagnetic Pulse
EO — Electro-Optical
E-Scan — Electronically Scanned
ESM — Electronic Support Measures
EW — Electronic Warfare
Excom — Executive Committee
F-22 SPO — F-22 System Program Office
FADEC — Full Authority Digital Engine Control
FBW — Fly-By-Wire
FCLP — Field Carrier Landing Practice
FCS — Flight Control System or Fire Control Sys.

FJCA — Future Joint Combat Aircraft
FLIR — Forward-Looking Infrared
FMRAAM — Future Medium-Range AAM
FMS — Full-Mission Simulator
FMV — Defense Materiel Administration (Sweden)
FMV:PROV — Swedish Defense Material Administration's Testing Unit
FOAS — Future Offensive Aircraft System
FOC — Full Operating Capability
FPA — Focal Plane Array
FQI — Fuel Quantity Indicator
FSO — Front Sector Optronics
FTB — Flying Test Bed
FUS39 — Flight Conversion System 39 (Sweden)
FY — Fiscal Year
GaA — Gallium Arsenide
GCI — Ground Control Intercept
GFRP — Glass-Fiber-Reinforced Plastic
GFSU JAS39 — Adv. Oper. Gripen Training (Sweden)
GFU — Basic Flying Training (Sweden)
GMTI — Ground-Moving Target Indication
GPS — Global Positioning System
GPWS — Ground-Proximity Warning System
GTA — Ground Telecommunications Amplifier
GTU — Basic Tactical Flying Training (Sweden)
HAS — Hardened Aircraft Shelter
HAV — High-Alpha Velocity Vectory
HDD — Head-Down Display
HE — High Explosive
High-Alpha — High Angle-of-Attack
HMD — Helmet-Mounted Display
HOTAS — Hands-On Throttle and Stick
HRR — High-Range Resolution
HUD — Head-Up Display
IAPO — Irkutsk Aircraft Production Organization
IA-PVO — Fighter Air Defense Forces (Russia)
ICAP-III — Improved Capability III
ICAW — Integrate Caution/Advisory/Warning
ICP — Integrated Core Processor
ICS — Internal Countermeasures Set
IFDL — Intra-Flight Datalink
IFF — Identification Friend-or-Foe
IIR — Imaging Infrared
ILS — Instrument Landing System
INS — Inertial Navigation System
IOC — Initial Operating Capability
IPA — Instrumented Production Aircraft
IR — Infrared
IRIS-T — Infrared Imaging System Tail
IRST — Infrared Scanner/Tracker or IR Search & Track
IRSTS — Infrared Search-and-Track System
ITV — Instrumented Test Vehicle
J/IST — Joint Integrated Subsystems Technology
JAS — *Jakt/Attack/Spaning* (Fighter/Attack/Recon.)
JASDF — Japanese Air Self Defense Force
JAST — Joint Advanced Strike Technology
JDAM — Joint Direct Attack Munition
JHMCS — Joint Helmet-Mounted Cueing System
JIRD — Joint Interim Requirements Documents
JOANNA — Joint Airborne Navigation & Attack
JORD — Joint Operational Requirements Docs.
JSF — Joint Strike Fighter
JTIDS — Joint Tactical Information Distrib. System
KEPD — Kinetic Energy Penetration & Destruction
KIAP — Shipborne Fighter Air Regiment
KLu — *Koninklijke Luchtmacht* (Dutch Air Force)
kN — Kilonewton
KnAAPO — Komsomolsk Aviation Enterprise
lb st — Pounds Thrust
LCD — Liquid Crystal Display
LDGP — Low-Drag General Purpose
LERX — Leading-Edge Root Extension
LFI — *Iyogkiy frontovoi istrebitel'* (Fifth-generation Light Fighter Project)
LGB — Laser-Guided Bomb
LIP — Low Probability of Intercept
LLTV — Low-light Television
LMTAS — Lockheed Martin Tactical Aircraft Systems
LO — Low Observables
LO/CLO — Low Observables/Counter Low Obsvbls.
LPLC — Lift-Plus Lift/Cruise
LRIP — Low-Rate Initial Production
LSO — Landing Signals Officer
LSPM — Large-Scale Powered Model
Luftwaffe — German Air Force
MACS — Modular Airborne Computer System
MAPO — Moscow Aircraft Production Association
MDC — Miniature Detonating Cord
MDPU — Modular Data Processing Unit
MFD — Multifunction Display

MFID — Multifunction Instrumented Display
MHDD — Multifunction Head-Down-Display
MICA — Combat and Self-Defense Missile (France)
MIDS — Multiple Information Distribution System
MIDS-LVT — MIDS - Low Volume Terminal
MIRFS — Multifunction Integrated Radio-Freq. Sys.
MMH/FH — Maintenance-Man-Hour per Flying Hour
MMIC — Microwave Monolithic Integrated Circuit
MMT — Multimission Trainers
MMTD — Miniature Munitions Technology Demnstr.
MoD — Ministry of Defence
MoU — Memorandum of Understanding
MTBF — Mean Time Between Failure
MTO(W) — Maximum Takeoff Weight
MWS — Missile-Warning System
NAS — Naval Air Station
NASAMS — Norwegian Advanced Surface-to-air Missile Systems
NATF — Naval Advanced Tactical Fighter
NBILSLT — Narrow-Band Interleaved Search & Track
NCTR — Non-Cooperative Target Recognition
NETMA — NATO Eurof. and Tornado Mgmt. Agcy.
NITKA — Aviation Research and Training Complex
NPKB — Nevskoye Design Bureau
NVG — Night Vision Goggles
OBIGS — Onboard Inert Gas-Generating System
OBOGS — Onboard Oxygen Generating System
OCU — Operational Conversion Unit
OEU — Operational Evaluation Unit
OKB — Design Bureau (Russia)
OSA — Open Systems Architecture
PIO — Pilot-Induced Oscillation
PIRATE — Passive Infrared Airborne Track. Equip.
PMFD — Primary Multifunction Display
PRF — Pulse-Repetition Frequency
PRTV — Production Representative Test Vehicle
PWSC — Preferred Weapon System Concept
RAE — Royal Aeronautical Establishment
RALS — Remote Augmented Lift System
RAM — Radar-Absorbent Material
RCS — Radar Cross-section
RF — Radio Frequency
RFI — Radio Frequency Interferometer
RMS — Reconnaissance Management System
ROE — Rules of Engagement
RSV — Eval. and Acceptance/Clearance Unit (Italy)
RW — Radar Warning
RWR — Radar Warning Receiver
SAM — Surface-to-Air Missile
SAR — Synthetic Aperture Radar
SDB — Small Diameter Bomb
SEAD — Suppression of Enemy Air Defenses
SES — Stored Energy System
SFIG — Standby Flight Instrumentation Group
SIGINT — Signals Intelligence
SIGINT/ELINT — Signals Intel./Electronic Intel.
SMFD — Secondary Multifunction Display
SPECTRA — Self-Protection Equipment Countering Threats of Rafale Aircraft
SPS — Secondary Power System
Stanags — Standard Agreements
STAR — Surveillance Target Attack Radar System
STOBAR — Short-Takeoff but Arrested Recovery
STOL — Short-Takeoff and Landing
STOVL — Short-Takeoff and Vertical Landing
T/EMM — Thermal/Energy Management Module
T/R — Transmit/Receive
TACAN — Tactical Aid to Navigation
TARAS — Tactical Radio System
TBO — Time Between Overhaul
TER NAV — Terrain-Referenced Navigation
TFLIR — Targeted FLIR
TRD — Towed Radar Decoy
TRN — Terrain-Referenced Navigation
TsAGI — Central Aero- and Hydrodynamics Inst.
TU JAS 39 — Oper. Test and Eval. JAS39 (Sweden)
TV — Television
UCAV — Unmanned Combat Air Vehicle
USSR — Union of the Soviet Socialist Republics
UFD — Upfront Display
UHF — Ultra High Frequency
VHF — Very High Frequency
VHSIC — Very High-speed Integrated Circuits
VOR — VHF Omnidirectional Range
VSWE — Virtual Strike Warfare Environment
VTAS — Voice, Throttle and Stick
VTOL — Vertical Takeoff and Landing
VVS — Russian Air Forces
WSO — Weapon Systems Operator
WVR — Within Visual Range